Detain and Deport

Detain and Deport

THE CHAOTIC U.S. IMMIGRATION ENFORCEMENT REGIME

NANCY HIEMSTRA

THE UNIVERSITY OF GEORGIA PRESS

Athens

© 2019 by the University of Georgia Press
Athens, Georgia 30602
www.ugapress.org
All rights reserved
Set in Minion Pro by Graphic Composition, Inc. Bogart, GA.
Most University of Georgia Press titles are
available from popular e-book vendors.

Printed digitally

Library of Congress Cataloging-in-Publication Data
Names: Hiemstra, Nancy, author.
Title: Detain and deport : the chaotic U.S. immigration enforcement regime / Nancy Hiemstra.
Description: Athens : The University of Georgia Press, 2019. | Series: Geographies of justice and
    social transformation | Includes bibliographical references and index.
Identifiers: LCCN 2018034206| ISBN 9780820354651 (hardback : alk. paper) | ISBN 9780820354637
    (pbk. : alk. paper)
Subjects: LCSH: United States—Emigration and immigration—Government policy. | Illegal
    aliens—Government policy—United States. | Detention of persons—Government policy—
    United States. | Deportation—Government policy—United States.
Classification: LCC JV6483 .H54 2019 | DDC 325.73—dc23
    LC record available at https://lccn.loc.gov/2018034206

For my parents,
Janet Wemer Hiemstra
and Roger Hiemstra

CONTENTS

ILLUSTRATIONS

ACKNOWLEDGMENTS

This book has been a long time in the making, and there are many acknowledgments to be made.

In Ecuador, Cuenca's Casa del Migrante welcomed me as a volunteer and incorporated me into its daily activities for nine months. Special thanks to Carmen Alvarado, who provided key support in the study design and conduct. The family members who trusted me to try to help them get information made this project possible. I am deeply grateful to the deportees who agreed to an interview, as well as the government and nongovernment interviewees who took time out of their busy schedules to speak with me.

The development of this project from dissertation to book followed my own journey from student to faculty member, and many people have offered guidance and assistance in many forms along the way. Alison Mountz has been there at many critical stages, as my dissertation adviser and mentor, and now colleague, from visiting me in Ecuador during fieldwork to offering incisive feedback at multiple points. Emily Billo buoyed me during fieldwork, helped work through methodological challenges, and always has an encouraging word. Many thanks to Deirdre Conlon, for being a sounding board, inspiration, and cheerleader. I also thank her for allowing me to draw on our joint project on the internal economies of detention for chapter 5 of this book. Kate Coddington, Lauren Martin, and Katie Wells read all or parts of the book manuscript at various stages and offered feedback that shaped the book in important ways. Doctoral committee members Don Mitchell, Joseph Nevins, Tom Perreault, and Jamie Winders were instrumental during the early stages of this project. For fact checking and clarification regarding my explanations of the legal processes of U.S. detention and deportation, I thank Austin Kocher and Shaun Mabry (but all errors remain my own). Thank you to Joseph Stoll of the Syracuse University Cartographic Laboratory for his fabulous maps. At Stony Brook University, colleagues in what is now the Department of Women's, Gender, and Sexuality Studies offered encouragement and advice at key moments, including Mary Jo Bona, Ritch Calvin, Lisa Diedrich, Melissa Forbis, Victoria Hesford, Teri Tiso, and Liz Montegary (with special thanks for sharing the junior faculty journey), as have others outside the department, including Tim August, Daniela Flesler, Tiffany Joseph, and Gallya Lahav. Other forms of mentoring, encouragement, and scholarly inspiration for this book have come from Shaul Cohen, Susan Coutin, Alexandra Délano Alonso, Brian Duff, Nick Gill, Tanya Golash-Boza, Susan Hardwick, Jen Hyndman, Emily Kaufman, Maria Lane, Jenna Loyd, Cetta Mainwaring, Dominique Moran, Lise Nelson, Marie Price, and Jill Williams.

At the University of Georgia Press, I am indebted to Press editor Mick Gusinde-Duffy, Jon Davies, and other talented editorial, design, and production staff. Special thanks to series editor Mat Coleman for his vision of what my work offers, careful readings of the manuscript, and enthusiasm.

This project was made possible by generous financial and material support. The research in Ecuador was funded by a National Science Foundation Doctoral Dissertation Research Improvement Fellowship, and the Syracuse University Department of Geography, Graduate School, the Maxwell School John L. Palmer Fund and Roscoe Martin Research Grant, and the Program on Latin America and the Caribbean. Valuable writing time for the book was provided by Stony Brook University's Arts, Humanities and Lettered Social Sciences Faculty Research Fellowship, as well as through a visiting scholar position at the Zolberg Institute on Migration and Mobility at the New School for Social Research.

Finally, my family has sustained and kept me sane throughout this project. Of special mention: the book truly would not have been possible without my parents, Janet Wemer Hiemstra and Roger Hiemstra. They provided unflagging support, including care for my children, manuscript assembly assistance, and unwavering belief in me. My children Kian and Saskia keep me anchored; when I take a dive into pessimism, their joy, smiles, and curiosity remind me there is good in the world worth working for. My partner and best friend, Sean Bowditch, has been there through it all—fieldwork, dissertation, junior faculty insanity, and getting this book finally finished—always radiating confidence that I would get it done. This book is really a collective effort; thanks to so many, and apologies to those I inadvertently failed to mention.

ABBREVIATIONS

AEDPA   Antiterrorism and Effective Death Penalty Act
A-Number Alien Registration Number
CCA   Corrections Corporation of America
DHS   Department of Homeland Security
EOIR   Executive Office for Immigration Review
ERO   Enforcement and Removal Operations
ICE   Immigration and Customs Enforcement
IIRIRA   Illegal Immigration Reform and Immigrant Responsibility Act
INS   Immigration and Naturalization Service
IRCA   Immigration Reform and Control Act
IRTPA   Intelligence Reform and Terrorism Prevention Act
NTA   Notice to Appear
ODLS   Online Detainee Locator System
PBNDS   Performance-Based National Detention Standards
SBI   Secure Border Initiative
SENAMI   Secretaría Nacional del Migrante (Ecuador's National Secretariat
                  of Migrants, no longer in existence)
USCG   United States Coast Guard
9/11   September 11, 2001 (attacks in the United States)

Detain and Deport

The need for critical studies of deportation and detention has never been more urgent, with use of these strategies for immigration enforcement on the rise around the world. The United States leads this global trend, deporting over four hundred thousand people per year and holding at least thirty-four thousand in detention facilities on any given day. Through research crossing national borders, *Detain and Deport* interrogates this massive system in the United States, with the aim of calling into question the conceptual pillars underlying the accelerating use of such practices globally.

While the current climate of openly anti-immigrant political discourse, as well as intentionally visible and cruel enforcement practices, tempts one to ascribe the contemporary detention and deportation machine in the United States to the current administration, that system has been in the making for more than thirty years, becoming bigger and stronger regardless of the political party in power. In 2016, Donald Trump was elected president on a platform in which he called immigrants murderers, rapists, and "bad hombres" and incited rally chants to build a border wall. As president, Trump has called for—and is working swiftly to enact—a sweeping agenda of policies targeting immigrants. However, while often shocking in its overt hostility, the Trump administration's embrace of deportation and detention is the continuation of a well-established approach to immigration enforcement. In fact, his predecessor Barack Obama took many steps to build out and solidify the detention and deportation infrastructure. When I began research for this book in 2009, President Obama was just taking office. During his campaign, Obama promised reform of the broken immigration system in the United States and a softer approach to immigration. But instead of scaling back the use of deportation and detention, the Obama administration increased it. Determined to grease the wheels for comprehensive immigration reform by showing Congress that U.S. borders could be and were being enforced, Obama earned the angry nickname of "Deporter in Chief," deporting over three million people during his presidency. Despite his approach, immigration reform

2 Introduction

didn't happen, the deep divide in the country about immigration remained, and resentment against immigrants continued to grow in parallel with frustrations about the economy and changing demographics. Donald Trump capitalized on these long-simmering resentments and frustrations to win the presidency.

While the numbers are, by far, the largest in the United States, deportation and detention are increasingly central to the migration and border-policing strategies of many countries. In response to more and more people around the globe on the move, destination countries adopt their own version of Trump's anti-immigrant rhetoric and rationales to mobilize the mass exclusion of particular groups of people. Destination as well as transit countries are building detention facilities and multilayered webs for ensnaring migrants. Bureaucracies orchestrating deportation and detention are developing in size and complexity, in seeming global adoption of the idea that these practices are necessary immigration enforcement strategies.

Detain and Deport examines both the drivers and consequences of this global turn to detention and deportation through a focus on the United States. Because of the U.S. role as a global leader in these policies, and because U.S. rationales are repeated in many other countries pursuing such policies, the U.S. system has implications for understanding immigration enforcement around the world. *Detain and Deport* asks how the United States arrived at this point, in which detaining and deporting undocumented immigrants is central to immigration enforcement. The book also investigates what is actually accomplished amid this relentless turn to detention and deportation. These are important endeavors at this critical point in time, as the United States—like many other countries—is working to further expand its capacity to incarcerate and expel immigrants.

Detain and Deport answers these questions by conducting a transnational ethnography of policy. It pairs research in the United States with research in a country of migrant origin, Ecuador, and foregrounds the everyday experiences of those who are deported or detained. Research in countries of migrant origin is critical for breaking down the smokescreen around immigration policies. By overlaying research in Ecuador with information gathered from inside the United States, we can expose the obscured truths of detention and deportation.

Hidden Truths

As someone who has worked with immigrants and studied deportation and detention for over two decades, I find that there are strong moral and practical arguments to be made against these policies as currently practiced by the United States. For one, the United States wastes tremendous talent, resources, and opportunities when it expels hard-working immigrants. These policies also create serious harm, not just for those detained and deported, but for their families, communities, and wider networks. Separating families—including some whose members are U.S. citizens—is unnecessarily cruel and violent. The United States has an obligation to protect the vulnerable and honor international agreements safeguarding human rights. But for many policymakers, politicians, and members of the general public, other arguments carry more weight and therefore justify deportation and detention. For example, some people argue that the United States shouldn't have to take responsibility for noncitizens, and abiding by international agreements regarding immigrants and refugees is burdensome and unfair. For many, immigrants are perceived as criminals and lawbreakers, and it is believed that immigrants come to the United States to take advantage of opportunities and benefits to the detriment of citizens. In this thinking, harsh policies are necessary to protect American security, and immigrants deserve punitive treatment. *Detain and Deport* takes on these opposing beliefs by presenting rational, evidence-based understandings of how deportation and detention came to dominate immigration enforcement approaches today, what they look like in practice, and what their consequences are. By making visible the truths underlying these policies, I counter some of the most prominent anti-immigrant arguments and demonstrate that there are strong reasons—both moral and practical—to shift away from deportation and detention.

A first truth is that the U.S. detention and deportation system is inherently chaotic—that is, confused or disordered. The massive system produces myriad chaotic geographies, or particular ways in which chaos is spatialized and temporalized. Through identifying and scrutinizing chaotic geographies of deportation and detention, we can better grasp both the drivers and the consequences of these policies. *Detain and Deport* refuses to accept the chaos of the system as a barrier to understanding the system, or as a proxy for immigration and immigrants in general. Despite the undeniable centrality of these policies to current immigration enforcement approaches, real information is scarce about how the system works, what happens inside it, and what its actual effects are. The "doing" of detention and deportation, in other words, is quite concealed from the general public, from immigrants experiencing and threatened by these policies, from families and advocates, from scholars, and even from policymakers. Through a focus on practice—the "doing"—this book brings attention to the chaos of detention and deportation to better understand how the chaos is created as well as what the chaos itself produces and obscures. Chaos can be understood as critical to the appeal and momentum of these policies. Identifying chaotic geographies means tracing how detention and deportation work through time (from how these policies came into being to scrutinizing their consequences over time) and space (from inside U.S. borders to inside countries of migrant origin). This focus on chaos thus provides an opening to get behind, and deconstruct, the rationales propelling deportation and detention and simultaneously to see what these policies do in practice.

Second, through its attention to chaos, *Detain and Deport* reveals that many of the fundamental beliefs about what detention and deportation accomplish are incorrect. Punitive approaches to immigration enforcement are grounded in the assumption that they deter future immigration. I argue that detention and deportation fail as deterrents. I do not mean that no migrants are dissuaded from trying to migrate. While that is certainly part of what I am arguing—that policies intended to deter often do not deter—it is undeniable that some people are discouraged from migrating, at least in the short term. Instead, this claim is anchored in the reality that detention and deportation fail to deter in the bigger picture, in the long game, so to speak. Immediate migration decisions may be influenced. But by not addressing the reasons that migrants are pushed and pulled to leave their home country, migration remains a possibility, an out, for many potential migrants. And I describe how in Ecuador these policies create insecurity in families and communities, insecurity that can spark immigration in the future. So while some people may be dissuaded, others are pushed in new ways to migrate. Following Wong (2015, 147), I suggest that *displacement* is a more accurate word to describe actual effects. Migration to the United States may be stopped at that particular moment, but that immediate stoppage may lead to migration to another place, or at another time, all with eventual consequences for the United States.

In addition to incorrect assumptions about their deterrence value, the transnational reverberations of deportation and detention are profoundly miscalculated. Policymakers give virtually no thought to consequences of detention other than discouraging migration, and deportation is grounded in the belief that it brings a definitive end to a deportee's migration journey and relationship with the United States. *Detain and Deport*'s multisited approach forces recognition that, to the contrary, detention and deportation are inherently transnational processes. Instead of cutting ties and permanently terminating migration, they can instead weave and deepen ties between the United States and countries to which people are deported. Detention can contribute to immediate and lasting insecurity in a detainee's country of origin, during and after the period of detention. And deportation is often not the end of a migrant's journey, as most migrants resolve to migrate again. What's more, for deportees who do not try to migrate again, the consequences of deportation stretch out temporally, and in widening impact rings of family, community, and region. Paradoxically, then, detention and deportation work to bind the United States to countries of migrant origin, both in the short and long term.

Third, detention and deportation are typically framed as policies that will cut down on illegal activities. I join others in arguing that restrictive border and immigration enforcement approaches instead add to illicit activities. As getting to and across the U.S.-Mexico border becomes more difficult, smugglers become nearly essential for the undocumented migrant. Their prices go up, and migrants become vehicles for profit. More corruption occurs along the route. Journeys become more dangerous. More people become involved in the business of illicit migration, and invested in continuing it. Migrants take on more and more debt to pay smugglers, debt that means no matter how bad the journey is, or how great their fears of detention and deportation are, they are permanently committed to somehow reaching and remaining in the United States. Efforts to make it harder for migrants at the same time as migrants are more determined to migrate, therefore, feed extralegal markets and activities.

A fourth hidden truth is that a lot of money is being made off detention and deportation. In addition to false assumptions of deterrence, detention and deportation are couched in logics of homeland security, economic necessity, and national identity. In other words, immigrants are portrayed as threatening American safety, taking American jobs, and threatening American identity. These portrayals work as very effective smokescreens for the domestic economic consequences of these policies. Economic consequences include how fear of detention and deportation keep immigrant workers vulnerable and their labor cheap, in ways that allow some employers to make more money. But more specifically here, I am concerned with how private companies, local governments, and individuals are profiting, and profiting healthily, from the process of detaining and deporting migrants. A growing web of entities and people are dependent on this enforcement approach, and very invested in the continuation of current policies. This web is a powerful driving force behind the U.S. embrace of detention and deportation, a reality starkly reflected in how private prison companies (whose services include immigration detention) saw their stocks shoot up immediately after the election of Donald Trump. The current approach to undocumented migration, in which detention and deportation are basically taken for granted as appropriate responses, has been carefully shaped and normalized by those who profit from it. This truth in particular underscores the urgency of fighting new expansions in detention and deportation infrastructure, because as more and more individuals and entities become financially tangled up in our current approach, the more difficult it will be to change course.

Finally, when you take all of these hidden truths into consideration, some of the moral and nationalistic justifications for deportation and detention unravel, and racism and xenophobia emerge as important foundations. For example, supporters of these policies often object to arguments that the United States should show compassion to vulnerable populations and show sympathy to migrants fleeing difficult conditions in origin countries. In response, they insist that it is not the United States' job to take care of the whole world, or that U.S. citizens should be taken care of before immigrants. Through the transnational ethnographic perspective engaged in this book, however, it becomes clear that the United States bears a large degree of responsibility for the arrival of those typically deemed unwelcome, after years and years of political, economic, and military intervention around the globe and immigration and border enforcement policies that contribute to insecurity and more migration. Incarceration and expulsion of immigrants are also justified by narratives that immigrants are criminals, that they forfeit their rights when they enter the United States illegally, and that they come to reap benefits that they don't earn. But these narratives of criminality, too, unravel with better understanding of how policies have developed and how they are enacted unevenly through time and space and among different groups of people. It becomes clear that immigration debates and laws—historically and today—have played a key role in criminalizing and racializing certain populations. Deportation and detention are revealed as part of a self-reinforcing loop: a particular group of immigrants is targeted by immigration enforcement, so members of that group are treated and made visible as criminals, so the public believes that it is morally justified and necessary to target that particular group. After tracing why and how immigration policies develop, what their actual consequences are, and who is benefiting by promoting deportation and detention today, racism and nativism emerge as undeniable drivers. In other words, who is targeted and how immigration laws are written are tightly linked to race-based ideas of American national identity. By spotlighting this often unspoken (yet fundamental) driver of deportation and detention, this book aims to disrupt typical anti-immigrant narratives and bring some supporters to revisit the validity of common justifications for these policies.

Outline

Chapter 1 sketches what a transnational ethnography of detention and deportation is, both theoretically and methodologically, and identifies Ecuador as the primary research site. Here I lay out the argument that the U.S. approach to immigration enforcement, instead of sealing and protecting U.S. borders, actually creates spatiotemporal links between the United States and Ecuador. I spell out definitions of *deportation* and *detention* that emphasize how these policies forge connections through space and time. Then I explain how key rationales driving the adoption of these policies—security and deterrence—fail to recognize these connections. Transnational ethnography, an approach that draws on feminist ideas of ethnography and embodiment, can counter these mistaken assumptions, and I explain how. Finally, the chapter provides an overview of the specific methods I used to capture the expansive spatiality of detention and deportation.

Chapter 2 takes the reader to Ecuador. Before considering how U.S. immigration enforcement policies reverberate to Ecuador, it is important to understand why Ecuadorians have migrated to the United States in the first place. We must understand that U.S. policies have shaped Ecuadorian migration to the United States since it began. This chapter traces the historical development of contemporary patterns of migration, scrutinizing political, economic, and social factors. Ecuadorians began to migrate to the United States in the 1950s, establishing networks that expanded with time and proliferated exponentially with an intense economic and political crisis in the late 1990s. It is clear the United States has played a critical role in shaping these patterns, through influence and involvement in Ecuador from the postcolonial period to the present day. The chapter then explores the causal lines between U.S. immigration enforcement policies and the booming—and now international—human smuggling industry in Ecuador. The intensification of policies intended to deter, such as transnational policing of migrants, hardening borders, and detention and deportation, are a boon to illicit industries that prey on migrants' need to move across borders.

I examine the historical, conceptual, and material infrastructure of the U.S. detention and deportation system in chapter 3. I ask, how did the United States arrive at the contemporary point in which deportation and detention are—often across political party lines—considered appropriate responses to undocumented migration? I first identify three persistent factors that have shaped the United States' reactionary, often punitive, and restrictive approach to immigration enforcement. These include the framing of immigration as a threat to national security, race-based ideas of who can be "American," and the scapegoating of immigrants in times of economic downturn. I then trace these factors through a targeted history of deportation and detention, beginning with the legal and material precedents set in the late 1800s through to the infrastructure of our current system. This historical accounting pulls out pivotal shifts, especially in the last four decades, that brought about the full-fledged institutionalization of deportation and detention. First, immigration was increasingly viewed through a "homeland" security lens that conceptually merged the idea of "immigrant as criminal" with "immigrant as terrorist." Second, policymakers unquestioningly adopted the belief that both detention and deportation work to deter immigrants. Third, a range of private and public entities and individuals came to see immigration enforcement as a profit-making opportunity and invested in strategies to develop the detention and deportation system. Particularly in the panic following the September 2001 terrorist attacks, these factors and shifts together drove an unprecedented, rapid expansion of the system.

The next two chapters explore the structure and mechanisms of the contemporary U.S. detention and deportation system. This system, today, typically projects a sense of chaos to immigrants caught up in it as well as to those on the outside: immigrants, families, advocates, and the general public. In chapter 4, I draw on my experiences in Ecuador assisting families of detained immigrants and interviews with deportees to break through the bureaucratic walls surrounding detention and deportation and explain how the detention and deportation system is organized and operates. I first walk the reader through a range of strategies

I used to "search" for detained migrants from Ecuador. Then the chapter provides an overview of the various legal paths that a detained migrant may follow between apprehension and deportation. Describing these various strategies and legal trajectories, including their inconsistencies and at times illogical operation, illustrates how and why the detention and deportation system is often perceived as impenetrable. Next, the chapter explores detention's weird spatiotemporality, by tracing and mapping how detainees can be transferred from facility to facility over widely varying periods of time.

Chapter 5 dives into how detention is experienced by those "inside" the detention system. While the collective chaos of detention and deportation may be partially the outcome of a number of uncoordinated, even accidental actions and processes, the resulting confusion and cloaking have significant consequences. In effect, the chaos works to funnel detainees toward deportation. Detainees are subject to multiple "undue processes" that curtail their access to counsel and other resources. They may also feel profoundly disoriented as a result of the dizzying number of transfers and uncertainty about how long they will be detained, at the same time as the detention system cuts off their access to family and support networks. Detainees are subjected to a constant barrage of dehumanizing conditions, including physical deprivation and forced labor. The role of the immigration industrial complex and the importance of profit making in driving the detention and deportation system are critical forces shaping detainees' experiences of detention. The chapter also examines how detention facilities—and the system as a whole—act as important sites for reinforcing dominant narratives of national identity, race, criminalization, and security.

Chapters 6 and 7 consider how detention and deportation stretch to Ecuador, contrasting policymakers' intentions and expectations regarding deterrence and security with realities on the ground in a country of migrant origin. Chapter 6 points to the irony—or, perhaps, intention, through the eyes of disciples of the deterrence paradigm—that policies enacted to protect U.S. "national security" tend to generate broad insecurity. I first focus on detention, enumerating the broad range of daily insecurities that families of detained migrants experience in Ecuador. These range from disruption of the patterns of everyday life to severe financial, material distress. Then the chapter explores the process of deportation and arrival for expelled migrants. The details of deportation are important, I suggest, because the process is one more space in which the U.S. government can attempt to dehumanize expelled immigrants and mark them as unwelcome.

Chapter 7 considers what happens after detention and deportation and interrogates the logic of deterrence that drives so much of U.S. immigration enforcement policy. I compare assumed policy outcomes with outcomes on the ground in Ecuador and argue that a mismatch occurs despite and because of the many insecurities produced by U.S. detention and deportation. I look at postdeportation realities in the everyday lives of deportees and their families.

Stress often mars returns to Ecuador, stemming from violent disruptions to the rhythms of daily life and family structures and from profound economic instability. Debt, both from economic conditions in Ecuador and directly tied to immigration, can contribute to sometimes extreme financial precarity. A wide range of everyday insecurities for deportees and their families push many Ecuadorians to migrate again, in moves that repeatedly illustrate both the shaky ground on which the deterrence paradigm rests and the links forged through detention and deportation across space and time.

In the brief final chapter, I pull together the arguments and findings presented in *Detain and Deport* and summarize how the conceptual and methodological strategies explored in this book can contribute to disrupting the turn to detention and deportation in the United States and beyond.

CHAPTER 1

A Transnational Ethnography of U.S. Detention and Deportation

I was standing off a busy street in Guayaquil, Ecuador, on a hot day in August 2009. A lumbering bus pulled off the street into the Ecuadorian Migration compound, carrying thirty-seven Ecuadorians who had just arrived after being deported from the United States. They got off the bus and lined up behind several tables. At one table, the deportees gave their identification information and answered a few questions. At another, they were reunited with possessions taken from them when they were first detained weeks or months earlier. An Ecuadorian government employee handed out small nylon knapsacks containing a few toiletry items, a thin blanket, and leaflets about government services. Deportees were also given a small sandwich and a cup of soda.

Another bus awaited to take deportees to Cuenca, about four hours away, and I climbed aboard with eighteen passengers. When the bus pulled away, there were several celebratory whoops. As we moved through Guayaquil traffic, some deportees marveled at how things had changed since they had last been there. Two men sitting near me had been in the United States for ten years. A man behind me said in perfect English that he had left Ecuador when he was fourteen years old, and he was seeing the country for the first time in sixteen years.

I pulled out my cell phone, and suddenly it seemed that everyone on the bus wanted to borrow it to announce their homecoming or to arrange a ride in Cuenca. The man next to me struggled to remember phone numbers, but eventually reached his daughter. He choked up as he told her he was back in Ecuador, to get the family together. As he handed the phone to me, he said quietly that he would only be able to recognize his children from photographs. A young woman said she would be so happy to see her children and her mother, but her husband was still detained somewhere in the United States, and she was worried about him. Other deportees talked about their experiences in U.S. detention facilities, about terrible food, denied requests to see doctors, cold rooms, and threats from guards to be put in the "hole." Many had struggled against anger, frustration, and desperation as their incarcerations stretched from weeks to months, not knowing when they would be released.

For several people on the bus, deportation was not a new experience. One young man said it was his third time. Most deportees said that they would go right back. One man explained, "What is there for me here? Nothing. I have to go back. I have to do it for my family." Throughout the trip to Cuenca, people got off at small towns and crossroads. At about 11 p.m., the bus pulled into the Cuenca terminal. The remaining riders exited into the darkened city streets—an odd, unremarkable homecoming.

▢ ▢ ▢

There is a particular spatiotemporal logic behind detention and deportation as key immigration enforcement strategies of the United States. Detention is understood as the physical containment of unwanted immigrants, and deportation as ejecting immigrants out of a national territory and ending their migration story. Both policies are intended to spread a transnational message of nonwelcome to potential migrants, deterring future migration. In other words, the logic behind detention and deportation is anchored in the idea that states are able to tightly control their borders, and it assumes a clear territorial break—in space and time—in terms of membership and belonging.

The opening anecdote from my fieldwork in Ecuador immediately refutes this logic. We see that instead of enforcing neat breaks and barriers in crossboundary movement, detention and deportation policies actually work to solidify and deepen ties between the United States and Ecuador through space and time. For many deportees, deportation is not over upon their arrival in Ecuador; in fact, it has just started, as migrants attempt to make their way in Ecuador amid great uncertainty. And deportation does not necessarily mean a permanent close to a migration journey; many deportees return to the United States, just as new migrants continue to go for the first time. However, in contrast to the reality conveyed in this anecdote, existing research and scholarship has largely been unable to shake the perception that detention and deportation work to enforce territorial borders or that they are necessary for the maintenance of a strong state.

Detention studies (Mountz et al. 2013) and deportation studies (Coutin 2015; Drotbohm and Hasselberg 2015) have emerged as important interdisciplinary fields that draw on, overlap with, and contribute to broader scholarship on immigration enforcement. Scholars have examined how and why detention and deportation have come to such prominence in the contemporary era. Some scholars see detention and deportation as products of the globally dominant political economic order (De Genova 2004; Hiemstra 2010; Peutz and De Genova 2010; Coleman and Kocher 2011), pointing to the role of capitalism (Golash-Boza 2015) and identifying neoliberal processes of privatization as a key driver

(Walters 2008b; Golash-Boza 2009; Conlon and Hiemstra 2014; Morris 2016). Other work ties the popularity of these practices to the emphasis on defining and protecting national sovereignty in the contemporary nation-state system (Walters 2002; Mountz 2010; Mountz and Hiemstra 2014; Wong 2015) or links these policies to processes of securitization and the criminalization of migration in the modern era (De Genova 2009, 2010; Zilberg 2011; Dowling and Inda 2013; Loyd, Mitchelson, and Burridge 2013; Moran, Gill, and Conlon 2013). Some of this scholarship builds on the work of theorists Giorgio Agamben and Michel Foucault to understand power, control, and the role of the state in detention and deportation. Agamben's (1998, 2005) theorizations of the "camp," spaces of exception, and bare life have been applied to practices and places of detention (e.g., Bigo 2007; Andrijasevic 2010) and to deportation (e.g., Walters 2002; De Genova 2010). Foucault's (1979, 1991, 2007) concepts of governmentality, discipline, and biopolitics have been particularly useful to scholars of detention and deportation (e.g., Bigo 2007; Peutz and De Genova 2010), especially to think through how, for example, detention performs state power and shapes how detainees see themselves (Gill 2009a, 2009b; Conlon 2010; Martin 2012; Bosworth 2014).

This scholarship has significantly advanced understanding of the causes and consequences of this detention and deportation "turn" and has provided vital ground for curbing its seemingly unstoppable momentum. Without devaluing or diminishing this work, I suggest that even the most critical scholars often inadvertently rely on—and reinforce—existing frameworks for understanding and responding to human mobility across territorial borders. As Toal (2000) notes, critical researchers can unintentionally give more life to the very target of their critique by resurrecting it, in a kind of deconstructive paradox. In this vein, in immigration scholarship there is a tendency to adhere to the nation-state scale when studying policy and to ignore the subnational and local scales, in what some have said amounts to a "methodological nationalism" (Wimmer and Schiller 2003, 576). By presenting a generally abstract picture of the border, scholarship often does not problematize who the subjects of border research are, nor where research on immigration policy takes place. Even innovative work that acknowledges the role played by immigration enforcement policy in constructing borders and ideas of belonging can reinforce the state-territorial frame through a border-centric approach. Immigration scholars may also take for granted the practices that constitute "immigration control" and in so doing limit understanding of how immigration control is exercised and experienced, as well as miss opportunities to challenge these practices (Coleman and Stuesse 2016). As long as the "doing" of detention and deportation remains relatively obscured and the belief that detention and deportation contain and separate persists, these practices will continue to be central in contemporary immigration enforcement. In addition, some scholars studying policy approach it "from above," that is, through research with those who make and implement policy and with a focus on stated intentions for policy (e.g., Peck and Theodore 2015). This can limit even critical scholars to policymakers' visions and metrics regarding a particular policy. In migration policy research, top-down approaches can involuntarily contribute to maintaining (and reinforcing) the dominance of territorial borders in policy imaginaries, as well as restricting understanding of policy outcomes.

Conscious of these risks for critical immigration scholarship, I ground *Detain and Deport* on the premise that we need to fundamentally change understandings of how detention and deportation work. This book calls for a broader lens when studying immigration policy, one not restricted or shaped by state territorial borders and centering attention on the everyday. I make the case for transnational ethnography to trace how immigration policies take shape and reverberate within and outside of the United States. Transnational ethnography is both a theoretical and methodological approach that aims to study policy "from below" by tracing policy from everyday, intimate spaces and places. This feminist approach engages both embodiment and ethnography to understand lived experiences of policy, with the goals of shaking loose the hold that state territoriality has over thinking about how immigration enforcement works, and splitting open the black box of knowledge about how it is practiced.

My transnational ethnography of U.S. detention and deportation, conducted in Ecuador, draws on research with detained migrants' families, deportees, Ecuadorian state and nonstate employees, and U.S. state and nonstate employees to broaden and deepen understanding of how U.S. immigration enforcement operates regardless of national borders. Through this approach, I argue for the reconceptualization of detention and deportation as creating spatiotemporal linkages across state borders, instead of containing or breaking them. Reframing these policies as inherently transnational means reconfiguring state power not in terms of an enforced disconnection, but instead in terms of an enforced connection between peoples and places on opposite—even nonproximate—sides of state borders.

A transnational ethnographic approach has important implications for both policymakers and scholars studying immigration enforcement. By emphasizing multiple and transnational sites of research, it contributes to disrupting frameworks of rigid territories and borders and pushes scholars to examine ways in which their work can inadvertently maintain the ideas of containment and partition that underlie detention and deportation. Transnational ethnography also facilitates more granular understanding of how these policies work in migrant origin countries as well as in the United States and why these policies are being so widely adopted today. It becomes clear that experiences of detention and deportation are not contained by detention facility walls or by national borders, and these policies bolster human smuggling networks as well as create local insecurities and instability that can galvanize new migration. This approach, too, helps fill in gaps in knowledge regarding how the complex and often opaque U.S. detention and deportation system works. We can then better recognize important influences behind today's detention and deportation turn, such as racist, nativist ideas of American national identity, financial incentives, and political ambition.

The goal for this chapter is to provide a comprehensive theoretical and methodological introduction to transnational ethnography and outline a framework for understanding detention and deportation as expansive and elastic within and across borders. I first work to destabilize the conceptual adherence to territorial borders and the false spatiotemporal imagination on which detention and deportation rest. The chapter then outlines the theoretical foundations for a transnational ethnographic approach to policy and explains how it contributes to dismantling this spatiotemporal imagination. Finally, I sketch the specific methods used in my transnational ethnography of U.S. detention and deportation policy from Ecuador.

Shifting Spatiotemporal Imaginings

Here I outline definitions of deportation and detention that emphasize the role of space and time in controlling particular populations, defining membership, and enforcing both conceptual and physical links between nation and territory. Then I examine two broad beliefs about what deportation and detention do—protect security and deter migration—and discuss how these beliefs are based on incorrect understandings of how immigration enforcement policies work in and through space and time.

(RE)DEFINING DEPORTATION AND DETENTION

Whatever the particular context in which detention and deportation are invoked—as approaches to immigration enforcement or practices and tactics of its execution—a failure to acknowledge their expansive spatiality contributes to policies that do not work as supposed, with negative consequences both for policymakers and for those subjected to these policies. I understand both deportation and detention as inherently transnational, or always operating across territorial borders, and refuse any ideas that fix and limit these practices and their consequences in time or space.

Detention is seen by geographers, among others, as "the use of space to control people, objects, and their movement" (Martin and Mitchelson 2009, 459). Martin (2015, 236) conceptualizes detention as "a lived process and a bundle of textual and embodied practices meted out through everyday enactments" and suggests that it is a "core spatial strategy" within immigration enforcement (233). Detention can be interpreted as any type of control over movement, such as through monitoring, use of check-in requirements, or even recommended behaviors (Martin and Mitchelson 2009; Conlon 2010; Mountz et al. 2013; Flynn 2016). Here, following the most common understanding in the U.S. context, I focus on immigration detention as the forced confinement of noncitizens (and sometimes citizens assumed to be noncitizens) for reasons related to their legal status of national belonging. This confinement typically takes place in designated, highly controlled, carceral facilities. The spatial reverberations of detention, however, are not contained to these facilities. For example, incarcerated detainees are connected to peoples and places beyond their site of confinement by virtue of their economic, social, and emotional relationships and networks outside the facility. Moreover, detention does (almost always) eventually end, and former detainees leave the place of confinement with various markers of detention inscribed on and carried by their bodies.

I understand *deportation* as the forced physical expulsion of an individual from one country to another. Typically, that individual is a noncitizen of the deporting country, but not always, as seen in cases in the United States of the deportation of citizens due to, for example, officials' denial of legitimate identity claims. Deportation is infused with a connective spatiotemporality. Drotbohm and Hasselberg (2015, 551) recognize that deportation "begins long before, and carries on long after, the removal from one country to another" and "crosses places and spaces, connects countries and nations" (see also Peutz 2006). I generally avoid, for the most part, the word *removal*—the official term used by the U.S. government—for several reasons. First, the practice of deportation is tied to the modern international order of nation-states and the very existence of territorial borders as a mechanism for defining and controlling populations (Walters 2002). Deportation has historically been understood as expulsion from one state to another, across territorial borders, resulting in banishment and exile (Walters 2002). Sites of exile, then, are necessary for the maintenance of state territorial borders and are strategically tied to the places from which people are exiled (Coutin 2016). Second, *removal* is a term employed by U.S. immigration officials that masks the actual practice of deportation by mixing "deportations" with "exclusions," both euphemizing deportation and making it harder to track. Third, *removal* sterilizes the violence done by and in the process of forcibly transporting someone with the stated goal of permanency from one state to another. The verb *deport* does more than "remove" to imply that the expulsion is being done by one person or group to another, that the action is not automatic or necessary, and that it requires intention and resources.

As an important point of clarification: while I often use *detention* and *deportation*" together, for example, "detention and deportation system," I do not view the two words as necessarily part of the same process, or as inevitably connected to one another. For one, as Martin (2015, 233) reminds us, "detention's primary role is often understood to be the enforcement of *deportation* . . . Yet for many, detention is part of the admission or entry process." For another, it is critically important to recognize that detention is strategically deployed in order to reach policy goals of deportation (Martin 2015). As this book explores in chapters 4 and 5, detention plays an important role in criminalizing and excluding noncitizens, as well as making it difficult for them to contest deportation (D. M. Hernández 2008; Gill 2016; Bosworth 2014; Martin 2015). By referring to the U.S. "detention and deportation system," I do not aim to normalize deportation as an automatic outcome of detention. To the contrary, my intention is to draw attention to the constructed and manufactured nature of U.S. immigration enforcement policy, or how processes are orchestrated to funnel migrants to deportation, without consideration of actual consequences of deportation.

THE FALSE SPATIOTEMPORAL LOGIC OF DETERRENCE AND SECURITY

In the expanding use of deportation and detention, assumptions of deterrence are interwoven with those of security (Mountz et al. 2013; Hasselberg 2014). These policies are supposed to bolster security by ridding the destination country of unwanted immigrants and defending sovereign borders. It is generally thought that deported migrants will remain in their countries of origin, and potential new migrants will be dissuaded. As Martin's (2012, 330) work on the efforts by Immigration and Customs Enforcement (ICE) to detain families and other vulnerable populations illustrates, "detention figures a transnational field of potential, future migrants" as policymakers use detainees' bodies to discourage entry. To some degree, then, policymakers expect—and indeed count on—consequences of these policies to expand through space and time, beyond U.S. borders. But there is a profound gap between expectations and real knowledge, and few attempts have been made to trace how detention and deportation shape daily life and choices both inside and especially outside of U.S. borders, in the short and long term. This shortsightedness is both conceptual and methodological, rooted in state-centric, territorially confined ideas of security, as well as a failure to consider consequences over time. This view, then, misses a core paradox of security-driven policies: that they tend to generate multiple insecurities, for multiple populations, within the policymaking country as well as outside it.

Security imaginaries are constructed on a fundamental privileging of some groups' security over others. The provision of security to particular members (in intentional opposition to not providing it to others) therefore links the very existence of territorial states with insecurity (Edkins 2003). Insecurity, then, is central to the general practice of statecraft (Dowler and Sharp 2001; F. Smith 2001; Hyndman 2004b). Actions taken in the name of protecting citizen security create insecurities for targeted populations, often migrants, who may understand security quite differently than states and hierarchically dominant groups (Staeheli and Nagel 2008). Nevins argues, "the production of security for 'us' in terms of immigration control is inevitably tied to the production of insecurity for others, or 'them'" (Nevins 2010, 196; Hyndman 2007; Staeheli and Nagel 2008). And especially with the post–September 11, 2001 (hereafter 9/11) adoption of the "homeland" security narrative, "the familial home/land is celebrated as a space of security" (Cowen and Gilbert 2008, 50; Kaplan 2003; Walters 2004). Through the depiction of the immigrant as Other, immigrants come to represent the inverse of, and a danger to, the American family, home, and way of life (Kaplan 2003; Walters 2004; Cowen and Gilbert 2008; Hyndman and Mountz 2008; De Genova 2009). Moreover, the concept of homeland security does additional work to heighten immigrants' daily experiences of insecurity by justifying more reactionary and extreme measures (Kaplan 2003).

Importantly, this security-insecurity paradox is also experienced by non-citizens outside U.S. borders, within the territories of origin and transit countries. In a world of high mobility and global social and economic networks, it is impossible to contain the effects of domestic actions to the domestic sphere. Security-driven policies predicated on protecting the intimate scales and spaces of the American home and family therefore generate insecurity at intimate scales and spaces outside of the United States. What's more, in the contemporary security milieu, states' efforts to protect "internal security" are no longer confined within national territorial borders. Instead, states routinely look beyond national borders in efforts to anticipate, interpret, and prevent security threats inside their own territorial borders (Bigo 2000, 2001; Mountz and Hiemstra 2012). Examples include policies made to prevent migrants and asylum seekers from ever reaching their desired destination (Collyer 2007; Hyndman and Mountz 2008), and—as critically explored in *Detain and Deport*—deportation to migrant-origin countries. Thus, security-driven immigration and border policies produce insecurity outside the state the policies were intended to protect (Golash-Boza 2015).

Transnational ethnography contests these conceptual foundations—security and deterrence—of deportation and detention. By focusing on places and people in a country of migrant origin and recognizing a range of experiences, I consider experiences beyond those referenced in dominant Western narratives, with scales "finer and coarser" (Hyndman 2004b, 315) than the nation-state. Critical awareness of the relationship between security and insecurity calls attention to contradictions between how policymakers believe "deterrence" policies work outside U.S. borders and how they really work. Certainly, deportation and detention have consequences in countries of migrant origin, as policymakers intend. But these policies do not always deter immigration, particularly because in many places human mobility has become a common recourse to address insecurity. We are able to see that policy is embodied across scales and national borders, and there is an inverse relationship between actions taken in the name of protecting the American home and "homeland" and experiences of insecurity for those who are excluded (Kaplan 2003; Cowen and Gilbert 2008; Hyndman and Mountz 2008; Staeheli and Nagel 2008; Pain 2010; Menjívar and Abrego 2012). In migrant origin countries, detention and deportation—and the threat of them—disrupt family members' daily lives to instill a constant sense of precarity and return deportees to the often unstable situations that pushed them to migrate in the first place (Menjívar 2006; Menjívar and Abrego 2012; Coutin 2016). These policies, dependent on the criminalization of immigrants and framed as necessary for maintaining the homeland security of the United States, produce insecurity precisely at the scale of the home in countries of migrant origin. Through transnational ethnography, we understand that these practices extend scales and spaces of insecurity, on and through detained and deported bodies, and miss the fundamental underlying insecurities that lead to migration. We can recognize that *deterrence* is largely a misnomer for their consequences. Instead, *displacement* is more truthful (Wong 2015, 147). These policies may have a chain reaction, deepening insecurities in countries of migrant origin in ways that compound rather than ameliorate factors driving migration. And when potential migrants are dissuaded from crossing U.S. borders, an unpredictable mix of other problems develop that may, sooner or later, reverberate into the United States.

Transnational Ethnography

Transnational ethnography, as employed here, brings a distinct feminist, critical, geopolitical awareness to the study of human mobility and immobility, one that demands attention to categories such as gender, race, and class that are often ignored even in critical analysis (Kobayashi and Peake 2000; Silvey 2005; Mountz 2010). Feminist geopolitical scholars insist that attention to a range of scales—such as the body, the household, the locality, and the supranational organization—is essential for more holistic readings of security (Mountz 2004; Hyndman 2004b, 2007a, 2007b; Pratt and Rosner 2006; Staeheli and Nagel 2008). Hyndman (2007a, 249), for example, insists, "Security is as much about people, households, and livelihoods as about state sovereignty or global economy." Targeted groups' experiences of insecurity are often anchored in daily life, in the restriction of everyday activities resulting from intensified state policing activities (Staeheli and Nagel 2008; Coleman 2009; Hasselberg 2014). Transnational ethnography as a methodological and theoretical approach thus rests on the idea that a multiscalar perspective is key to assessing the actual consequences, as opposed to those desired or assumed, of detention and deportation, and it draws on the strategies of embodiment and ethnography.

As a research strategy, the concept of embodiment "centers the body . . . in the analysis of complex processes as social and geographical worlds are made and experienced" (Dyck 2011, 358). Researchers employing embodiment consider ways in which phenomena are experienced by bodies as they influence and are incorporated into daily life. I draw in particular on the rich work in feminist geography that focuses on scales and spaces often overlooked by traditional research methods, those regarded as too banal or private to merit consideration. Feminist geographers have engaged the body as a principal scale of analysis to study complex social, economic, and political processes (Pratt 1998, 2004; Moss and Dyck 2002; Wright 2006; Dyck 2011). I am particularly interested in the use of embodiment as a tool for studying the state, institutions, and policy (Mountz 2004, 2010). Embodied political analyses endeavor to identify and understand how laws and discourses associated with them are given form, become lived experiences, and shape people's everyday realities (Nast and Pile 1998; Pratt 1998; McDowell 1999; Nelson 1999; Dowler and Sharp 2001; Hyndman 2004b; Mountz 2004, 2010; Lind and Williams 2012).

Ethnography is a methodological strategy attractive to researchers interested in exploring "the tissue of everyday life" (Herbert 2000, 551; Katz 1996; Megoran 2006; Mountz 2010; Billo and Mountz 2015) and "transgressing boundaries" (Katz 1996, 171). For Coutin (2016, 12), ethnography can be seen "less as a 'research method' than as a way of knowing." Ethnography demands attention to individual stories, the body, and daily life (Dodds 2001; Dowler and Sharp 2001; Mountz 2004, 2010; Billo and Mountz 2015). Interpretations of what exactly constitutes ethnography vary from discipline to discipline, but it is broadly understood to employ close observation—and methods such as interviews, participant observation, and detailed fieldnotes—to access "the *processes* and *meanings* that undergird sociospatial life" (Herbert 2000, 550). By drawing on personal experiences, taking emotions into account, and privileging the knowledge of the "researched," the ethnographic researcher does not just record what he or she sees, but also reinterprets and adds to its meaning in ways that produce new knowledge.

While ethnography has long been employed in a variety of disciplines, it is a relatively novel tool for understanding the state and policy (Herbert 2000; Mountz 2004, 2010; Megoran 2006; Billo and Mountz 2015). By "shatter[ing] the hard surface of officiality" (Heyman 1995, 264–265), ethnographic methods have the potential to pry open the state on an intimate level, revealing ways in which it is diversely constituted and contested (Mountz 2004, 2007, 2010), as well as the varied, subjective, and often contradictory range of influences shaping how the state manifests in daily life (Gupta 1995; Heyman 1995; Herbert 2000; Hansen and Stepputat 2001; Mountz 2007, 2010). Consequently, as Herbert (2000, 555) posits, "The veneer of a seamless, transcendent entity is stripped away via intensive analysis, to reveal the processual, messy and ever-contingent reality of everyday state action." Ethnography thus takes on the way the state positions and narrates its policies and actions by providing multiple, alternative lenses. Ethnography therefore offers critical scholars of policy a methodological approach with the potential to avoid the deconstructive paradox (Toal 2000) of unintentionally reproducing the state's framing of immigration enforcement and the spatiotemporal assumptions on which it rests.

A truly ethnographic lens on policy expands inquiry beyond elite discourses and brings into focus those who actually experience policy (Megoran 2006). Simply claiming the use of ethnography does not make research ethnographic (Billo and Mountz 2015). For example, Peck and Theodore (2015) state that they conducted ethnographic research on "fast policy," or the worldwide spread of particular approaches to social and labor market policies. Relying principally on interviews conducted with policymakers, this work does little to assess policy consequences for those experiencing policy. While it provides an important analysis of how and why particular policies are adopted by states, this work does not address the "tissue of everyday life" (Herbert 2000, 551). It presents, instead, a largely uniscalar—and therefore partial—view of policy (Mountz 2010), accepting and inadvertently reinforcing state logics. Ethnography that actually traces policy from those who intimately experience it can offer a differently textured understanding, one that has the possibility of contesting state narratives. As De León writes (2015, 43), "By focusing the ethnographic lens on the migrant experience, we can start to add a graphic reality to federal policy discourse."

Ethnography is not an inherently feminist approach; it is the "conscious drawing on feminist theory" in the linking of theory and practice that makes ethnographic inquiry feminist (Dyck 1993, 53). Feminist scholars conducting ethnographies of the state and political power have drawn on the idea of institutional ethnography as developed by feminist sociologist Dorothy Smith (1987). Understanding institutions as dispersed and the power of institutions as traceable through situated experiences and institutionally produced texts, researchers employing institutional ethnography can uncover ways in which political and institutional power plays out in daily life (Mountz 2004, 2007, 2010; Billo and Mountz 2015). This attention to the scale of the body "reveals processes, relationships, and experiences otherwise obstructed" (Mountz 2004, 328). Institutional ethnography "has explicit critical or liberatory goals in its exploration of processes of subordination" (Billo and Mountz 2015, 200) that enmesh well with my goals of disrupting detention and deportation policies.

My approach to U.S. detention and deportation policies draws on both institutional ethnography and embodiment, which, used in concert, extend political analysis beyond the scale of the state and shift focus to people and the ways in which they experience state policies. My approach, however, endeavors to open access to institutions and policies previously closed to researchers. The conduct of institutional ethnography is limited to institutions to which researchers can obtain access; it requires, at least to some extent, that the state allows an entry point for collecting information through which power can be traced. The institutions of state immigration enforcement can be notably difficult to research ethnographically. Not only do these institutions actively refuse and even obstruct access, but their practices are uneven, often dispersed into mundane, seemingly unremarkable events, and challenging to verify because criminalized immigrant populations are pitted against law enforcement agencies (Coleman and Stuesse 2016). The practices of detention and deportation, and the institutions carrying them out, are notoriously slippery to researchers. In addition to the state's intentional blocking of entry, I suggest that this slipperiness is due to the ingrained acceptance of territorial thinking about how these policies work. That is, scholars' efforts to fully trace the operation and effects of these policies are thwarted by their adherence to the idea that detention and deportation operate according to border logics and effectively accomplish spatiotemporal containment and exile. They therefore are unable to pry open these institutions, provide alternate assessments, and contest dominant narratives. In my approach, in contrast, I trace the bodies detained and moved by these policies to create a new point of access to the institutions of detention and deportation where one did not previously exist. I seek to parse out how specific policies are embodied through attention to spaces and times where these policies are experienced, irrespective of state boundaries and dominant assumptions. I focus on how the intended targets of detention and deportation—migrants and their broader communities—experience policy. Instead of studying institutions from a privileged point within, this approach comes at institutions from outside, an outside that refuses to be defined and limited by territorial borders.

Building on Mountz's development of a methodology for a "transnational ethnography of the state" (Mountz 2007, 2010), I call my approach transnational ethnography of policy. I focus on policy by bringing together research with detained migrants' families and deportees in a country of migrant origin with research on the people influencing and enacting detention and deportation policies in a migrant destination country.[1] *Transnational*, to me, captures the idea of continuous mobility and the contemporary instability of migrant settlement (e.g., Xiang, Yeoh, and Toyota 2013) better than other popularly used terms such as *international*. *Transnational*, then, is employed to emphasize research across space, to signal the inherent unterritoriality of policy, and to question neat ideas of distinct, containable nation-states, as well as the idea that bodies within them can and should be immobile.

Transnational ethnography of policy offers a powerful methodological tool for researching seemingly mundane policies whose effects supersede national borders and for bringing academic and public attention to how immigration policies actually work. I am not suggesting that the use of ethnography to study immigration is new; in fact, ethnography is a frequent tool in migration studies.

There is a strong precedent of ethnographic research on migration using trans-national frames, often paying attention to countries of migrant origin and destination (e.g., Mountz and Wright 1996; Menjívar 2000; Mountz 2010; Boehm 2012; Abrego 2014; De León 2015), including important studies of the consequences of detention and deportation (e.g., Fischer 2013, 2015; Golash-Boza 2015; Coutin 2016; Drotbohm and Hasselberg 2015). Drotbohm and Hasselberg (2015) emphasize that ethnographic perspectives reveal how deportation extends through space and time, regardless of the placement of marked national borders or expectations of the territorial limits of belonging. My emphasis here is on the power of feminist, ethnographic methods to study policy both within and outside of U.S. borders, thus extending previous ethnographies of the state in several critical ways. Earlier work conducted under the name of state ethnography has been (for the most part) geographically located inside the physical boundaries of the state under scrutiny (e.g., Gupta 1995; Heyman 1995). Here, by applying ethnographic methods to a policy, I stretch the siting and analytic possibilities of state ethnography. Like previous work, this ethnography of policy focuses on the actions of bureaucrats and policy design (e.g., Gupta 1995; Heyman 1995; Mountz 2004, 2007, 2010; Bosworth 2014; Gill 2016). As methodological additions, my ethnography of a policy also includes attention to ways in which policy is experienced outside the policymaking state's borders, by people who are not members of the state performing the policy.

My project, with its simultaneous, intimate attention to the United States and Ecuador, analyzes the form and functioning of the U.S. detention and deportation system and its geopolitical reverberations through time and space. By engaging ethnographic methods in Ecuador on U.S. detention and deportation, *Detain and Deport* breaks through obstructionist barriers surrounding the detention and deportation system and also pulls back the curtain on how the system routinely and regularly produces serious harms in countries of migrant origin. In other words, transnational ethnography brings academic and public attention to how detention and deportation actually work, making critical links between what goes on inside U.S. detention facilities and cross-territorial consequences. In so doing, it adds to existing knowledge on U.S. immigration enforcement policies, further fostering the development of a multiscalar, multisited understanding of both detention and deportation. My approach also provides additional attention to migrants' families and communities—especially the understudied consequences of detention in countries of origin—and facilitates an assessment of policy outcomes alongside stated policy rationales.

Additionally, by anchoring my research at the level of the practices and everyday processes that constitute what is often mistaken as the state and state power, as well as centering research conducted outside the policymaking state, I illuminate a paradoxical relationship between macro-level conceptualizations of security and micro-level experiences of insecurity. This approach also triggers new and different measures regarding the success of security-driven policies. My use of embodiment to study policy counters the apparent opacity of detention and deportation by considering the role of individuals' actions and decisions in policy implementation (Heyman 1995; Mountz 2004, 2010). I build understandings of how laws, ideas, and narratives linked to security imaginaries are fleshed out, turned into personal experience, and shape people's lives. Furthermore, transnational ethnography shows that despite and because of the daily insecurities produced, detention and deportation do not work as effective deterrents to migration. In fact, and contrary to the fundamental rationale of punitive immigration policies, detention and deportation are linked to return—and new—migration to the United States.

Methods for a Transnational Ethnography of Policy

My research methods include participant observation, interviews, and document and media review. These methods do not in and of themselves constitute ethnography or, especially, transnational ethnography. What makes my project a transnational ethnography is the way in which I harness these methods to understand how U.S. immigration policies are embodied at multiple scales and in diverse sites. I examine how the U.S. detention and deportation system is organized and operated, while simultaneously tracing how these policies are materialized outside of U.S. borders, in a country of migrant origin, in daily life.[2]

Ecuador today has a population of nearly 16 million people. Ecuadorians have been migrating to the United States in significant numbers since the 1970s. The U.S. census puts the number of Ecuadorians living in the United States now at almost 450,000 (Jokisch 2014), though unofficial estimates are typically much higher. Today, Ecuador is the eighth highest receiver of immigrants deported from the United States (U.S. DHS 2017).[3] The city of Cuenca, Ecuador (population of around 400,000), serves as the regional metropolitan hub for the Andean provinces of Azuay and Cañar (see map 1). While today people migrate internationally from all over Ecuador, due to historic and contemporary migration patterns, "the greater Cuenca region is Ecuador's emigration system writ large" (Whitten 2003, 10).

Between November 2008 and August 2009, I lived in Cuenca, with occasional short trips to Quito and Guayaquil.[4] In January 2009, I began to volunteer at the Casa del Migrante, House of the Migrant, an agency opened by the municipal government of Cuenca in 2007 that is charged with aiding migrants and their families.[5] I worked with Carmen Alvarado, the lawyer in charge of Legal Assistance at the time. People came in to Legal Assistance with a variety of inquiries, including questions about obtaining visas, problems paying migration debts, and issues with human smugglers. The most common requests, how-

MAP 1. Ecuador, with primary region in which research was conducted indicated

ever, came from family members asking for help acquiring information about Ecuadorian migrants detained in the United States. Before I arrived, Carmen usually handled these inquiries by sending an email to an Ecuadorian consulate in the United States or to the Ecuadorian Ministry of Foreign Relations—and she rarely received replies. Carmen quickly put me to work addressing these requests.

Four to five days per week, I would set up my laptop computer in an unused meeting room, connect to the Casa's wireless internet, and open the calling program Skype. During my eight months at the Casa, I worked on over eighty-five cases of detained migrants. While some of the family members seeking assistance came into the Casa only once, others returned repeatedly and checked in frequently while we pursued information for them. My efforts to "search" for detained migrants entailed hundreds of phone calls to ICE offices and detention facilities, private detention centers, and county prisons. Personnel with whom I spoke included ICE officers, county jail officers and administrators, private jail facility contractors, social workers, police officers, lawyers, and members of activist groups working to support immigrants in detention and deportation proceedings.

This volunteer work at the Casa became the cornerstone of my ethnographic approach, inviting a new gaze at the U.S. state and its policies. A primary method was participant observation, an ethnographic method "concerned with developing understanding through being part of the spontaneity of everyday interactions" (Kearns 2000, 108). By producing data via the researcher's personal experiences and impressions, it is a key method for "access[ing] embodied forms of knowing" (Nairn 2002, 150). Participant observation can also be particularly useful for studying the state (Gupta 1995; Megoran 2006; Mountz 2007). My efforts to locate and follow the cases of detained Ecuadorians critically contributed to my understanding of how detention and deportation are embodied, both in the United States and in Ecuador. My work with family members allowed me to observe firsthand how U.S. policy infiltrates and influences life in Ecuador.[6] I witnessed a range of daily experiences of detention-related insecurity. At the same time, through verbal interactions with system personnel, I learned about day-to-day operations, inconsistencies in the system, and actors involved.[7]

Interviews were another important component of my transnational ethnography. Researchers conduct interviews to examine the complexities inherent to behavior, gain access to a range of perspectives and experiences, and fill gaps in knowledge left by other methods; it is a method that potentially empowers and honors participants (Bloom 1998; Dunn 2000). The data gathered through my interviews served as important windows into both how U.S. detention and deportation policy is enacted and what consequences result from it in Ecuador.

I conducted semistructured interviews with two major groups: people who worked with migration in Ecuador in some capacity and people who had been deported from the United States.[8] Interviewees in the first group totaled twenty-five and included municipal government employees and elected officials in Cuenca and surrounding cities and towns; religious leaders; employees of federal, regional, and local groups; Ecuadorian federal government employees in Cuenca, Quito, and Guayaquil, and one ICE official at the U.S. embassy in Quito.[9] My goal for these interviews was to better understand the Ecuadorian government's approach to migration, the relationship between the U.S. and Ecuadorian governments in matters of migration, U.S. government activities in Ecuador concerning migration, and Ecuadorian perceptions of U.S. detention and deportation.

The second set of interviews, of forty deportees, was planned and conducted as a joint effort with the Casa del Migrante between March and August of 2009. Carmen Alvarado and I collaborated with the goal of, in addition to generating data for my specific research project, producing information of use to the municipality and other Ecuadorian agencies and organizations working with migration issues. Carmen made the initial contacts with many of the interviewees, I conducted the interviews, and together we prepared a summary report of findings that was presented at a press conference at the Casa in December 2009 (I participated from the United States via Skype). Participants had been deported from the United States between April 2008 and August 2009.[10] My interviews of deportees were more structured than those of the first group in order to establish patterns and provide a basis for comparison of deportees' experiences.[11] Most deportees were contacted through the family members who came to the Casa seeking assistance while they were detained. Carmen's assistance was critical to making these contacts. We attempted to contact approximately seven migrants for every interview that took place.

Interviews of people who worked with migrants and issues of migration generally reflected more systemic consequences of the policy in Ecuador, as well as national, regional, and community responses. Interviews of deportees provided lenses into ways in which detainees embody detention and deportation policy, how genealogies of immigration enforcement in the United States shape detainee interactions with system personnel, and transnational reverberations after deportation at the scales of the individual, household, and community. Interviews, together with participant observation, also facilitated assessment of actual policy consequences alongside stated policy objectives.

A third primary research method for this project was analysis of Ecuadorian and U.S. news media and government documents. I reviewed, on an almost daily basis between July 2007 and December 2009, three Cuenca-based newspapers available online, scanning for articles or announcements regarding migration.[12] Research also included regular perusal of U.S. online media and government websites for news and information regarding immigration policies and laws, and websites with information pertinent to the larger research project, such as sites of Ecuadorian government agencies and organizations and those of migrant associations and organizations that support migrants and their families in some capacity. In addition, in Ecuador I collected a variety of documents that had to do with Ecuadorian migration, such as government propaganda, government and NGO brochures, and conference papers and agendas. Review of all these documents deepened my understanding of migration-related events, debates, and responses at multiple scales in Ecuador. It fostered a sense of the many ways in which migration permeates daily life in Cuenca, and it was critical in my efforts to understand the experiences of detained and deported migrants and their families. It also facilitated my interpretation of ways in which people working in migrant detention talk about and interact with detained migrants.

Finally, the strategy of data analysis I employ is consistent with the idea of transnational ethnography, for the way in which it relies on a careful assembly of a variety of lenses. To establish patterns as well as to organize and process the large amount of data collected, I coded research notes, interview transcripts, and documents collected. I constructed tables and made maps. I draw on work by other researchers, on relevant bodies of theory, and on a wide range of reports. Fieldwork is spatially and temporally extended through the process of analysis and "writing up" the project. As Coutin (2005, 202) observes, "the moment of writing thus becomes part of the moment of fieldwork." Indeed, my understanding and interpretation of fieldwork conducted in 2008 and 2009 has shifted along with the intensification of detention and deportation in the U.S. policies since then.

Conclusion

Both a methodological and a conceptual approach to immigration enforcement policy, transnational ethnography broadens the places and scales of analysis employed when considering ways in which immigration policies work. My transnational ethnography of policy, conducted in and from Ecuador, brings together research on policymakers and policymaking in the United States with research on people in a country of migrant origin directly living the consequences of the policies made. By foregrounding the reality that policies do not adhere to territorial borders, it shows that detention and deportation create spatiotemporal linkages across borders. This approach contributes to disrupting taken-for-granted assumptions regarding how detention and deportation work and with that the state-territorial frame that sustains and animates these policies. Transnational ethnography thus fundamentally challenges how policymakers think about detention and deportation and suggests that we must rethink what detention and deportation are and do, from the ground up. Policymakers, and often scholars, do not recognize that policies such as deportation and deterrence have more of a displacement effect than one of deterrence. Such alterations in understanding can contribute to shifting the debates around detention and deportation.

Transnational ethnography has a number of broader implications for the generation of knowledge about policy. First, it calls for a transnational approach to the study of policies typically considered to be domestic public policies. Second, it offers a model for bringing together bottom-up and top-down approaches in the study of policy, for pairing data on policymakers and policymaking with data on those who experience policy. Third, it deploys feminist, ethnographic methods to explore the logics and consequences of public policy "from below." To be clear, I am not suggesting all researchers of immigration policy should begin their projects outside of the policymaking country. Instead, I posit that transnational ethnography can expand critical researchers' methodological toolboxes in valuable ways, by pushing scholars to seek out new methodological strategies to policy that refuse territorially grounded ideas of state power, open access to apparently closed institutions, and incorporate attention to the intimate spaces of home and community.

The next chapter immediately stretches our spatial and temporal perspective on U.S. immigration and immigration enforcement. It traces the historical development of the contemporary relationship between Ecuador and the United States, with a focus on the role U.S. policies play in shaping Ecuadorian migration patterns and lived realities.

CHAPTER 2

Ecuadorian Migration, U.S. Policy, and Human Smuggling

Santiago had just been deported from the United States for the second time. I interviewed him at his home in a rural sector outside Cuenca, together with his wife, Rosa, and his mother-in-law. Santiago had reached sixth grade before leaving school to farm full-time on his family's land. He and Rosa married as teenagers and eventually had nine children. Even though Santiago often took on temporary labor jobs to supplement his farm income, his family still struggled to get by.

One day, a woman who lived nearby paid them a visit. She was a *coyota*, a human smuggler, and she painted a pretty picture of how Santiago would easily make a lot of money if he just went to the United States. She assured him she had the contacts and experience to get him there safely and quickly, for just $15,000. They could borrow the money for the journey against their land.

Santiago and Rosa talked it over. In Cuenca and the surrounding areas, evidence of the rewards of migration is everywhere, like flashy four-wheel drive trucks and big new homes. They decided it would be worth the investment. "I decided to go," said Santiago, "because of the economy here. To see if we could help our children get a better education. Also, to save for our old age." Rosa added, quietly, "Because of poverty."

▢ ▢ ▢

Most immigrants do not easily make the decision to migrate, nor do they choose their destination arbitrarily. This chapter focuses on why Ecuadorians migrate to the United States. While there is a panorama of reasons, it becomes clear that in Ecuador, as in immigrant origin countries around the world, the policies of the destination country play a central role, both historically and today. In fact, the long-standing, intimate relationship between U.S. policies and Ecuadorian migration contributes to the fact that Ecuadorians continue to emigrate in the face of continually more punitive and restrictive U.S. immigration enforcement strategies. Important, too, is how this relationship has contributed to the growth of an increasingly sophisticated and international human smuggling network.

The mismatch between policy objectives and actual geopolitical reverberations is a theme that continues into the focused study of detention and deportation in the chapters to follow.

I take a "synthetic approach" to understanding Ecuadorian migration, one that draws on a wide range of theories and perspectives to gain a comprehensive understanding of reasons (Massey, Durand, and Malone 2002, 21). My approach is partially informed by a substantial subset of literature in traditional migration studies that explores causes of international human mobility. For example, neoclassical economic models see migration as the result of rational decision making based on maximizing personal wealth. World systems theory explains migration as a consequence of the expansion of markets into new areas. Social capital theory suggests that migration leads to more migration, as future migrants draw on the connections and lessons of previous migrants. Ideas of cumulative causation posit that as migration patterns become entrenched, migration flows are only more likely to increase (Massey, Durand, and Malone 2002). Scholars also frequently frame migration in terms of push-pull factors, the "push" factors determined by conditions and events in a country of origin, such as poverty, violence, and environmental disaster, and "pull" factors referring to things that draw migrants to a particular destination country, such as employment, security, and family ties (Koser 2007).

In addition to these classic theories and framings, my synthetic approach to comprehending Ecuadorian migration relies heavily on critical scholarship that interrogates how constructed categories create difference and divide in the service of power. My work is grounded in feminist perspectives that not only center gender in analyses of why people migrate; they also call attention to scales and places previously ignored and foreground the experiences and voices of a broad range of individuals (e.g., Lawson 1998; Hyndman 2004a; Silvey 2005). Scholarship in queer studies reveals how migration decisions and experiences are inextricable from heteronormative family forms and calls into question the role of taken-for-granted identity categories and the structures that sustain them (e.g., Luibhéid 2014). I am also influenced by an interdisciplinary range of critical scholarship that centers race, ethnicity, and class and views migration as integral to global economic systems, from colonial relationships to contemporary neoliberal global capitalism. Restricted human mobility across national borders is linked to the relatively unrestricted flows of capital, with racialized differences as a lynchpin in facilitating and justifying inequalities (e.g., Radcliffe 1999; Nevins 2008; Golash-Boza 2015). Collectively, these critical perspectives in migration studies provide important tools for focused study of the role of U.S. policies in Ecuadorian migration.

Ecuadorian migration can be understood as an example of mobility from less to more economically successful countries, a logical outcome of the formation of transnational ties related to trade, militarization, political forms, and cultural influence (Sassen 1988; Castles and Miller 2003). The critical synthetic lens employed in this chapter fosters additional scrutiny of U.S. policies and influence. For example, the decision of Santiago, the Ecuadorian with whom we began this chapter, to migrate to the United States was made for a number of reasons. The most obvious reason is poverty in Ecuador contrasted with seemingly unlimited opportunity in the United States. This poverty is linked to how colonial and neo-colonial structures and foreign influence have critically shaped contemporary Ecuador. Today, relationships of interdependence are generated between states against the backdrop of globalization (Sassen 1988; Bauder 2006; Golash-Boza 2015). Scholars identify the critical role of U.S. trade policies in the last forty years in producing Latin American migration flows to the United States, with recognition of the importance of neoliberal trade and economic policies (e.g., Bacon 2004; Nevins 2010; Golash-Boza 2015). Santiago's decision was also influenced by other U.S. policies. Ecuador has been of interest to the United States, historically and today, for reasons that include the objective of control over its neighbors in the Western Hemisphere, protection of U.S. economic interests, and its strategic geographical location. Consequently, U.S. economic, political, and immigration policies have long made the borders between the two countries fuzzy and permeable, in ways that profoundly shape contemporary patterns of Ecuadorian mobility.

A critical focus on policy also highlights outcomes antithetical to stated policy goals. Another key factor in Santiago's decision was the smuggler's act of recruitment. The robust smuggling industry that has developed in Ecuador would not exist without U.S. border and immigration enforcement policies that produce ever more robust illicit operations to get around them. There is a clear link between hardening territorial borders and increasing illicit activities (Heyman and Smart 1999; Andreas 2000; Abraham and van Schendel 2005). Scholars argue that the state plays a key part in the development of human smuggling operations, emphasizing the feedback relationship between heightened immigration enforcement and smuggling (Salt and Stein 1997; Chin 1999; Andreas 2001; Koser 2001, 2008; Kyle and Dale 2001; Kyle and Koslowski 2001; Abraham and van Schendel 2005; Doomernik and Kyle 2004; Spener 2004; Mountz and Hiemstra 2012). Instead of deterring extralegal migration, more border and immigration policing forces smuggling routes to more remote areas, increases smuggling fees, and generally heightens risk (Kyle and Dale 2001; Spener 2001; Cornelius and Lewis 2005). Restrictive policies also drive more people into smuggling and related activities and lead to large, sophisticated, and criminally oriented operations (Andreas 2000, 2001; Kyle and Dale 2001; Spener 2001). A critical approach to understanding migration illustrates the role of U.S. policies in the evolution of Ecuador as a global smuggling center. It also sets the stage for discussions in chapters to come regarding why detention and deportation are largely unsuccessful as deterrence strategies.

This chapter first sketches the history of Ecuadorian migration to the United States, examining global to local factors, with detailed attention to the exponential increases in the number of Ecuadorian emigrants in the last two decades. It then explores how U.S. policies intended to fortify U.S. borders and police migration farther and farther away from its own territory have fueled the human smuggling industry in place today.

Tracing Immigration from Ecuador to the United States

The critical ways in which foreign governments have influenced Latin American migration can be traced all the way back to post-independence relationships. At the end of colonial rule in the early 1800s, Latin American countries were urged by the United States and Europe to develop commodities for export (Hillman 2001). In Ecuador, the subsequent transformations in national economies had two important consequences. First, the Ecuadorian economy became dependent on and oriented to foreign markets. Second, this development of export-based industries encouraged previously unknown domestic labor mobility between the highlands, Amazon region, and coast in the production of, for example, cacao, sugar cane, bananas, and, in later decades, petroleum, shrimp, and flowers (Jokisch 1997; Camacho 2004). After World War II and the devastation wrought by the global economic crash, economists advised Latin American governments to develop industries that produced goods for consumption within their own countries in a strategy known as import substitution industrialization (Carriére 2001; Hillman 2001; Perreault and Martin 2005; Peet and Hartwick 2009). In Ecuador, the subsequent growth of small city-based industries spurred considerable rural to urban migration (Jokisch 1997). This widespread domestic migration laid the conceptual foundation for eventual international migration. For Ecuadorians already uprooted from their communities and families, moving abroad seemed less of a radical move than it otherwise would have been (Kyle 2000).

The first Ecuadorian migrants to the United States arrived in the 1950s from Azuay and Cañar provinces, as an immediate response to the decline of a key export-driven industry in that region: "Panama" hats (see map 1 in chapter 1). While agricultural products were the primary exports for many areas of the country, local elites in the southern Andean provinces had developed the straw hat industry—known as Panama hats due to passage of the export through Panama—beginning in the mid-1800s (Kyle 2000; Jokisch 2001; Gratton 2006). The hats enjoyed great success in international markets, particularly in the United States, and many household incomes in Azuay and Cañar came to be dependent on some aspect of their production (Kyle and Liang 2001). Then, during the Great Depression, the hat industry was among those that experienced a sharp drop, and it never recovered (Kyle 2000). The resulting destabilization of the regional economy led some hat exporters to use international connections established through the hat market to migrate to the United States in the 1950s (Jokisch 2001). These first migrants, almost entirely men, formed the roots of expanding migration networks between Ecuador and the United States (Kyle 2000; Jokisch 2001; Camacho 2004).

U.S. political involvement in Ecuador during the Cold War also set the stage for future international migration. In response to the Cuban Revolution of 1959 and fears of spreading communism, in the 1960s and 1970s the U.S. government sponsored agrarian reforms throughout Latin America (Grindle 1985). Ecuador instituted land reforms in 1964 and 1973 with the goals of preventing communist sentiment from gaining traction in the countryside, promoting capitalist modernization of agriculture, and increasing food production to feed a growing urban population (Jokish 1997; Korovkin 1997). These reforms effectively dissolved a semifeudal rural labor system, but the small parcels of land allotted to families were not sufficient to sustain a household (Jokisch 1997; Kyle 2000). More men and now women, too, around the country engaged in domestic migration to supplement meager farming incomes (Borrero and Vega 1995; Jokisch 1997; Gratton 2006) and became poised to make the leap to international mobility.

Ecuadorian emigration to the United States grew gradually for two decades, accelerated in the 1980s and early 1990s, then exploded in the late 1990s. These trends were framed by the global geoeconomic context. In the 1960s and 1970s, the world's oil dependence grew, and oil-producing countries deposited their soaring profits in banks of the Western world. Eager lenders looking to invest excess capital encouraged countries of the "developing" world, including in Latin America, to borrow heavily and offered low interest rates as an incentive (George 1988; Harper and Cuzán 2001). These countries then borrowed to finance development projects, from these banks as well as international lending organizations such as the International Monetary Fund and the World Bank. This borrowing led to the Latin American debt crisis that occurred after the worldwide oil shocks in the late 1970s, corresponding jumps in interest rates, and the 1982 oil market crash (George 1988; Harper and Cuzán 2001). The United States in particular influenced Latin American governments' responses to the crisis through direct pressure as well as its position of power in lending agencies (Gerlach 2003; Whitten 2003). Under the neoliberal capitalist banner, indebted governments were forced to prioritize repayment over domestic well-being by dismantling protections for domestic industry, privatizing public sector industries, and implementing harsh "structural adjustment" measures (Carriére 2001; Acosta, López, and Villamar 2004).

This global context shaped Ecuador's political and economic landscape. Oil had been discovered in the Ecuadorian Amazon in 1968, and Ecuador began exporting oil in 1972 upon completion of an Amazon-to-coast pipeline. Ecuador was not one of the countries depositing oil profits in Western banks, but the government that took power in 1972 borrowed significantly from these banks and international lending organizations to increase military spending, develop internal infrastructure, and implement a range of domestic subsidies (Carriére 2001). When oil markets crashed in 1982, Ecuador, like many Latin American countries, was in serious trouble (Gerlach 2003; Sawyer 2004). A devastating earthquake in 1987 resulted in additional debt (Carriére 2001; Gerlach 2003). Ecuador became increasingly beholden to foreign lenders, and the cost of servicing its external debt consumed ever greater portions of export revenues. Successive Ecuadorian governments, following neoliberal doctrine, entered a cycle of imposed austerity measures, rising inflation, and growing poverty.

The resulting everyday hardships provided strong incentives for Ecuadorians countrywide to emigrate (Carriére 2001; Marconi 2001; Acosta, López, and Villamar 2004).[1] Household incomes dropped and the cost of living increased, at the same time as many government subsidies and assistance programs were cut (Jokisch 2001). Concurrently, in the United States neoliberal ideology promoted reduced regulation of trade and business in ways that encouraged employers to search for ever-cheaper labor (Bauder 2006; Leitner, Peck, and Sheppard 2007; Peck and Tickell 2007). Ecuadorian migrants (mainly men) consistently found employment upon arrival, typically in the construction and service industries (Jokisch 2001). In Azuay and Cañar, daily struggles stood in stark contrast to displays of the material rewards of earlier migrations to the United States, such as the construction of large houses and purchase of goods such as electronics and clothes (Jokisch 2001; Jokisch and Pribilsky 2002). Consequently, by 1990 approximately 34 percent of all households in south-central Ecuador reported that at least one family member had left for the United States, and more women began to emigrate (Borrero and Vega 1995; Jokisch 1997; Jokisch 2001). Migration to the United States was becoming routine for many Azuay and Cañar families (Jokisch and Pribilsky 2002).

Then, in the late 1990s, Ecuador experienced what was known as *la crisis*. Already by the mid-1990s, financial and political circumstances were precarious. The deficit, unemployment, and inflation rates were at record highs, while oil prices reached record lows, and debt servicing consumed 41 percent of the government's budget (Carriére 2001). Ecuador engaged in an expensive border war with Peru in 1995, and in 1997 and 1998 El Niño storms caused costly damages to infrastructure (Camacho 2004; Jokisch and Kyle 2008). The political situation was likewise characterized by instability. Corruption was on the rise, and public protests increased (Carriére 2001; Gerlach 2003). The country made its way through a rapid succession of presidents. In 1998, President Jamil Mahuad, already unpopular after being elected by a razor-thin margin, initiated a new round of austerity measures in an effort to keep paying Ecuador's external debt (Carriére 2001; Acosta, López, and Villamar 2004). In 2000, Mahuad began a national process of *dolarización*, or currency conversion to the U.S. dollar, a glaring example of the fuzziness of borders between the two countries in its creation of total dependence on U.S. monetary policies. And while dollarization did eventually stabilize the economy, it was immediately disastrous for citizens across the economic spectrum. Inflation jumped as high as 300 percent (Acosta, López, and Villamar 2004). Nationwide protests led by indigenous leaders forced Mahuad out of office on January 21, 2001 (Gerlach 2003). Federal government power was temporarily held by a group of army colonels, but under U.S. pressure they stepped down, and the former vice president took power (Carriére 2001; Gerlach 2003). Both the Ecuadorian economy and government were in turmoil.

The cumulative effect of this crisis was devastating for Ecuadorians of all classes. Between 1995 and 2000, Ecuadorians experienced the most rapid and extreme impoverishment in the history of Latin America as the proportion of the population living in poverty grew from 34 to 71 percent (Acosta, López, and Villamar 2004). Rising poverty was accompanied by a general deterioration in human security, experienced as the closure of businesses; employment loss; erosion of working conditions and worker rights; and decreased government spending on health, education, housing, and community development. Ecuadorians' daily lives were marked by increased crime, violence, and precariousness (Acosta, López, and Villamar 2004).

Emigration rates grew explosively. From 1999 to 2005, between 1.4 and 1.6 million Ecuadorians left the country (Herrera, Moncayo, and Garcia 2012, 35). The view of migration as a logical escape mechanism was no longer limited to the region around Cuenca, as migrants began to leave from all over the country, from a range of classes and professional backgrounds, and including women as often as men (Acosta, López, and Villamar 2004; Kyle and Jokisch 2005; Jokisch and Kyle 2008).

For many who left as part of this exodus, Europe, not the United States, became the new "promised land" (Jokisch and Pribilsky 2002, 82). This expansion of migration to Europe occurred against the backdrop of Europe's aging population, general upward socioeconomic mobility, and changing roles of women — factors that created a shortage of unskilled laborers particularly in southern Europe (Camacho 2004; Cornelius 2004; Calavita 2005; Herrera 2006). Spain was the primary European destination, with smaller numbers of Ecuadorians going to Italy, France, and the Netherlands (Jokisch and Pribilsky 2002). Due to the demand for domestic and personal care services, initially more women than men migrated to Europe (Camacho 2004; Cornelius 2004; Herrera 2006). Also, while lower-skilled Ecuadorians from more rural areas led migration to the United States, the 1990s crisis spurred professionals to migrate first to Europe, followed by Ecuadorians from lower educational backgrounds (Marrero 2004). By 2005 approximately 500,000 Ecuadorians were in Spain (Actis 2006), and as many as 120,000 (Jokisch 2007) in Italy.

The United States, however, remained the most common destination for Ecuadorians from Azuay and Cañar provinces, due to the networks already in place.

Conservative estimates (based on the U.S. census) suggest that between 2000 and 2010, the Ecuadorian population in the United States more than doubled, from 260,559 to 564,631 (Herrera, Moncayo, and Garcia 2012). Estimates by the Ecuadorian government and media articulated a significantly higher number, of at least one million (Marrero 2004; Jokisch 2007).

Following historic patterns, the majority of Ecuadorians went to the New York City area, but others also settled in and around the cities of Chicago, Columbus (Ohio), Los Angeles, Miami, Minneapolis, Boston, and Philadelphia (Kyle and Jokisch 2005; FLACSO 2008; Jokisch and Kyle 2008). During the crisis-spurred exodus, the numbers of Ecuadorian women and men in the United States evened out (FLACSO 2008). Ecuadorians in the United States continued to find employment relatively easily (Gratton 2006).[2] The wage differential was profound, especially in the context of the Ecuadorian crisis; Kyle (2000, 42) noted "an Ecuadorian in New York City . . . can earn the equivalent of the Ecuadorian monthly wage in one day, or even a few hours."

Today, between 1.5 million and 2 million Ecuadorians live abroad (Jokisch 2014). Research for this book was conducted in Azuay and Cañar provinces; approximately 6 percent of Cañar's population and 3.9 percent of Azuay's have left Ecuador, ranking them as first and second for the country in percentages of migrants abroad (Herrera, Moncayo, and Garcia 2011). More detailed geographic analysis at the *cantón* level (equivalent to the U.S. county) illustrates how migration patterns have been concentrated in certain areas.[3] A comparison of remittances also reflects the importance of migration in Azuay and Cañar, which in 2010 were the second and fourth highest remittance-receiving provinces in the country (Herrera, Moncayo, and Garcia 2011).

Migration patterns from Ecuador to the United States reflect the long-standing political and economic ties between the two countries. The United States has consistently treated Ecuador's territorial borders as porous and broachable in terms of U.S. involvement. Likewise, and in a linked process, international migrants come to understand the borders between the countries as proximate and connected. In other words, the physical distance between the United States and a country of migrant origin is collapsed through years of influence and intervention.

U.S. Policies, Migration Strategies, and Human Smuggling

Approximately 70 percent of migration from southern Ecuador to the United States during and in the years immediately following the crisis was undocumented (Falconí and Ordoñez 2005). This is in stark contrast to Ecuadorians migrating to Europe during this time, who did so via legal or quasi-legal means.[4] The different migration policies of destination countries play a critical role in Ecuadorians' individual and family migration decisions and plans (Herrera 2008).[5]

Exploring Ecuadorians' strategies for reaching the United States further illustrates the immense role that U.S. policies play in migration patterns, shaping journeys, and—significantly—fueling the development and entrenchment of a human smuggling industry.

U.S. MIGRATION AND BORDER POLICING

U.S. immigration laws at the time of the crisis (and today) worked to discourage legal migration by making it extremely difficult to obtain a visa for legal entry to the United States. For work or tourist visa applications made in Ecuador, decisions to grant or not were made in person at the U.S. embassy in Quito or the consulate in Guayaquil, far from home for many Ecuadorians. Applicants were required to pay repeated, hefty, nonrefundable application fees. Then, visa applications were often denied based on subjective decisions of consular officials, hinging on an opaque range of grounds for exclusion. Even Ecuadorians with legitimate family claims became discouraged by the considerable investment of time and money required (Herrera 2008).[6] By 2008, U.S. citizens and permanent residents had to wait ten years for family reunification applications to be processed (because the number of applications filed greatly exceeded the quota permitted by the 1965 Immigration and Nationality Act) (Herrera 2008). The resulting surge of illicit migration north occurred precisely when the United States was escalating and geographically extending immigration and border enforcement efforts.

In the 1980s and 1990s, immigration to the United States from Latin America and the Caribbean grew significantly. The increasing numbers of non-European immigrants sparked xenophobia and nativism among a public that failed to recognize U.S responsibility for these new patterns of human mobility. These dynamics are unpacked in the next chapter, as are the punitive and restrictive domestic immigration policies that they unleashed. Here, we focus on how, especially in the 1990s and after the attacks of September 11, 2001, the U.S. government increasingly pursued border and immigration enforcement strategies that extend outside U.S. territorial borders, in terms of the conceptualization of the strategies' effects as well as on-the-ground activities. A belief that more policing and harsher enforcement measures would deter future migration provided the rationale for many of these strategies (Nuñez-Neto 2008; Flynn 2014; Bruzzone 2016). In 1994, the U.S. Border Patrol, under President Bill Clinton, adopted the "Prevention Through Deterrence" strategy, which aimed to push migrants away from popular border crossing spots to less hospitable territory, under the assumption that harder crossings would discourage migrants. While this strategy was first applied at the U.S.-Mexico border, it was eventually extended further south (Flynn 2014).

One strategy to extend U.S. policing was to enlist countries in the region to apprehend, detain, and deport U.S.-bound migrants through offers of financial and logistical aid (Jokisch 2001; Kyle and Liang 2001; Flynn 2002; Ramírez and Álvarez 2009; Peutz and De Genova 2010; Falconí and Ordóñez 2005; Coleman 2007b). This entailed the initiation and coordination of regional measures. In 1996, the United States led the formation of the Regional Conference on Migration (RCM, also known as the Puebla Process), creating a forum for member nations to share strategies and "best practices" for fighting migrant smuggling and to facilitate joint activities (Falconí and Ordóñez 2005). For example, Operation Global Outreach, initiated in 1997, was a coordinated effort to intercept migrants and smugglers before they reached the U.S. border (Coleman 2007b; Flynn 2002). Another part of this strategy, stepped up after 9/11, was to directly train and fund individual countries for migrant interception. Mexico increased its immigration policing on both the U.S-Mexico border and its southern border with Guatemala, consequent to the 2001 Plan Sur and the 2002 bilateral Border Partnership Action Plan (Flynn 2002; Coleman 2007b). Guatemala initiated Venceremos 2001 (We Shall Overcome), a plan to apprehend and deport migrants on their way north that was directly funded by the United States (Peutz and De Genova 2010).

A second strategy was the expansion of migrant interception activities at sea, in both geographic scope and frequency. In response to the Mariel boatlift of Cuban migrants and growing Haitian migration, the U.S. Coast Guard (USCG) mission shifted from primarily search and rescue to more of a partner with the Immigration and Naturalization Service (INS) (and later Immigration and Customs Enforcement and the Border Patrol) for purposes of drug interdiction and immigration enforcement (Palmer 2009; Flynn 2005). In 1999, the U.S. military established three "Forward Operating Locations" in Latin America: in Manta, Ecuador; El Salvador; and the Dutch Antilles (Flynn 2005).[7] After 9/11, the USCG came under control of the newly formed Department of Homeland Security (DHS), and the USCG and U.S. Navy cooperated to make migrant interception a top activity in the Eastern Pacific (Finley 2004; Flynn 2005). The United States signed bilateral agreements with at least twenty-six countries in Central and South America, which allowed the United States to patrol territorial waters of other countries and investigate suspected smuggling activities (Finley 2004; Flynn 2005; U.S. Congress 2009). While these agreements focused on counternarcotics interdiction, migrant interdiction often occurred at the same time (Finley 2004; Flynn 2005). Intercepted migrants were landed in transit countries such as Guatemala and Mexico with which the United States had agreements, and these countries then detained and deported the migrants to their country of origin (El Tiempo 2008).

These extraterritorial U.S enforcement efforts ramped up precisely as Ecuador descended into political and economic crisis. The increasing difficulty of getting to the United States likely influenced the migration decisions of the many Ecuadorians who chose Europe instead of the United States as their destination (Jokisch 2001; Marrero 2004). Most migrants leaving from Azuay and Cañar during that time, however, still chose the United States. Given the impossibility of legal migration, many of these migrants decided that contracting with a smuggler was the easiest, fastest, and often only way to reach the United States (Herrera 2008). As Kyle and Liang (2001, 208) explain, "The U.S.-Mexico border enforcement and anti-smuggling policies have done little to deter a substantial flow of illegal migrants from Ecuador." What U.S. immigration policing strategies did accomplish, instead, was to ignite the meteoric growth of the human smuggling industry and make Ecuadorian migration north more costly, dangerous, and time consuming.

EVOLUTION OF AN INDUSTRY: HUMAN SMUGGLING IN ECUADOR

The earliest Ecuadorian migrants, whatever their legal status, simply flew to the United States. When the United States began to increase entry requirements in the 1970s, undocumented migrants flew instead to Mexico, then crossed the U.S.-Mexico border by land (Jokisch 1997; Jokisch and Pribilsky 2002). The system that developed in Ecuador to facilitate these migrations served as the foundation for the much more complex industry to come. *Pasadores* assisted migrants by making travel arrangements and obtaining documents such as a falsified U.S. visa or passport or legitimate visa for Mexico. They also connected migrants with local high-interest moneylenders, called *chulqueros*, to finance the journeys (Jokisch 1997; Kyle and Liang 2001).

As the United States pressured Mexico and Central American countries to step up their enforcement practices in the late 1980s, 1990s, and 2000s, Ecuadorians' migration endeavors became progressively more complex. Increasing U.S. immigration policing abroad increased Ecuadorian demand for human smugglers, as their expertise became nearly essential to negotiate the quickly changing geography of illicit migration (Kyle and Dale 2001; Kyle and Liang 2001; Falconí and Ordoñez 2005). The pairing of Ecuadorians' need to travel with smugglers' determination to continue doing business resulted in the growth of smuggling in Ecuador at one of the fastest rates for such operations in the world (Thompson and Ochoa 2004).

Smugglers adapted to new policies designed to target particular mobility patterns by changing routes and methods. For example, after Mexican visas became difficult to obtain, U.S.-bound Ecuadorians could no longer fly to Mexico (and cross the U.S.-Mexico border from there). Smugglers started routing migrants to Central American countries either by land or air, then by land into Mexico and across the U.S.-Mexico border. At the time of *la crisis* in the late 1990s, migrants faced increasing obstacles in Central America as the United States put pressure on transit countries to step up their migration policing. A new route emerged to accommodate the surge of Ecuadorians: by sea from Ecuador to Guatemala, Nicaragua, or (until 2002) Mexico, and then north by land (Jokisch 1997; Jokisch and Pribilsky 2002; Ramírez and Álvarez 2009). The popularity of this route was reflected in the sudden jump in 1999 of Ecuadorians intercepted at sea by the U.S. Coast Guard patrolling in the Eastern Pacific (Jokisch and Pribilsky 2002; Garcés 2005; U.S. Coast Guard 2015).[8] A preferred route in 2008 and 2009 (while I conducted my fieldwork) was to fly from Ecuador to Honduras, taking advantage of a Honduran law allowing Ecuadorians to enter without a visa and then travel north by land. Alternatively, many Ecuadorians traveled all the way from Ecuador to the United States by land. With the participation of more countries in policing, there were reports of Ecuadorians being deported from Bolivia, Colombia, Costa Rica, Guatemala, Mexico, Nicaragua, and Panama (Jokisch 2001; Flynn 2002; Falconí and Ordoñez 2005; Ramírez and Álvarez 2009; Herrera, Moncayo, and Garcia 2012).

While tougher and more geographically expansive enforcement regimes did not necessarily deter migration, they did heighten risk and danger for migrants en route (Nevins 2010; Meissner et al. 2013; Slack et al. 2015; Bruzzone 2016). Many Ecuadorians migrating to the United States during the crisis and in the following years recalled experiences of fraud, robbery, and being held hostage to extract more money from their families (Thompson and Ochoa 2004; Falconí and Ordoñez 2005; Ramírez and Álvarez 2009). Some were victims of fraud even before leaving Ecuador, indebting themselves to a smuggler who disappeared with their money before the trip ever began (Falconí and Ordoñez 2005). Others reported physical abuse, inhumane conditions, hunger, dehydration, temperature extremes, and fear. Women especially faced additional risk of sexual violence (Thompson and Ochoa 2004; Camacho and Hernández 2005b; Ramírez and Álvarez 2009). Some journeys even ended in death, due to physical conditions of the journey or acts of brutality (Falconí and Ordoñez 2005). The sea route, largely out of use by 2008, was particularly deadly due to overcrowding and the use of unseaworthy vessels; hundreds of Ecuadorians died attempting that leg (Thompson and Ochoa 2004). Ecuadorian migrants also experienced the escalating violence related to gang activity in transit countries, as when an Ecuadorian was among the seventy-two migrants murdered in northern Mexico in August 2010 (AFP 2010; Archibold 2010).

Increased risk and more circuitous paths were accompanied by rising cost and more time en route. In the 1970s and early 1980s, the cost of an illicit trip to the United States was approximately $1,200 (Jokisch 1997). In 1995, smuggled migrants paid around $6,000 (Jokisch 1997); in 2001, $7,000 to $9,000 (Jokisch 2001); and in 2005, over $13,000 (Jokisch and Kyle 2008). During my fieldwork in 2008 and 2009, $15,000 was a typical price.[9] While some migrants were able to pay for their journey with funds provided by family already in the United States, the majority took out high-interest loans from local lenders, as did Santiago in the account at the beginning of this chapter. Interest rates between 5 and 8 percent monthly meant that migrants could end up owing thousands of dollars more than their original loan, making repayment a difficult, extended process (Jokisch 2001). Failed journeys led to the loss of property and homes put up as collateral.[10] While smooth trips could take as little as ten days, many migrants reported journeys of weeks or even months (Jokisch and Kyle 2008). Smugglers came to expect that some migrants would be detained and deported en route or at the U.S.-Mexico border, and they included multiple attempts as a selling point (Jokisch and Kyle 2008).[11]

With the swift development of the "business" of human smuggling (Salt and Stein 1997) in Ecuador, the country became the South American center for illicit human mobility. Ecuadorian smuggling operations grew more sophisticated, internationally connected, and entrenched. Local *coyoteros*, or coyotes, developed business relationships with a network of smugglers throughout Ecuador and then Central America and Mexico as they facilitated the increasingly complex migration journeys of more and more Ecuadorians. Rarely did an Ecuadorian smuggler travel all the way to the United States; instead, migrants were handed off from one group of smugglers to another (Kyle 2000; Thompson and Ochoa 2004; Ramírez and Álvarez 2009; De León 2015). Migrants of other nationalities began to tap into the Ecuadorian networks, as evident in reports of Peruvians, Colombians, Chinese, Nepalis, and Saudi Arabians on north-bound Ecuadorian vessels (Flynn 2002).

A number of policies implemented by leftist president Rafael Correa contributed to Ecuador's role as an international smuggling center. In 2008, Correa promoted the idea of "universal citizenship," stating that all persons have the right to free international mobility, by removing visa requirements for foreign visitors, a policy unmatched in South America. Almost immediately, international smugglers took notice, as evidenced in the arrival of approximately twelve thousand Chinese migrants in the six months after the policy change (Bowditch 2009b; Hiemstra 2012). Reports also indicated that increasing numbers of Indian and Pakistani migrants were being plugged into Ecuador's networks (Marosi and Becker 2011). While Correa's government did make some policy changes in 2010 to curtail such entries, another move in 2012 significantly lowered requirements for obtaining Ecuadorian citizenship to two years of residence (Hiemstra 2012).

With its emergence as both a leading source of South American migrants and an international smuggling hub, Ecuador made U.S. officials nervous. Americans grew increasingly concerned that dangerous migrants from Pakistan, Iran, Iraq, Afghanistan, and countries of East Africa could use Ecuador as a springboard to the United States (Bowditch 2009b; Farah and Simpson 2009; Farah 2011; Marosi and Becker 2011; Reich and Vazquez Ger 2012). The United States increased patrolling at sea in the Eastern Pacific region (also for purposes of drug interdiction) and used the U.S. base in Manta, Ecuador, for activities related to migrant interdiction (Flynn 2005).

The United States also tried to extend immigration policing within Ecuador's borders, largely through Immigration and Customs Enforcement (ICE) offices in the Quito embassy and Guayaquil consulate. ICE worked with a unit of the Ecuadorian National Police, called the Anti-Contraband Operative Unit (Cuerpo Operativo Anti-Contrabando, or COAP), in efforts to prevent trafficking, smuggling, child pornography, and prostitution. ICE periodically instructed COAP to send agents to migrant exit hotspots (i.e., certain coastal cities) in response to tips, to detain potential migrants, and to verify their identities. In these operations, non-Ecuadorians were detained and deported to their country of origin, and Ecuadorians were usually released. During one interview in 2007, I learned that in order to reduce smuggling out of Ecuador, ICE also pressured the Ecuadorian government to improve its national identity cards so that it was more difficult for foreigners to obtain an Ecuadorian identity card and use it to reach a country closer to the United States for which Ecuadorians do not need visas, such as Honduras.

U.S.-Ecuador relations progressively deteriorated, particularly after the 2007 election of President Correa. Many factors contributed to this souring, but issues to do with human mobility played a prominent role.[12] Correa was immediately outspoken in his objections to U.S. (and European Union) policies regarding immigration and border enforcement. From his perspective—and that of many Ecuadorians—U.S. migrant policing activities at and within Ecuador's borders were an affront to Ecuadorian sovereignty. The U.S. base in Manta became a major source of controversy, largely due to its involvement in migrant interdiction, and Correa refused to renew the base's lease in 2010 (Hiemstra 2012). ICE activities inside Ecuador were interpreted as interfering in Ecuador's internal affairs, and they were abruptly terminated in 2009 after Correa accused an ICE official of using foreign aid to attempt to control the police and expelled him (El Universo 2009).

TRANSNATIONAL POLICING, MIGRATION, AND SMUGGLING TODAY

The sense of absolute crisis that permeated Ecuador in the late 1990s and early 2000s gradually dissipated, and emigration rates eased (Herrera, Moncayo, and Garcia 2012; Jokisch 2014). Economic conditions stopped their steep decline by the mid-2000s, and the government has been relatively stable since President Correa's 2007 election and through the 2017 election of President Lenín Moreno. After the global economic recession in 2008, there has even been a considerable amount of return migration (Herrera, Moncayo, and Garcia 2012; Jokisch 2014).[13] Still, Ecuadorians continue to migrate to the United States (and elsewhere) (Herrera, Moncayo, and Garcia 2012; Jokisch 2014). Much of this migration is documented; for example, nearly eleven thousand Ecuadorians annually were given legal permanent resident status in the United States between

2010 and 2013 (Jokish 2014). But undocumented migration to the United States persists (Herrera, Moncayo, and Garcia 2012; Jokisch 2014; De León 2015) for a number of reasons, many of which continue to be connected to U.S. policies (discussed in chapter 7).

With the difficulty of migrating legally, family reunification is a primary goal of undocumented migrants (Herrera 2008; Herrera, Moncayo, and Garcia 2012; Jokisch 2014). And for many Ecuadorians, migration continues to offer an unmatchable opportunity to improve individual and family financial circumstances. Employment options in Ecuador, while better than during the crisis years, remain limited, and salaries are still significantly lower than in the United States. In addition, new patterns of migration into Ecuador have altered the employment landscape. Ecuador's 2000 adoption of the U.S. dollar, which contributed to Ecuadorian emigration, also made Ecuador attractive to its regional neighbors, particularly Peruvians (Jokisch and Kyle 2006).[14] Violence in Colombia, much of it linked to the U.S.-led "War on Drugs" and Plan Colombia (Rojas 2004), forced roughly 150,000 Colombians to flee to Ecuador (Jokisch 2014). The willingness of these new in-migrants to work for less than Ecuadorians generates complaints that they bring down wages and increase competition in the Ecuadorian labor market (Jokisch 2007; Bowditch 2009a), in ways that may fuel additional out-migration of Ecuadorians (Bowditch 2009a).

At the same time as Ecuadorians feel compelled to migrate, the escalation of U.S. immigration and border policing throughout Latin America is unrelenting. U.S. officials continue to view the southern border as a gateway for security threats and categorize all undocumented migration as potentially dangerous.[15] For example, the surge beginning in 2014 of Central American women and children, including unaccompanied minors, largely fleeing violence was generally met with alarm instead of compassion. Against this backdrop, the United States pursues ever more geographically expansive policies.

One prong of this expansive approach is continued investment in policies aimed at deterring migration. The Prevention Through Deterrence strategy for border enforcement has been intensified, since 2011, to the "Consequence Delivery System" suite of policies, aimed at making migration more difficult, dangerous, lengthy, and costly (Slack et al. 2015; Bruzzone 2016). The Department of Homeland Security has continuously pushed its activities farther beyond U.S. borders. The U.S. Coast Guard and U.S. Navy continue to police migration at sea. ICE has developed an extensive global presence, with staff in approximately seventy-one offices in forty-seven countries (Peaco 2012); a stated goal of one of its initiatives is to "extend operating borders." The U.S. military, too, has an active presence throughout the region through joint military operations, special training, and agreements to use foreign bases. Additionally, the United States has further developed "partnerships" with origin and transit countries. To target the roughly three hundred thousand migrants who pass through Mexico yearly en route to the United States (Barahona 2016), the focus is on Mexico and the "Northern Triangle" countries of El Salvador, Guatemala, and Honduras. Through agreements and regional security initiatives such as the Mérida Initiative, Plan Frontera Sur, and the Central America Regional Security Initiative, the United States supplies money, equipment, and training to source and transit countries to stop U.S.-bound migrants before they reach the U.S. border (as well as to interdict other illicit activities) (Meyer and Seelke 2015; Meyer et al. 2016).

Scrutiny of the consequences of these "deterrence" policies south of the U.S. border supports the argument that "displacement" is a more accurate framing. First, we can evaluate DHS claims under President Obama that a drop in border apprehension and detention numbers are proof that deterrence strategies are working. While 2016 numbers in the United States were the lowest they had been in years, detention was reaching new highs in Mexico (Barahona 2016; Martínez 2015). It is also important to note that these "security partnerships" contribute to ignoring—and the United States escaping the blame for ignoring—the most vulnerable populations (Villegas and Rietig 2015; Suárez, Knippen, and Meyer 2016). For example, in 2014, "Mexico deported almost six times more unaccompanied minors than the United States" (Villegas and Rieteg 2015, 9), and Mexico's rate for granting asylum is significantly lower than that of the United States.

Second, in this paradox of intensifying U.S. immigration policing against continued resolve to migrate, Ecuador's smuggling industry remains robust. During the crisis, smuggling came to be an integral part of the Ecuadorian economy. Those involved in and dependent on smuggling include not just local *coyoteros* (coyotes) and moneylenders, but many individuals and organizations at points throughout the migration journey, such as drivers, people housing and feeding migrants, vendors selling goods and services to migrants (typically at inflated prices), banks and other organizations facilitating money transfers, and corrupt government officials and police officers (Ramírez and Álvarez 2009). And as Santiago's story at the beginning of this chapter shows, smugglers play a role in perpetuating Ecuadorian migration by recruiting new migrants in order to maintain and grow their business (Kyle and Liang 2001; Falconí and Ordoñez 2005).

Ecuador's smuggling industry has also continued to attract migrants from around the world. Though the government added visa requirements for some nationalities, Ecuador is still comparatively easy to enter, and smugglers are adept at negotiating changing border policies. Most recently, for example, there was a surge of Cubans passing through Ecuador.[16] Many other foreign nationals have arrived in Ecuador, and while some likely remain, most probably tap into smuggling networks to the United States (Herrera, Moncayo, and Garcia 2012). Herrera, Moncayo, and Garcia (2012, 61) reported that in 2010, nationals arrived in Ecuador from Afghanistan, Angola, Bangladesh, Cameroon, Congo,

Ethiopia, Haiti, India, Indonesia, Iraq, Kenya, Nepal, Nigeria, Pakistan, Senegal, Sri Lanka, and Ukraine. There are also reports of human trafficking in Ecuador, particularly the sex trafficking of women and children, with Ecuador as source, transit, and destination country (Jokisch 2014).

Third, human smuggling industries in Latin America continue to grow in step with this always escalating enforcement and policing. For example, in 2010 smuggling in Central America generated $6.6 billion (Sandoval 2013). What's more, increased smuggling entails a number of disturbing trends, including a rise in government corruption; migrants being forced to take more dangerous routes; more violence, abuse, and death of migrants (Sin Fronteras 2014; Smyth 2015; Barahona 2016); and increases in other illicit industries such as illegal adoptions and sex trafficking (Sandoval 2013; Smyth 2015).

Conclusion

This chapter's account of Ecuadorian migration to the United States highlights the important role played by countries of destination in migratory decisions and patterns, despite the tendency to ignore or deny responsibility. U.S. policies reverberate beyond the United States' physical territory in ways that deviate significantly from policymakers' expectations, blur borders, and produce connective corridors. In Ecuador, foreign influence and involvement first provoked domestic migration, which paved the way for later international migration. Importantly, policies expressly deemed immigration policies are not the only ones that influence migration from countries of migrant origin. Economic and foreign policies enacted by the United States with the objectives of shaping global markets and protecting U.S. interests in the hemisphere have also influenced Latin American economic and political landscapes in pivotal ways. In Ecuador, the collective result is a host of consequences that appear antithetical to U.S. objectives, primary among them entrenched migration networks and the development of an international smuggling industry.

This chapter also serves as a study of the consequences of hardening, increasingly extraterritorial immigration and border policies. The Ecuadorian case illustrates that regardless—and because—of the severity and extent of U.S. immigration control efforts, migration from Ecuador to the United States continues. Scholars have found that migration policies of destination countries often have little to no influence on personal migration decisions (Black et al. 2006; Collyer 2007; Nevins 2008). As Nevins (2007, 241) writes, "That many individuals choose to migrate in the face of the ever-hardening boundary between the United States and Mexico and associated risks speaks to the power of the forces driving migration." While increased border enforcement and policing frequently fail to halt migration, they do tend to alter the spaces and times of migration patterns, in terms of routes, tactics, danger, duration, and cost, and to cultivate ever more complex and extensive human smuggling networks.

The book now turns to additional policies at the heart of the contemporary U.S. approach to immigration enforcement: deportation and detention, which operate like U.S. foreign intervention and influence to collapse physical distance between national borders. Once undocumented Ecuadorians are apprehended at or within U.S. borders, the U.S. government increasingly responds with incarceration and expulsion. Before exploring consequences of these strategies in Ecuador, *Detain and Deport* scrutinizes the detention and deportation system itself. We begin with the historical development and contemporary drivers of the system.

CHAPTER 3

The Making of a Massive System

On the bus transporting just-arrived deportees in Ecuador from the airport, one man asked me, in a half-joking, half-serious tone, "Why don't they like us there in your country?" This chapter explores the U.S. "dislike" of certain immigrants as experienced through their incarceration and expulsion. It traces the development of the U.S. detention and deportation system, from its precursors to the present day.

While it was not until the 1980s that detention and deportation became increasingly central and permanent mechanisms of the U.S. immigration and enforcement approach, they have been used throughout U.S. history. There are three key factors consistently buttressing the use of deportation and detention, historically and today: the linking of immigration to national security, racialized ideas of national identity, and fluctuating economic climates.

First, while the specific narratives shift over time, logics of security consistently undergird detention and deportation. The concept of national security (and the need to protect it) has long been invoked as rationale for a wide range of U.S. political strategies at home and abroad. Indeed, the invocation of security provides policies with an air of untouchability. As Nevins (2008, 173) notes, "'Security' in the United States is what some have referred to as a 'God-word'—something universally embraced, and insufficiently questioned—at least among supporters of the status quo." *Securitization* is the definition and conceptualization of something as a national security threat (Waever 1995; Doty 1998). To securitize any phenomena is to elevate it, to prioritize it as an existential threat requiring exceptional attention, and justifies the marshaling of significantly more resources than it would have been given otherwise (Buzan, Waever, and Wilde 1998; Edkins 2003; Williams 2003; Sheehan 2005). "By uttering 'security,' a state representative moves a particular development into a specific area, and thereby claims a special right to use whatever means are necessary to block it" (Waever 1995, 55). Migration has been securitized throughout U.S. and European history at times when territorial borders and national identity were perceived as under threat (Walters 2008b;

Chebel D'Appollonia 2012). In the United States, security concerns have been used to justify and normalize exceptional measures such as detention and deportation.

Second, throughout U.S. history, struggles over immigration have been intertwined with racialized conceptions of national identity, specifically the anchoring of Americanness to "whiteness" (Honig 1998; D. M. Hernández 2008; Nevins 2010).[1] Citizens understand their membership in a specific state in relation to a perceived "Other" who does not belong. Laws regarding who can and cannot become American thus police constructed boundaries of national identity, especially regarding race, but also according to gender, sexuality, religion, language, and other markers. And by effectively placing entire groups of people outside legal boundaries, exclusionary laws also serve to criminalize these groups and seemingly justify their incarceration and exclusion (Stumpf 2006; C. C. G. Hernández 2015). Detention and deportation are within a suite of mechanisms used to maintain racist ideas of the "white" American citizen (D. M. Hernández 2008; Nevins 2010; Moloney 2012) by constructing immigrants as the "anti-citizen" (Khosravi 2009, 40). These practices link somewhat easily with national security concerns by creating "Others" who are visually identifiable and available to be marked as security threats, contained, and expelled.

Third, economic frustrations and aspirations overlap with and augment fears over security and racialized ideas of national identity, creating a powerful suite of reasons to oppose immigration and support exclusionary practices like deportation and detention, in three distinct if related senses. The health of the national economy critically influences citizens' perceptions of immigrants. Nativist sentiments rise in times of economic recession, when citizens typically blame financial woes on immigrants, and subside during times of growth, when immigrant labor is recognized as an important engine of economic prosperity (Takaki 2008; Nevins 2010). The use of deportation has clearly mirrored these fluctuations, increasing during times of financial uncertainty (De Genova 2005; King, Massoglia, and Uggen 2012). While immigrant workers may be recruited from abroad and welcomed by some employers to fill labor shortages, economically frustrated citizens embrace the belief that expelling immigrant workers—typically groups singled out according to racist criteria—will relieve pressure on the labor market.

Then, the persistent possibility of incarceration and expulsion works to maintain a vulnerable, flexible, and cheap workforce for certain segments of the economy (De Genova 2004, 2005; Coleman 2008, 2009; Golash-Boza 2015). As De Genova (2004, 161) contends, "Some are deported in order that most may ultimately remain (un-deported)—as workers, whose particular migrant status has been rendered 'illegal.'" The workers being controlled are irrefutably those who fall outside the conceptualization of national identity as white, making it a "system of racialized social control" (Golash-Boza 2015, x; De Genova 2005; Nevins 2008, 2010).

And finally, in the last thirty years, detention has figured into the economic milieu in a somewhat different sense: as a generator of revenue. In these neoliberal times made uncertain by deindustrialization, privatization of formerly government-run institutions such as prisons, minimal government oversight of privatized industries, and decreased federal government support at the state and local levels, detention has provided an increasingly important source of income—and a growth opportunity—for the private prison industry, as well as for state and local governments. In the context of the pervasive and unrelenting securitization of immigration, and racialization and criminalization of immigrants, the tremendous influence of those making money off of detention is easily masked.

This chapter provides a targeted history of U.S. deportation and detention, one that deliberately traces how these factors have worked together to sustain and expand the use of deportation and detention throughout U.S. history. This is not intended to be a comprehensive account, and it does not attempt to discuss all instances of these practices.[2] Instead, the goal is to strategically identify key moments that will provide the reader with an understanding of why and how the contemporary system came to be, and to emphasize recurring factors as well as pivotal moments of change. I begin with the earliest uses of deportation and detention, then pay particular attention to critical shifts in the 1980s that laid the groundwork for the contemporary deportation and detention "turn": the emergence of the "homeland" security narrative, rise of the "immigration industrial complex," and embrace of deterrence logic.

Antecedents: Deportation and Detention until the 1980s

Antecedents to deportation and detention today demonstrate the recurring interweaving of national security concerns, racist sentiments, and fluctuating economic climates as drivers of exclusionary efforts. Striking early examples include episodes now disavowed as black marks in U.S. history, such as the Indian Removal Act, fugitive slave laws, and schemes for expelling African Americans (Kanstroom 2007a). Since its founding, the United States has used race and class markers to delineate citizenship. The direct legal foundations of contemporary mechanisms can be traced to Chinese exclusion laws. Large numbers of Chinese immigrants had answered the U.S. need for cheap labor during the mid-1800s era of westward expansion, but when the U.S. economy dipped into a series of depressions in the late 1800s, the public view of Chinese immigrants grew increasingly hostile (Kanstroom 2007a; Silverman 2010; Coleman 2012). In response, in the 1880s to early 1900s, the government passed a series of laws that blocked new Chinese immigration, targeted already-present Chinese for deportation, and established a framework for both pre-entry and pre-deportation detention (Chacón 2007; Kanstroom 2007a; Lee 2007; Nevins 2010; Coleman 2012). In court cases attempting to challenge various aspects of Chinese exclusion, the government successfully presented national security as a guiding rationale of immigration law and invoked security to insulate deportation from judicial review and regulation (Coleman 2012). Judicial decisions also established race as a legitimate basis for exclusion. During this era, the government detained individuals targeted for deportation, immigrants deemed "alien enemies" (citizens of countries with which the United States was at war), and for pre-entry inspection (D. M. Hernández 2008). Ellis Island, for example, was established in the 1890s to detain arriving immigrants, making it the first permanent immigrant detention facility.

Racist anti-Mexican sentiment and hysteria regarding Mexicans as a presumed threat to national security spurred more use of deportation and detention in the early 1900s. As a consequence of Chinese exclusion, many employers turned to Mexican workers. Given that the existing U.S.-Mexico boundary cuts through what was, until 1848, Mexican territory, Mexicans and Mexican Americans had long passed back and forth between Mexico and the United States. The boundary was largely unregulated and unmarked until the early 1900s (Nevins 2010). To meet World War I–driven agricultural labor needs, the federal government even instituted programs recruiting Mexican laborers (Kanstroom 2007a). However, rising economic instability again led to racist resentment and violence, and tough-talking politicians criminalized Mexican workers (Nevins 2010; Kanstroom 2007a; K. L. Hernández 2010). The first policies targeting Mexican entry into the United States were enacted with the 1917 Immigration Act (Nevins 2010).[3] Mexicans crossing the U.S.-Mexico border were automatically detained and forced to undergo degrading medical examinations and quarantine before being allowed entry (D. M. Hernández 2008; K. L. Hernández 2010).

Around World War I and the postwar Red Scare, and in a climate of heightened racial violence, racist discourse often merged with alarmist security fears. The 1917 Immigration Act also broadened grounds for deportation (Kanstroom 2007a). It became a tool to keep labor in check and silence activists holding views perceived to be ideologically opposed to the U.S. government (Kanstroom 2007a). The Bisbee, Arizona, deportations in 1917 offer a prime example of using deportation to control labor. Under the discursive guise of protecting national and local security, employers and the government collaborated in the deportation of immigrant workers of eastern and southern European origin who protested poor wages and working conditions (Kanstroom 2007a; Benton-Cohen 2011).[4] The Palmer Raids of 1919 and 1920 likewise targeted labor activists and anarchist leaders of, again, primarily eastern and southern European descent (Kanstroom 2007a). Those targeted for deportation were detained, typically, in local jails and prisons (Silverman 2010).

Widespread financial hardship together with a persistent sense of threatened national security maintained a sharp anti-immigrant climate throughout the 1920s. The Immigration Act of 1924 (also called the National Origins Act) created a permanent immigration quota system that blatantly favored northern Europeans, effectively defining them as the only legitimate "white" immigrants

(Chacón 2007; Nevins 2010). Interestingly, the 1924 Act exempted the Western Hemisphere from this quota system. Mexicans were therefore not included, and "the exclusion and deportation systems thus evolved to become the primary legal means to regulate this movement of people" (Kanstroom 2007a, 157). The Border Patrol was created at that time to monitor the U.S. borders with Canada and Mexico (Nevins 2010; K. L. Hernández 2010). Between 1921 and 1930, over 92,000 people were deported to Mexico (Kanstroom 2007a). Deepening economic hardship led to further intensification of deportation efforts targeting Mexican immigrants, and in 1929 unauthorized entry was made a misdemeanor and reentry after deportation a felony (Ngai 2005; Chacón 2007). Then, during the Great Depression in the 1930s, a campaign of forced "repatriation" resulted in the deportation to Mexico of roughly 500,000 Mexican immigrants and U.S.-born Mexicans, including many U.S. citizens (De Genova 2004; Kanstroom 2007a; D. M. Hernández 2008; Nevins 2010).[5]

A dramatic shift in policy took place with agricultural labor shortages brought about by World War II. In 1942, the government initiated the Bracero Program. Before the program ended in 1964, over four million Mexican workers were brought to the United States on temporary work contracts. The social networks established during the program, together with solidification of employers' dependence on Mexican labor, served to maintain immigration patterns even after the program's termination (Calavita 1992; Massey, Durand, and Malone 2002; Nevins 2010). During this period, deportation became the primary way to regulate fluctuating labor needs (Kanstroom 2007a; D. M. Hernández 2008). Kanstroom (2007a, 224) writes, "The remarkably symmetrical relationship between labor recruitment and the deportation system is illustrated by the fact that, up to 1964, the number of braceros, nearly 5 million, was almost exactly the same as the number of deportees" (see also Nevins 2010).

During World War II, racism and national security logics again merged to propel a pivotal precursor to contemporary detention practices: the internment of over 33,000 "enemy aliens": primarily people of Japanese descent (including U.S. citizens), but also some of Italian and German backgrounds, from 1942 to 1946 (Kanstroom 2007a). The first large-scale detention project, these internments entailed the designation and building of facilities solely for detaining immigrants (and descendants of immigrants), the development of new cooperative relationships between various government agencies (INS, Bureau of Prisons, and Border Patrol), and a profound reimagining of the INS to include long-term detention (Kanstroom 2007a; Ridgley 2011). Japanese internment starkly illustrated social and judicial "acceptance of racial stereotyping and detention of noncitizens" (Kanstroom 2007a, 213).

In the Cold War, anticommunist context of the late 1940s to 1960s, deportation was further institutionalized as part of the U.S. immigration enforcement system. Citing concern for national security, deportation was once more used to target labor leaders, political activists, and liberal writers and artists (Kanstroom 2007a; Ridgley 2011). The Internal Security Act of 1950 broadened grounds for deportation to include any present or past membership in the Communist Party. In subsequent court cases, the government was given broad powers to deport practically anyone it targeted (Kanstroom 2007a). While the Immigration and Nationality Act of 1952 (also known as the McCarran-Walter Act) is often praised for eliminating explicit racial criteria for immigration, it also set up a restrictive quota system according to nationality (TRAC 2006a). The act also broadened the grounds for deportation and further limited judicial review (Kanstroom 2007b). Security panic together with labor regulation aims fueled another massive effort to deport Mexicans in 1954: Operation Wetback, which entailed the detention and forced removal of roughly one million individuals (Calavita 1992; K. L. Hernández 2010).

While in some respects the government appeared to dial back on its use of detention during this era, key pieces of the contemporary detention framework were being put in place. In 1954, the INS announced it was eliminating detention except for immigrants facing deportation who were considered flight risks or a danger to public safety (Dow 2004). For the next nearly three decades, most arriving immigrants were simply excluded at the border or immediately deported, and immigrants facing deportation charges in the U.S. interior had numerous options available to help secure their release from detention (Miller 2003b; Dow 2004). The pronouncement about eliminating detention, however, was in the same year as Operation Wetback, which "led to the highest number of persons ever held in detention by the INS in a single year, at over one-half million" (D. M. Hernández 2008, 51). Wetback included the opening of new INS facilities with the express purpose of holding migrants prior to deportation and illustrated a continued willingness for large-scale detention projects (D. M. Hernández 2008). Furthermore, court decisions in the 1940s and 1950s reinforced the government's power to detain immigrants throughout deportation proceedings, no matter how long they lasted (Kanstroom 2007a).

There were few significant changes to detention and deportation policies in the 1960s and 1970s, but important developments set the stage for the dramatic changes that began in the 1980s. The Immigration and Nationality Act of 1965 (also known as the Hart-Cellar Act) put an end to the national-origins quota system, and it is generally hailed as a liberal reform for introducing a supposedly egalitarian system and emphasizing family reunification (Miller 2003a). The 1965 reforms, however, cumulatively had a restrictive effect particularly on Latino migration by setting a limit of 120,000 immigrant visas per year for the Western Hemisphere. This highly unrealistic number is identified as a principal reason for the massive undocumented immigrant population of today (De Genova 2004; Kanstroom 2007a; Golash-Boza 2009). In addition, after U.S involvement in Cold War proxy wars, President Jimmy Carter ushered in legislation that allowed the arrival of increasing numbers of refugees from Cambodia and Vietnam. While these refugees were initially generally well received, events in the 1980s began to warp many Americans' perceptions of (nonwhite) refugees in general.

1980s to 2001: Racial Panic, Deterrence, and Privatization

Critical historical developments and conceptual shifts in the 1980s and 1990s spurred the shift from the periodic use of detention and deportation in response to particular moments of perceived crisis to, today, detention and deportation as permanent and central features of the country's approach to immigration enforcement. Primary reasons for the emergence of immigration as a key public issue at that time mirrored key reasons from the past: panic stemming from challenges to racialized ideas of national identity, economic recession, and the portrayal of immigration as a threat to national security. Additional catalysts that appeared over these two decades paved the way for the contemporary period of mass detention and deportation: adoption of the deterrence rationale and the conversion of detention and deportation into profit-making opportunities.

Beginning in the mid- to late 1970s, not only did immigration rates grow dramatically but arriving immigrants fell visibly outside the idealized "white" U.S. citizen. After President Carter facilitated the admittance of significant numbers of Cambodian and Vietnamese refugees, the U.S. Refugee Act was passed in 1980, and in that year alone over 200,000 Southeast Asian refugees came to the United States (Igielnik and Krogstad 2017). Also in 1980, Cuban leader Fidel Castro declared that anyone who wanted to leave Cuba could do so from Mariel Harbor. During the "Mariel boatlift," in a six-month period over 125,000 Cubans entered the southern United States, until an agreement was negotiated stopping the movement (Miller 2003a). That same year, dire political and economic conditions in Haiti drove 25,000 Haitians to undertake risky ocean crossings to reach the United States. Also, after taking office in 1981, President Ronald Reagan pursued neoliberal trade policies and military interventions in Central America that led to a jump in immigration from Latin America. Approximately one million refugees seeking asylum from El Salvador, Guatemala, and Nicaragua made their way to the United States (Kahn 1996; Dow 2004). Mexican immigration, too, increased after the 1982 collapse of the Mexican economy and the financial hardship created at the local level due to the loosening of trade regulations with the United States (and again after the 1994 implementation of the North American Free Trade Agreement) (Massey, Durand, and Malone 2002; Miller 2003a; Bacon 2004; Fernandes 2007). Among a public oblivious to the fact that U.S. economic policy and Cold War wrangling was largely responsible for these migration patterns, the growing numbers of nonwhite immigrants "fueled a racial panic about refugee streams which were feared to be black and Latino, criminal, ideologically left, and diseased" (D. M. Hernández 2008, 51; Kahn 1996).

These significant shifts in immigration trends overlapped with a domestic economic downturn and heightened security fears. In the 1970s, numerous sectors of the economy, especially those associated with industry, entered a sustained period of decline that generated deep frustration among wide swaths of working-class Americans around the country. Predictably, many citizens directed their frustration at certain immigrant groups, along race-based criteria. Anti-immigrant hysteria grew subsequent to the first attacks on the World Trade Center in 1993, the Oklahoma City bombing in 1995 (though perpetrated by a white American citizen), the 1993 arrival of 286 smuggled Chinese migrants on the *Golden Venture,* and the discursive linking of the War on Drugs to immigrants (Welch 2002; Miller 2003a; Dow 2004). The "tough on crime" attitudes and other political initiatives occurring at this time, such as welfare reform and increasing incarceration rates (despite decreasing crime), further influenced negative attitudes about immigrants (Welch 2002; Miller 2003a; Dow 2004).

At the same time, broad new social and political anxieties emerged in the 1980s that intensified the securitization of immigration in public and political discourse (Doty 1998; Nevins 2008, 2010). Amid a growing sense of globalization, some Americans sought to shore up ideas of national identity by targeting racialized immigrants. The post–Cold War vacuum and rush to identify new security issues was also an important factor. Beginning in the 1980s with the loss of one easily definable enemy, state officials, security professionals, and scholars began to reshape and broaden ideas of security. Migration became a new focus of securitization in this broadening. Security professionals searching for a new focus played a pivotal role in the escalation of anti-immigrant sentiments and the shift to practices such as detention and deportation (Walters 2008a; Bigo 2000, 2001, 2002).

It was in this context of fear, frustration, and panic regarding immigration that deterrence emerged as a key goal and rationale of evolving policies. Policymakers embraced the belief that detention and deportation serve deterrence goals. Deportation had long been understood as ending migration journeys (despite patterns of reentry indicating otherwise). Now, the idea that detention itself works to deter immigration became popular. Policymakers came to count on the threat of future incarceration and expulsion to work across borders and influence the decisions of potential migrants, essentially aiming to prevent migration before it occurs (Martin 2012; Mountz and Loyd 2014). Policymakers imagined that detained and deported bodies broadcast the promise of failed migration, both within the United States and into countries of migrant origin. In other words, assumptions regarding the pre-entry control value of detention and deportation are as important as the post-entry control functions for understanding the increasing investment in these strategies.

The contemporary detention and deportation system began to take shape.[6] The new Reagan administration initiated the first massive expansion in detention capacity in 1981, declaring that any immigrants seeking asylum would be detained while their decisions were pending. A two-part strategy was adopted specifically in response to Cuban and Haitian migration: interdiction of migrants before they reach U.S. territory and detention in transit countries and U.S.-held Guantánamo Bay Naval Base in Cuba (Flynn 2014; Mountz and Loyd 2014). The Reagan administration and INS officials repeatedly justified the new emphasis on detention by stating that it would deter future migration (Welch 2002; Dow 2004), and lawmakers framed detention of asylum seekers as essential for deterring fraudulent asylum claims (Siskin and Wasem 2005; Nuñez-Neto 2008; Haddal and Siskin 2010). Expanding detention capacity, then, was linked to an important shift from the perception of detention as simply a de facto aspect of deportation to the understanding of detention as a "spectacle of state power" (Martin 2012, 325) with deterrent value in and of itself. In turn, the incarceration of targeted groups of refugees reinforced racialized public beliefs that immigrants were unsafe and criminal.

It is no coincidence that the increasing emphasis on detention in immigration policymaking occurred in tandem with the expanding prison system. Throughout the 1980s and 1990s, rates of criminal incarceration in the United States grew rapidly, spurred not by increasing crime rates but by laws that massively broadened grounds for incarceration, the War on Drugs, and heightened criminalization of people of color. Private prison corporations, businesses that supply prisons in various ways, and politicians and government entities that benefit from these relationships—what has been called the *prison industrial complex* (Davis 2003)[7]—played key roles in these shifts. Growing numbers of local jails and private corporations (such as the Corrections Corporation of America, Wackenhut, and GEO Group) recognized immigration detention as a source of revenue with great potential (Welch 2002). What's more, in this neoliberal era of shrinking federal support, the building of both criminal prisons and detention facilities was undertaken as a strategy to help counties and localities out of tough financial times (Welch 2002; Doty and Wheatley 2013; Martin 2016). The cultural and political emphasis on deterrence and security served to justify and necessitate reliance on private companies and local governments to expand detention capacity (Kahn 1996; D. M. Hernández 2008; Mountz et al. 2013).

In fact, government efforts to expand detention capacity were made possible only by the involvement of private companies and local governments who saw immigration detention as a revenue-generating opportunity (Kahn 1996; D. M. Hernández 2008). For example, after Reagan's shifts to mandatory detention, existing INS detention facilities were immediately filled beyond capacity with Cubans, Haitians, and Central American refugees (Kahn 1996; D. M. Hernández 2008).[8] The five immigrant prisons on the U.S.-Mexico border, where Central Americans typically crossed into the United States, became severely overcrowded, and conditions were atrocious (Kahn 1996; Dow 2004; D. M. Hernández 2008). The INS contracted the private prison operator Corrections Corporation of America to open facilities in Houston and Laredo and reopen a facility in Florence, Arizona.[9] INS also contracted with the local government of Oakdale, Louisiana, to build a new facility with a capacity of six thousand (Kahn 1996). The 1986 Immigration Reform and Control Act (IRCA), passed in an effort to decrease the undocumented immigrant population, was the first legislation to condone the use of criminal penalties for immigration violations (Miller 2003a). In so doing, it contributed significantly to the continued growth in detention (Welch 2002). Then, in 1989, under the new administration of President George H. W. Bush, the Justice Department made detention mandatory for any immigrant whose refugee claim was denied, with the aim of discouraging possible claimants from migrating in the first place (Kahn 1996). This move led to the initiation of "the biggest detention project since it had imprisoned Japanese Americans during World War II" (Kahn 1996, 13) and involved rapid expansions in INS capacity as well as more contracting with private and local governments.[10]

Propelled by the anti-immigrant socioeconomic climate and the influence of a growing number of interested businesses and local governments, the turn to detention and deportation only accelerated in the 1990s. In 1994, under President Bill Clinton, the Border Patrol explicitly articulated its rationale of Prevention Through Deterrence for the strategy adopted at the southwest border that entailed increased patrolling, surveillance, and apprehension efforts, as well as expanding the capacity to detain migrants caught crossing the U.S. border (Nuñez-Neto 2008; Martin 2012; Meissner et al. 2013; Flynn 2014; Bruzzone 2016). As discussed in the previous chapter, the Clinton administration also extended the Prevention Through Deterrence strategy outside U.S. borders, orchestrating and funding the interception and detention of migrants en route to the United States in transit countries throughout Latin America (Flynn 2014).

In 1996, two sweeping pieces of legislation were passed that both established the legal framework of the current detention and deportation apparatus and led to its immediate expansion: the Illegal Immigration Reform and Immigrant Responsibility Act (IIRIRA) and the Antiterrorism and Effective Death Penalty Act (AEDPA). Together, these laws vastly enlarged immigration officials' powers to detain and deport migrants by "redefining the boundaries of criminality" (Miller 2003b, 221). They broadened the list of criminal offenses resulting in detention and deportation, made new categories of immigrants vulnerable, curtailed immigrants' rights to fight deportation, and eroded judicial discretion (Miller 2003b; Kanstroom 2007a; D. M. Hernández 2008). Importantly, IIRIRA established the "expedited removal" procedure, originally applied only in certain areas along the U.S.-Mexico border, through which immigrants are subject to mandatory detention and are ordered deported by an immigration official in lieu of a judge (Siskin and Wasem 2005).

Deportation and detention numbers skyrocketed. Between 1900 and 1990, deportation rates had been fairly constant, at approximately 20,000 per year

(Hagan, Eschbach, and Rodriguez 2008). Between 1990 and 1995, they rose to approximately 40,000 deportations per year (Hagan, Eschbach, and Rodriguez 2008). After implementation of the 1996 legislation, that number jumped to more than 180,000 per year (Hagan, Eschbach, and Rodriguez 2008). Detention rates escalated in a parallel manner. In 1994, the INS detained 5,532 migrants. In 1997, this number tripled to 16,000, and by 2000, it had grown to 188,000 detainees per year (Miller 2003a). The punitive approach solidified in the 1996 laws reinforced racialized public perceptions of immigrants as criminal, dangerous, and threatening to national security (Welch 2002; D. M. Hernández 2008; Martin 2012). And more and more companies, local governments, and individuals became financially dependent on the escalation of immigration enforcement and the institutionalization of detention and deportation.

After 2001: Homeland Security, Crimmigration, and the Immigration Industrial Complex

By the turn of the century, there was a growing sense among some lawmakers that the 1996 laws had gone too far, especially regarding implications for deportation and detention. Then, however, the attacks of September 11, 2001, instantly derailed nascent reform attempts (Miller 2003a). Instead, the administration of President George W. Bush initiated a rapid enlargement of the legal and physical infrastructure to detain and deport, which—as in previous periods in U.S. history—had vastly disproportionate consequences for nonwhite immigrants. Here, I first provide an overview of post-9/11 policies and then discuss how these policy shifts demonstrate a continuation and intensification of recurring influences and discourses.

Detention and deportation were central to post-9/11 responses. Passed immediately after the attacks, the USA PATRIOT Act gave the attorney general new powers of indefinite detention (Dow 2004; Fernandes 2007; Haddal and Siskin 2010). Over twelve hundred Muslim immigrants were detained for extended periods in abusive, isolated conditions, and then the framework for indefinite detention was applied broadly throughout the immigration enforcement system (Dow 2004; Nguyen 2005). The Homeland Security Act of 2002 created the Department of Homeland Security (DHS), which replaced INS with the new Bureau of Immigration and Customs Enforcement (ICE). ICE's budget was vastly greater than that of the INS, thus generating new potential for increasing detention (Siskin et al. 2006). In 2003, ICE issued the "Strategic Plan, 2003–2012 Detention and Removal Strategy for a Secure Homeland," also known as "Operation Endgame," which detailed steps for deporting all "removable" immigrants. To assist ICE in this removal goal, in 2004, Congress provided for eight thousand new detention "beds" each year between 2006 and 2010, in the Intelligence

Reform and Terrorism Prevention Act (IRTPA) (D. M. Hernández 2008; Haddal and Siskin 2010). IRTPA together with the REAL ID Act of 2005 also expanded provisions for deportation as well as definitions of terrorism in ways that netted additional categories of immigrants (Siskin et al. 2006). And in 2004, DHS announced expedited removal would be applied to migrants caught within one hundred miles of the U.S.-Mexico land border, driving its application—and the power to deport without an immigration hearing—deep inside U.S. territory along the southern border (Coleman 2012).

Moves to increase border policing and enforcement continued to center detention and deportation. In 2005, DHS launched the Secure Border Initiative (SBI), which focused on the southern border and involved numerous government agencies, the use of "Smart Border" technology, more personnel to enhance border surveillance and immigrant apprehension, and "expanded detention and removal capabilities to eliminate 'catch and release' once and for all" (U.S. DHS 2005, opening statement; Siskin et al. 2006; Fernandes 2007; Núñez-Neto 2008). As Martin (2012, 313) discusses, the increasing use of detention was central to these approaches, as "loopholes" were closed allowing the detention of "a whole range of individuals who previously would not have been detained in order to effect deportation—including arriving asylum-seekers, Central Americans who could not be quickly deported, and 'vulnerable' populations, such as families." Furthermore, as part of SBI, in early 2006 the DHS made expedited removal applicable to any undocumented immigrants apprehended within one hundred miles of all land borders and coastal areas, putting immigrants living in many major metropolitan areas at risk (U.S. DHS 2004; Siskin and Wasem 2005; Kanstroom 2007a; Coleman 2009, 2012). The DHS secretary called for additional detention capacity to facilitate the use of expedited removal (U.S. CBP 2005).

Another important characteristic of the immediate post-9/11 era was increasing cooperation between federal immigration officials and state and local law enforcement officers, which make more immigrants vulnerable to detention and deportation, particularly in the U.S. interior. Key to this was the 2002 "inherent authority doctrine" by Attorney General John Ashcroft, which permitted non-federal law enforcement officers to enforce immigration law (Coleman 2007a, 2009). Ashcroft's declaration became law in the Clear Law Enforcement for Criminal Alien Removal Act and the Homeland Security Enhancement Act, both passed in 2005 (Coleman 2007a). Inherent authority allows increased cooperation between local and federal authorities in immigration enforcement efforts, the linking of local and federal databases registering criminal and immigration violators, and the extension of the authority to initiate deportation proceedings (Coleman 2007a, 2009; Núñez-Neto 2008). A previously little-used clause of the 1996 IIRIRA legislation, 287(g), was promoted by the Bush administration to foster cooperation with local law enforcement agencies willing to participate (Coleman 2009). Bush also piloted Secure Communities in 2008, a "deportation program" aimed at integrating federal, state, and local databases and expanding cooperation with the goal of identifying immigrants for deportation. In addition, there was an increase in initiatives aimed at apprehending undocumented immigrants in the interior, such as Operation United Front in 2007, which supposedly targeted employers but resulted in the detention of hundreds of migrant workers (Kanstroom 2007b).

Discourses of national security provide the fundamental rationale for all of these post-9/11 policy initiatives. The rise of the homeland security imaginary, however, has markedly deepened the securitization of migration and normalized what were previously seen as exceptional measures. Kaplan (2003, 87, emphasis in original) explains, "The meaning of *homeland* has an exclusionary effect that underwrites a resurgent nativism and anti-immigrant sentiment and policy." While the word *homeland* was used in government and military forums in the 1990s, it was introduced to the general public by the George W. Bush administration in tandem with its aggressive response to the 9/11 attacks (Kaplan 2003). The fusion of *homeland* with *security* yielded a phrase heavy with meaning that works to anchor a powerful normative discourse (Walters, 2004; Kaplan 2003). As Bialasiewicz et al. (2007) emphasize, there is a deeply performative element to homeland security: the characteristic of stating a particular reality and then bringing that reality into existence through discourse and action (Butler 1997). The term itself works to produce a "radical insecurity" (Kaplan 2003, 85) grounded in the profound differentiation between citizen and foreigner. In the contemporary context of homeland security fears, the immigrant comes to be regarded as a key enemy of the nation.

The narrative of homeland security centers the figure of the racialized immigrant, who not only is portrayed as un-assimilable and threatening to national security but is also actively conflated with the terrorist figure. In this imaginary, all nonwhite immigrants come to represent the inverse of, and a danger to, the American family, home, and way of life (Kaplan 2003; Walters 2004; Cowen and Gilbert 2008; Hyndman and Mountz 2008; De Genova 2009). The homeland security imaginary intersects with the criminalization of immigration initiated in the 1980s and 1990s. All (racialized) immigrants are thus morphed into the criminal/terrorist figure in the minds of the nervous, jumpy public, crystallizing today in the permanent intersection of immigration and criminal law, or what scholars have called "crimmigration" (Stumpf 2006; C. C. G. Hernández 2015). Crimmigration has led to the normalization of "cruel and brutal immigration policies" (Fernandes 2007, 30), with detention and deportation prime among them. And against the backdrop of post-9/11 hysteria, the need to disguise racialized assumptions regarding the criminality of immigrants dissipated (Chacón 2007). For example, in 2003, the Justice Department made racial profiling permissible (and encouraged) in cases involving national security concerns (Chacón 2007).

Framed as necessary for protecting security, policies and practices expanding detention and deportation are legally insulated from judicial oversight. As in previous eras, "the linkage of immigration with national security tends to support excessive judicial deference and jurisdictional-preclusion statutes that dangerously empower the executive branch" in ways that make detention and deportation protected from review (Kanstroom 2007b, 1919). The Bush administration orchestrated numerous expansions of the executive branch's power to detain immigrants (Miller 2003a). Court decisions continued to amplify the plenary power (power not constrained by the Constitution) of Congress to regulate immigration (Miller 2003a; Coleman 2007a; Kanstroom 2007a). This exceptionalism is significant because it contributes to the high degree of impenetrability—and apparent chaos—surrounding the contemporary detention and deportation system architecture.

In the immediate post-9/11 era, security logics continued to be intertwined with those of deterrence (Meissner et al. 2013; Mountz and Loyd 2014). Policymakers, for example, framed mandatory detention of asylum seekers as a way to discourage potential claimants from making the migration journey in the first place (Nuñez-Neto, Siskin, and Viña 2005) and extolled the deterrent value of further expanding expedited removal. The importance of deterring "Other-than-Mexicans" was stated as a principal reason for increasing detention capacity (Nuñez-Neto, Siskin, and Viña 2005). Prevention Through Deterrence logics continued to frame Border Patrol strategies, such as Operation Streamline initiated in 2005, aimed at deterring future undocumented immigration by criminally prosecuting apprehended migrants (Gambino 2010).

Finally, the role of entities and individuals profiting in the post-9/11 buildup cannot be underestimated. Private contractors, through "extensive lobbying, contributions to political campaigns, and membership of powerful organizations" (Doty and Wheatley 2013, 436; Fernandes 2007), influenced the planning and implementation of the federal government's immigration enforcement policies after the 2001 attacks, including requirements for increased detention capacity (Fernandes 2007; Barry 2009a; Cervantes-Gautschi 2010).[11] For example, lobbying played a pivotal role in DHS's 2006 policy shift to charge immigrants with crimes considered aggravated felonies, such as identity theft and fraud for carrying falsified documents, a move that massively expanded the potential detention population (Cervantes-Gautschi 2010). Lobbying efforts also contributed to the maintenance of weak regulatory frameworks (Flynn and Cannon 2009), allowing detention providers to increase profit by providing a minimum of basic services for detainees (Welch 2002; Dow 2004; Barry 2009b). The term *immigration industrial complex* has been used to describe this "confluence of public and private sector interests in the criminalization of undocumented migration, immigration law enforcement, and the promotion of 'anti-illegal' rhetoric" (Golash-Boza 2009, 296; Fernandes 2007; Doty and Wheatley 2013).

From Obama to Trump: The Institutionalization of Detention and Deportation

All of these post-9/11 policy changes led to steady increases in detention and "removal" numbers throughout the administration of George W. Bush. Immigrants and immigrant advocates initially had high hopes that President Barack Obama would reverse course on the reactionary, punitive post-9/11 approach to immigration and border enforcement. Instead, Obama continued the expansion, with largely unquestioning adherence to the twin rationales of security and deterrence.

Border and immigration enforcement policies during the Obama era effectively constructed the massive deportation and detention apparatus in effect today. In 2009, Congress put in place what has come to be known as the "detention bed mandate," essentially requiring DHS to have 33,400 immigrants in detention at all times; this was raised to 34,000 in 2011.[12] The bed mandate drove a new expansion in detention capacity. While this quota has been a continuing subject of debate in Congress, with a number of proposals made to eliminate it, it remains in place today. The DHS also expanded the roll-out of Secure Communities, aiming to enroll all state, county, and local police jurisdictions by making it mandatory. While the program was adopted in many places, it faced significant resistance from state and local authorities for the ways in which it ensnared many noncriminal immigrants and eroded trust in law enforcement; eventually around 330 jurisdictions refused to participate.[13] In addition, the Obama DHS continued the Bush-era practice of periodic raids, but under criticism it shifted emphasis to "criminal aliens." However, undocumented immigrants of color with no criminal records were frequently swept up in these operations, and there is evidence that the DHS actively employed strategies of racial profiling to target immigrants (Lazare 2017). In 2011, DHS implemented the "Consequence Delivery System" plan (discussed in chapter 2), which entails an even more aggressive approach to deterrence, with policies expressly intended to intensify consequences for migrants and their families as a supposed deterrent. The new plan is remarkable for its overt emphasis on creating lasting harms that are felt in the United States and in countries of origin (Slack et al. 2015; Meissner et al. 2013; Lowen 2016).

The Obama administration also greatly expanded the practice of and capacity for detaining families and children. Family detention appeared to be on the decline with the closing of the Hutto Family Detention Center in Texas in 2009. But in response to a "surge" of women and children fleeing extreme violence and poverty in Central America beginning in 2014, DHS opened a number of new detention facilities by contracting with private companies and local governments and worked to expeditiously deport unaccompanied minors and families. The Obama administration presented this approach as crucial for discouraging additional migration and fought in court—citing homeland security concerns—to maintain these vulnerable populations in detention, even defying court orders to immediately release them. In 2016, the DHS also conducted a series of raids aimed at apprehending and deporting recent Central American arrivals, particularly mothers and children (Burnett 2016).

This is the conceptual and material infrastructure that Donald Trump inherited upon taking office. Rising to power during a period in which key factors are again recurring—acute security concerns, fear of the racialized Other, and a sense of economic decline—Trump was elected largely on the time-honored strategy of scapegoating immigrants, by promising to "crack down" on all (non-white) immigrants. Trump and his advisers are following and promoting the belief that ruthless, reactionary immigration policies will protect national security and deter future immigration. Trump's actions from the first days of his administration have demonstrated that he plans to build on this infrastructure to breathtaking new degrees, to the celebration of companies and local governments invested in detention and deportation (e.g., Fang 2017).

Indeed, the immigration industrial complex remains a central driver of the ongoing institutionalization of detention and deportation. Today, immigration detention is a thriving industry, sustained and galvanized by a complicated web of individuals, entities, and communities dependent upon it. Currently, over two hundred facilities around the United States detain immigrants for ICE. For every "bed" filled, contracted facilities are paid on average $124 per day (Detention Watch Network 2017). Sixty-two percent of these facilities are run by private companies (Detention Watch Network 2017) and make substantial profits. For example, between 2007 and 2014, the Corrections Corporation of America (recently renamed as CoreCivic) saw profits increase by almost 50 percent, and GEO Group's profits increased by 244 percent (Carson and Diaz 2015, n.p.). More and more counties have come to see immigration detention as a revenue generator, contracting directly with ICE and working with private companies in the construction of new facilities (Barry 2009b, 2010; Martin 2016). In addition, many other kinds of companies are involved, from phone companies to food service providers to physicians (Fernandes 2007; Golash-Boza 2009; Barry 2010; Doty and Wheatley 2013; Conlon and Hiemstra 2014; Hiemstra and Conlon 2016, 2017). Examples abound of government officials involved with security policymaking who serve on corporate boards or have personally invested in companies profiting from immigrant detention (Fernandes 2007; Barry 2009a; Cervantes-Gautschi 2010; Hodai 2010). There is also a significant number of individuals who move between working in the design and implementation of immigration enforcement policy and working in private industry (American Friends Service Committee 2010; Cervantes-Gautschi 2010; ACLU 2011). These webs of dependence interweave with imaginaries in which racialized immigrants are both criminals and threats to homeland security (Doty and Wheatley 2013), in ways that propel detention and deportation system growth.

The detention and deportation machine must also be understood in the context of the broader global economic system, which depends on a constant supply of cheap, disposable labor and uses constructions of race as a sorting mechanism. Golash-Boza (2015, x) argues that "mass deportation is critical to the sustainability of global capitalism" and a central component of the "neoliberal cycle," in which global inequality, undocumented immigration, low-wage work, popular feelings of insecurity, and increased policing of racialized populations are all connected. Contemporary processes of "crimmigration"—particularly the massive escalation in detention and deportation—work to broadly control all workers who can be racialized as nonwhite (Chacón 2007; D. M. Hernández 2008; Golash-Boza and Hondagneu Sotelo 2013; Golash-Boza 2015).

Golash-Boza and Hondagneu-Sotelo (2013) label the U.S. deportation machine a "gendered racial removal program," pointing out that post-9/11 deportations have overwhelmingly focused on black and Latino men. The homeland security climate coincides with an economy in which there is a shortage of workers to fill jobs gendered as female, such as care work, cleaning, and other service jobs, and an excess of workers to fill jobs gendered male, such as construction; this economic reality was only heightened with the U.S. financial crisis of 2007–2008 and its aftermath. While in some previous periods women were often the focus of efforts to control immigration and deport immigrants (Luibhéid 2002; Chavez 2008), in the current context deportation is a tool to control labor supply through a focus on deporting men—racialized and criminalized immigrant men (Golash-Boza and Hondagneu-Sotelo 2013; Golash-Boza 2015). Then, in a self-reinforcing cycle, detention and deportation of immigrants strengthen public perceptions of them as outsiders and criminals, seemingly justifying their physical containment and removal (Miller 2003a, 2003b; Bosworth 2008; D. M. Hernández 2008; Khosravi 2009; Silverman 2010), linking to exclusive notions of home, and heightening non-immigrants' sense that national security is endangered (Chacón 2007; Coleman 2008; Nevins 2010; Mainwaring 2012).

Without denying the responsibility of specific political administrations, it is important to remember that the present-day detention and deportation system is the product of multiple factors and influences: exclusive race-based ideas of national identity, the securitization of migration, the deterrence paradigm, global economic relationships, the scapegoating of immigrants for economic problems, and the emergence of the immigration industrial complex. Together, these factors have led to explosive growth in the detention and deportation system. This system often projects a sense of chaos, a chaos that materializes over and over again throughout the contemporary organization and operation of the system, with important consequences inside and outside of the United States. The next chapters explore this chaos, with the aims of putting some order to it and disrupting some of the factors that have produced the system itself.

CHAPTER 4

Ordering Chaos
System Organization and Operation

The United States operates the largest detention and deportation system in the world. In recent years, the United States has deported over four hundred thousand immigrants annually. Every day, there are over thirty-four thousand immigrants detained in ICE custody. They are held in approximately two hundred facilities around the country, which are owned and operated by ICE, state and local governments, and private companies (Detention Watch Network 2017). For those detained as well as family members and advocates on the outside, this massive detention and deportation machine is experienced as baffling, opaque, and disorienting—in short, chaotic.

My transnational ethnography of the U.S. detention and deportation system—conducted from Ecuador—facilitates a view of various chaotic geographies produced by this massive system of incarceration and expulsion, or the ways in which chaos is spatialized and temporalized. Eyal Weizman (2007, 8) writes regarding the disordered settlement strategy pursued by the Israeli government, "Chaos has its peculiar structural advantages." I ask: what are the "peculiar structural advantages" of detention and deportation? Through identifying and scrutinizing chaotic geographies of deportation and detention, we can better grasp both the drivers and the consequences of these "popular" policies. Their popularity is not because they are effective policies but because distasteful truths are hidden and powerful interests are served, ranging from the interests of individuals to the maintenance of economic, social, and political orders.

In my attention to these chaotic geographies, I walk a tricky, thin line between understanding the chaos as accident or intention. The chaos of detention, deportation, and their aftermath is, to be sure, largely the result of circumstance. The system's inconsistent logic and indecipherability is without a doubt partly due to its rapid expansion over the last two decades—as explained in the previous chapter—amid a lack of central coordination and oversight (Belcher and Martin 2013). Much of the appearance and experience of chaos, therefore, is tied to the ad hoc manner in which policies have been implemented, as practitioners scramble to respond to changes (Wadhia 2015). It would thus be a mistake to say that policymakers sit and craft suites of policies intended to generate chaos (Belcher and Martin 2013). At the same time, however, we must not overlook the fact that the chaos inherent to deportation and detention has important consequences, many of which are recognized and desired by policymakers. In brief, the chaos contributes to achieving system goals: increasing deportation numbers and (policymakers assume) deterring future migration. It also becomes clear that the perception of chaos depends on who and where you are. That is, the chaotic geographies of detention and deportation are not experienced uniformly, and perhaps that unevenness—that strong connection between positionality and chaos—is where the power of chaos lies.

Transnational ethnography is an important methodological approach for balancing assertions of intention behind policies with the circumstantial momentum and effects of chaos. By studying detention and deportation from Ecuador, this research creates cracks in the concealing barriers that chaos has built around detention. It illuminates not just how the U.S. detention and deportation system works, but also consequences of this chaos in a country of migrant origin.

This chapter sketches the system's organization and operation, showing one "advantage" of the chaos of detention and deportation to be the creation of seemingly impermeable bureaucratic walls. Processes of bureaucratization are fundamental to carceral expansion (Mitchelson 2014; Gill 2016; Martin 2016; Hiemstra and Conlon 2017). By commodifying incarcerated bodies, bureaucratization works to justify and propel continuous growth in carceral regimes (Mitchelson 2014; Martin 2016). Martin (2016) argues that in the U.S. detention system, the public-private relationships formed through contracting between ICE, county governments, and private companies contribute to the normalization of detention. Bureaucratization also works to dehumanize detainees, simultaneously rendering them deserving of detention, distancing them from citizens, and erasing negative conditions of confinement (Mitchelson 2014; Gill 2016; Martin 2016; Hiemstra and Conlon 2017).

I first describe the process of "searching" for immigrants detained in the United States from a country of migrant origin. In addition to conveying a sense of the confusion typically felt by family members in Ecuador, I want to illustrate the thick layers of bureaucracy encircling the U.S. detention and deportation system. Next, again from the perspective of family members, the chapter provides an overview of the basic legal procedures that detainees are put through in detention, aiming to show how this is anything but a straightforward, predictable, easy-to-understand process. Then, I explore the chaotic spatiotemporality of detention, by mapping interviewees' transfers from facility to facility and exploring how detainees' physical paths do and do not line up with total time detained. I introduce and explore this spatiotemporality as a critical characteristic of the detention and deportation system. In chapter 5, I consider specific consequences for detainees.

Searching for Order amid the Chaos, or the Problem of "Gobbledygook"

I waved at the security guard as I entered Cuenca's Casa del Migrante, or House of the Migrant, then walked through the central courtyard of the old colonial house and ascended the creaky wooden steps to the second floor. There were already two women sitting in the office of Legal Assistance, one holding a squirming baby. The lawyer who ran Legal Assistance, Carmen Alvarado, was taking information on the women's husbands, Santiago and Jorge, brothers-in-law who had left Ecuador one month earlier to travel to the United States. Santiago had made a very short call sixteen days ago to say that they were detained in Arizona, but the women had not heard anything since then. It was the second migration attempt for both men; their attempt one year earlier had resulted in deportation. The women wanted to know what was happening: Where were they? Were they okay? Would they be deported? If so, when?

As I shrugged off my backpack, Carmen introduced me and asked, "Can you call right now?" "Sure," I answered, "let's go across the hall." The two women followed me to the empty meeting room and watched as I pulled out my laptop computer, turned it on, and plugged in my calling headset. I looked over the information Carmen had written down and asked for a few more details, opened the calling program Skype, and began dialing U.S. numbers. After an initial call that went immediately to voicemail, I realized that this "search"—like most— could take a while. I promised to call the women when I had more information, and they gave me contact information and left.

With this anecdote, you enter the U.S. detention and deportation system as family members in Ecuador do, and as I did in my capacity as a volunteer at the Casa del Migrante. To outsiders—particularly those in countries of origin—the detention and deportation system projects impenetrability and confusion. In this section, I guide the reader through the process of "searching" for detained immigrants from Ecuador. What I refer to as *searches* entail not just locating a detained migrant but also following her or his case until release from detention, which in my experience was almost always through deportation to Ecuador. My goals here are twofold: to illustrate the arbitrary, uneven, unordered nature of detention and deportation but also to bring some order to the appearance of chaos, to see—and see through—cracks in the system.

FINDING AN ENTRY POINT

With access to multiple federal and state agency databases, ICE (as an agency of DHS) has a wide range of powerful tools to find and track migrants in (and out of) detention. But for outsiders—be they family members, lawyers, or other people like myself attempting to assist detainees and family members—establishing a point of entry to the detention and deportation system can be a real challenge.

My position of privilege—as an American, a speaker of English, familiarity with U.S. bureaucracy, and the time and resources to spend hours making international calls and sorting out how the system works—made it possible for me to try to break through the material and perceived barriers surrounding this system. During my months at the House of the Migrant, I discerned basic rules and procedures of operation, appropriate questions to ask of both family members and system personnel, and how to navigate uneven practices between and among detention facilities and ICE offices.

Searches often started with just a few pieces of information, which I used like the prisms and mirrors in a periscope, trying to position them at just the right angles to permeate the bureaucracy shielding detention and deportation from outsiders' eyes (Hiemstra 2017). After much trial and error, I found the easiest starting point to usually be the detainee's Alien Registration Number, or A-Number, a nine-digit number assigned to noncitizens in the United States. In my searches, an A-Number was usually the first thing requested of me when I explained that I was trying to locate a detained migrant, and many places had automated answering systems requiring one to enter an A-Number in order to proceed. Unfortunately, relatives in Ecuador rarely had this information, due to a total absence of communication between detainees and family members, brief phone calls, or detainees not understanding that they should communicate their A-Number to family members.

Another point of entry, then, is biographical information. The ICE has the capability to use additional pieces of personal data, including date of birth, detainees' parents' names, and country of origin, to search for registered migrants. Some employees with whom I spoke would conduct a search with just a first and last name, and if they found that name they could then use birth date and parents' names to confirm identity. But some employees would not proceed without an A-Number, typically providing reasons like it was "policy," "the only way to do it," and "you won't get anything with just a name anyway." This points to a frustrating conundrum for families: the DHS assigns detainees an A-Number that may be the only way to find a detainee in the system, but employees can refuse to give the number out. Additionally, personnel proficiency in navigating the computerized system varied tremendously. Many employees seemed to be trained to search only within specific geographic areas, or even just within one detention facility. In some instances when I did have an A-Number, the county prisons housing migrants for ICE (two-thirds of the detention infrastructure) did not use the assigned A-Numbers, using instead an identification system specific to that facility.

A common problem further complicating searches was the incorrect entry of detainee information into databases, which I came to think of as the problem of "gobbledygook," after one obviously skilled officer remarked to me that no matter how good one is at searching for a migrant name, "you have to work ahead of people in the field who don't care how names go in, if it's gobbledygook" (author's research journal, May 25, 2009). Spanish name conventions include at least two first names and two last names, and confusion can result when just one of each is entered (resulting in multiple combinations that can be searched for). Also, Spanish style for dates is to write "day/month/year," whereas English style is "month/day/year," and this can result in the month and day of a detainee's birth date being flipped when registered (for example, a birthday of August 10 being recorded as October 8). Misspelled names could likewise result in dead-end searches. In the process of a complicated search, the officer quoted above explained that there are ways to do "super queries" with "sounds like" for the name, and at the same time enter other qualifying information like country of origin and birth date.[1] I rarely encountered this advanced skill in my searches, meaning that the gobbledygook recorded at the moment of apprehension resulted in many dead ends. Another problem is detainees purposely giving false information to try to avoid deportation or to be deported to a country closer to the United States than their origin country (in the hopes of a shorter journey in subsequent attempts to migrate). This strategy rarely works today with the contemporary use of fingerprints and other biometric data, but some detainees have been told otherwise by smugglers or migrants from earlier times.

An additional point of entry to the detention system is geographic location, of apprehension or of detention. This approach could be relatively simple if family members had a facility phone number or name. Unfortunately, such information was not always helpful. Due to the practice of frequently transferring detainees (discussed below), the migrant was not necessarily still at the place of detention for which the family had information. And we again encounter the problem of gobbledygook: on several occasions, the person's name was incorrectly spelled on the facility roster or in ICE records so that even though the migrant was at the facility, that fact proved difficult to verify. Also, important details were often lost in translation. In one case, for example, family members knew only that a migrant was detained in "Paiconti"; it took me a while to ascertain that this meant Pike County, Pennsylvania.[2] Also, phone numbers could be recorded incorrectly by family members for a number of reasons, such as poor phone connections or the omission of area codes.

Another difficulty with the location approach was that it was much more common for a family member to have only a vague idea of where the migrant was taken into custody, such as the state—like the women in the earlier anecdote knowing only "Arizona"—or, often, "on the border." In these cases, I began by calling an ICE office near the approximate place of apprehension or somewhere along the border. But this can be a complicated strategy due to the regional geography of ICE office jurisdiction. For example, one might be detained in New Mexico, but the field office with jurisdiction is in Texas.

If I was able to locate a detainee, then I tried to also determine additional details that family members wanted to know, such as if the detainee was to be deported and, if so, the date of arrival in Ecuador. The degree of information attained varied tremendously according to the people with whom I spoke and the type of facility or office. Calls made to an ICE office or ICE-operated detention facility typically yielded a higher degree of detail about a detainee's situation than calls to a privately contracted detention facility or a county prison housing detainees for ICE. This could perhaps be due to contract guidelines regarding what information could be released or limits on contract facilities' access to databases and search engines. While basic administrative personnel at a contracted facility were often able to confirm or deny a migrant's location, they usually could not provide the additional details that an ICE officer could.

If I had been able to obtain an A-Number, another potential source for details of a detainee's case is the Executive Office for Immigration Review (EOIR), an agency within the Department of Justice that adjudicates all immigration decisions. There is one centralized, automated, toll-free EOIR number for all the immigration courts around the country. If a migrant has ever appeared or is scheduled to appear before an immigration judge, then by entering the A-Number on the EOIR line one should be able to access information about court date, decision, place, and time remaining for filing an appeal. The EOIR number could be a very helpful tool, though I often encountered significant delays in the updating of information available through that service.

In most cases, obtaining any degree of information at all depended on actually talking to someone. In my searches, I encountered many busy signals and never-answered rings. Calls frequently ended with recorded messages saying that there was no one available to take the call and to try again later or that the voice mailbox was full. Often, after being transferred to a particular person (sometimes by selecting an automated option) I was given the opportunity to leave a voicemail. These messages were rarely returned. The low callback rate may have been due partially to me being in Ecuador. Because I was calling using Skype, I could only leave my Ecuadorian cell phone number, the House of the Migrant number, and my email. These options were perhaps difficult or impossible to respond to because of the international call required or reluctance to use email. When I was back in the United States and able to leave a domestic phone number, approximately 25 percent of the calls were returned.

In 2009 as I concluded my fieldwork, ICE initiated the Online Detainee Locator System (ODLS), which allows anyone with internet access to search for a detainee by A-Number, or by biographical information including name, date of birth, and country of birth. I have attempted to use ODLS on several occasions since then (in occasional searches for House of the Migrant), all of them without success, perhaps for the same reasons of gobbledygook. And it is telling of the inconsistency and impenetrability of the system that despite the open online access to searches using just biographical information, employees at some detention facilities and ICE offices still insist that they must have an A-Number to proceed with a search.

CASE STUDIES: SANTIAGO, JORGE, AND ROLANDO

To walk the reader through how a search for a detained immigrant can play out—including the many possible twists, turns, and frustrations—I return to Santiago and Jorge from the anecdote at the beginning of this section and then introduce another detained Ecuadorian, Rolando.

Santiago's and Jorge's wives had supplied their husbands' names and basic biographical information and knew that the men were detained in the state of Arizona. While the women were still at the House of the Migrant, I began by calling the ICE office in Florence, Arizona, where there is a major migrant detention center, listed on the DHS website. (The women left after this call went to the information desk voicemail, and I realized the process could take a while.) An hour later I tried the Florence ICE office again, with the same result. I then called the Phoenix ICE office, and the man who answered said that he could only search "the system" if I had the men's A-Numbers. I explained that their family members in Ecuador did not have that information, but he firmly repeated that it was policy to only search with an A-Number. Next, I tried the Florence Detention Center, and a woman with whom I spoke responded very differently: she quickly checked the inmate roster, said that both men were there, gave me their A-Numbers, and explained that their prior deportation orders had been reinstated and travel documents already requested. "Finding" Santiago and Jorge proved to be relatively quick and easy.

Finding Rolando was somewhat more difficult. In June 2009, Rolando's wife, Lucinda, came in to the House of the Migrant. She had received a call from a friend in the United States to tell her that Rolando, who had been living in Massachusetts for twenty-one years, had just been detained. Lucinda did not know her husband's birth date, and when I explained that it was hard to search without that, she said she would find the information and return. She returned the following day with Rolando's birth date as well as his full name.

Because he had been living in Massachusetts, I began the search for Rolando by calling an ICE office in that state. The man with whom I spoke said that he could do nothing without an A-Number. I then called the ICE number in Buffalo, and a woman found Rolando in her database using his name and birth date. She would not give me his A-Number but did tell me the name of the county jail in which he was detained near Boston. I called that county jail, and with his name and birth date I was able to confirm that he was there. The woman with whom I spoke gave me his A-Number but said that for any details regarding his immigration case I would have to talk directly with ICE. I could now tell Lucinda where her husband was but not the status of his case.

At this point, I called the automated number for EOIR and by entering the A-Number learned that he had been ordered removed in Boston in 2003. The EOIR was obviously reporting a previous appearance by Rolando in one of their courts, and because he already had a deportation order I knew that it was possible that the order would simply be reinstated and he would not appear in court prior to deportation. I then called the ICE number for Massachusetts again and was told to call back in forty-five minutes to speak with the duty officer. Because I knew from past experience that responses often depended on the speaker, I called back immediately and spoke with a different person who suggested I call back in twenty minutes. I called ICE Buffalo again and spoke with a man who used the A-Number to report that Rolando had been ordered removed. He added that I would have to speak with ICE in Massachusetts to determine exactly how the deportation process works there. I immediately called the ICE in Massachusetts (approximately five minutes after my previous call to the same number) and spoke with a man who confirmed that Rolando was going to be deported and that the office was in the process of obtaining travel documents for him, which would likely take at least a couple of weeks.

The searches for these three Ecuadorians show the U.S. detention and deportation system to be vast, unwieldy, and difficult to navigate. Pieces of information required to even initiate a search can be hard to come by. The many offices and facilities within the system do not follow uniform procedures. Employee skill, knowledge, and degree of cooperation varies. Search mechanisms are flawed. In these cases, to obtain information that they keenly wanted, family members had to be willing to share personal family information with me, a stranger and a (privileged) American. As a researcher dedicated to the task, I had time to make multiple calls, I accrued knowledge of how the system works, and I speak English. I also possessed a computer and a Skype account that makes international calls cheaply. These opportunities and resources are unattainable for many of the Ecuadorians I encountered and for whom, then, the chaos of detention and deportation presents an impenetrable wall.

Funneling: From Detention to Deportation

In March 2009, four Ecuadorians driving together in a car near Scranton, Pennsylvania, were pulled over by local police for, according to one of the Ecuadorians, "looking *moreno*" (brown skinned). The men were originally from the small town of Santa Luisa outside of Cuenca.[3] Unable to produce acceptable documentation, within an hour they were in Pike County Correctional Facility in Lords Valley, Pennsylvania, a county-run prison that detains migrants for ICE in addition to criminal justice system prisoners.[4] Despite their identical circumstances of capture, each man was detained for a different period of time—from six weeks to four and a half months—and were deported according to distinct types of removal orders and legal procedures. Here, I provide a brief overview of the range of possible legal paths down which migrants can be forced, between detention and deportation; then I come back to these four Santa Luisans to explain how these processes can play out to create such different—and disorienting—experiences. To be clear, I am not a lawyer nor a legal scholar, and this is not meant to be a comprehensive overview and explanation of all the legal procedures and possibilities migrants face.[5] I no doubt oversimplify the process and omit a great deal. However, my aim in this chapter is to make an incredibly complex, often baffling array of procedures more understandable, from the perspective of family members in migrants' countries of origin. In the next chapter, I explore how detainees experience this process, including common rights violations.

What happens to a migrant after being detained is difficult to fathom and follow for family members in a country of migrant origin and, indeed, for nearly anyone not working within the detention and deportation system. To make it more comprehensible, I learned to explain it as a series of three steps. First, the migrant goes through the legal and procedural processes leading to an order of removal. Second, he or she must obtain required travel documents. Third, the migrant waits for a seat on a plane to Ecuador. In reality, these three steps often multiply or collapse into each other, but I believe the division—however artificial—is useful for deciphering detained migrants' possible trajectories. While deportation is not a completely inevitable outcome of detention, it is by far the most common and—as discussed further in the next chapter—is tied to how the system's structure and operation work to funnel detainees to deportation.

STEP ONE: RECEIVING A REMOVAL ORDER

This step, being "given" a deportation order, or "removal" order, is typically the most complex. The time required to pass through step one varies greatly, depending on factors such as the kind of removal order received, whether a migrant is waiting to see an immigration judge, how quickly paperwork is processed, the volume of migrants being processed at a particular location, and whether the detainee appeals a removal order.

The process for the most common removal order begins with a Notice to Appear (NTA), issued by the Department of Homeland Security, and ends with an immigration judge working for the Department of Justice issuing the removal order. NTAS can be issued in person to immigrants, but many are sent through the mail, leading to a common problem that immigrants never receive their NTA, for a variety of reasons.[6] Migrants are not required to be present in immigration court to receive a removal order, so if the migrant fails to appear, the judge may decide to proceed in absentia, often at the request of DHS trial attorneys. In such cases, the migrant may be unaware that he or she has been ordered deported (Kocher 2017). Once an immigrant receives an NTA, the immigration judge in charge of their case may use discretion to decide a range of outcomes that include granting temporary or permanent legal status in the United States or issuing a removal order. Despite wide variability across courts and judges, removal orders are the most common outcome. If there are no other aggravating factors, a removal order automatically carries a ten-year bar to legal entry to the United States.

There are additional kinds of removal orders. In the case of a *stipulated removal order*, a migrant who has received an NTA signs a paper stating that he or she does not wish to contest removal and thereby cedes the right to appear before a judge (Koh 2013). These papers are presented to migrants by immigration officials, such as Border Patrol personnel or ICE officers, not by an immigration judge. An *expedited removal order* was explicitly designed to prevent migrants from appearing before an immigration judge and does not require the migrant's consent. It can be issued immediately upon determining that the migrant is inadmissible and in the country for less than two weeks. Categories of migrants to whom expedited removal orders can be issued have been continuously expanded since it was introduced in 1996. While initially it could only be applied to migrants at ports of entry or the border, today immigration officials can apply expedited removal to migrants apprehended within one hundred miles of all land borders and coastal areas (which includes many major urban areas in which there are significant immigrant populations). President Trump has proposed allowing expedited removal to be applied anywhere in the United States for migrants in the country up to two years. A *reinstatement of removal* is applied to migrants who are found to be in the United States without permission after a previous removal. A migrant's initial removal order is "reinstated," and he or she is permanently banned from legal reentry.

A migrant can file for discretionary relief from removal. In my fieldwork at the House of the Migrant, I encountered cases of detainees seeking two different forms of relief (there are others): *asylum* and *voluntary departure*.[7] To even be allowed to apply for asylum, a migrant must pass a "credible fear" interview. Reports show that in some cases immigration agents refuse migrants this request. After passing a credible fear interview, an asylum seeker must then demonstrate to an EOIR judge "well-founded fear" of persecution in her or his country of origin. The process of obtaining asylum typically takes more than a year, during which time the migrant often remains detained (if detained at the time of application for asylum). At the House of the Migrant during my fieldwork, there were several cases of Ecuadorians seeking asylum due to domestic abuse or fear of retaliation from smugglers or debt holders. There were more cases in which detained migrants sought voluntary departure. Voluntary departure is most commonly granted to undetained migrants, but it can also be awarded to detainees. While it is technically "relief" from removal, the migrant still has to leave the United States.[8] Migrants may see voluntary departure as preferable because it does not carry a bar on reentry, and migrants believe that with voluntary departure they will have a better chance of receiving a visa for legal admission. What they often do not understand, however, is that they will still receive a bar for being unlawfully present and are likely still considered inadmissible for other reasons.[9] Detained migrants granted voluntary departure have to arrange for their own travel documents and purchase their own plane tickets within specific location and date guidelines. They remain detained until the flight unless a judge allows them to be bonded out (and they are able to pay the bond).

Note that within these legal twists and turns, immigration officials and judges have a considerable amount of discretion. This starts at decisions about what kind of removal order to pursue and continues throughout the process. In addition, though restricted by mandatory detention provisions, judges also have discretion to allow detained migrants to be released from detention (Wadhia 2015; Kocher 2017). The uncertainty and unevenness surrounding the use of discretion greatly add to the chaos of detention and deportation for detainees, family members, and supporters.

STEP TWO: OBTAINING TRAVEL DOCUMENTS

After a migrant is ordered removed, Enforcement and Removal Operations (ERO), a branch within ICE, must obtain the paperwork necessary to deport her or him, including confirmation of nationality and permission to travel. Possessing a valid passport significantly facilitates the process, but in the majority of cases on which I worked, Ecuadorians did not have one.[10] In such cases, ERO has to work with the migrant's origin country consulate to verify nationality. Delays can occur at this step for a variety of reasons. One problem is incorrect personal information about the detainee being sent to the consulate, or the gobbledygook problem.[11] One interviewee, Franklin, believed that the bulk of his extended detention period (four months) could be attributed to the misspelling of his name by the intake officer when he was first apprehended.

Another factor prolonging Ecuadorians' detention appears to be the (slow) speed of processing on the part of Ecuadorian consulates. I repeatedly heard comments in my conversations with ICE personnel that they were "just waiting on paperwork from the Ecuadorian consulate" and that Ecuadorian consulates seem to take longer than those of other countries. Interviewees' statements support these comments. Santiago was told by an ICE officer that the Ecuadorian consulate does not work quickly and because of that Ecuadorians were detained longer than people from other countries. Ecuadorian government employees with whom I spoke attributed this deficiency to a mismatch between available resources and the increasing numbers of Ecuadorian deportees. For example, the consulate may have to conduct an interview in person or by video to verify identity, and while ICE may be responsible for some delays in initiating these interviews, one issue appears to be the number of consulate staff available.

STEP THREE: WAITING FOR A FLIGHT

Once paperwork is in order, a migrant must wait for a deportation flight, either an ERO flight or a commercial flight. Most Ecuadorians caught near the U.S.-Mexico border are deported on ERO flights, which usually leave from states along the U.S.-Mexico border, in recent years primarily from Louisiana (from the Oakdale, Louisiana, facility constructed in the late 1980s). If Ecuadorians are detained in the U.S. interior, they may be transferred to ERO departure locations for deportation, or, less frequently, they are placed on commercial flights to Ecuador.

While this final step may move swiftly, some migrants are stuck in it for weeks or even months for a variety of reasons. ERO typically flies one plane of deportees to Guayaquil, Ecuador, every two or three weeks. If there is a backlog of Ecuadorians waiting for a flight, then a migrant must wait through the departures of numerous flights to Ecuador. In two cases at the House of the Migrant, Ecuadorians waited so long for an ERO flight that (according to ICE officials with whom I spoke) their paperwork expired, and the ERO had to reapply for the travel permission—essentially sending them back to step two. In several other cases, departures were delayed due to medical quarantines imposed on a facility during the 2009 AH1N1 (swine flu) scare.

CASE STUDY: FOUR SANTA LUISANS

Now we return to the four Ecuadorians from Santa Luisa to show how these three steps can play out in quite different experiences for detainees, in both legal processes and time detained. The four men were Remigio, Gabriel, Victor, and Iván. Family members of Iván and Remigio came into the House of the Migrant, independent of each other, soon after their capture, with inquiries regarding their whereabouts and situation. I therefore followed the four cases and interviewed Iván and Remigio after their deportation to Ecuador.

Remigio was deported to Ecuador after six weeks in detention. He had been caught four and a half years earlier crossing the U.S.-Mexico border and released from custody with a Notice to Appear. When he did not appear in court, he was ordered removed in absentia. When Remigio was caught in Pennsylvania, the original removal order was reinstated. He then proceeded relatively quickly through steps two and three.

Gabriel and Victor arrived in Ecuador approximately two and three months, respectively, after capture in Pennsylvania. Because neither of these men had been apprehended before, they were granted voluntary departure. Gabriel was able to meet all the conditions of voluntary departure while he remained detained, which include obtaining the necessary travel documents and buying a full-price, changeable ticket within strict time limits, and he returned to Ecuador after eight weeks total. Victor, however, could not meet all the conditions of voluntary departure within the time allowed, and the voluntary departure was automatically converted to a final removal order. He therefore spent an additional month in detention than did Gabriel while the ERO obtained his travel paperwork and he waited for a flight.

Iván was detained for four and a half months before being deported. Like Remigio, Iván had been caught at the U.S.-Mexico border in his first migration attempt in 2005. Unlike Remigio, however, Iván had actually been deported. His second migration attempt six months later was successful, and he lived in Connecticut for four years until his capture in Pennsylvania. The ICE office housed in Pike County Correctional Facility opted to charge Iván with the criminal felony charge of illegal reentry, punishable with three to twenty years in jail.[12] After three months, the U.S. Attorney's office dropped the case, and Iván was given a final order of removal. Now finally in step two after three months, he was scheduled for a flight in late June. Unfortunately, Iván was then caught in a swine flu quarantine at one detention facility, causing him to miss his scheduled flight and become stuck in a flight backlog. These incidents added an additional five weeks to his detention.

To reach the physical moment of deportation, detainees much pass through a mine-filled void of legal processes, in which seemingly miniscule circumstances can trigger different legal procedures and significantly alter how long someone is detained. In 2013, the average detention stay was thirty-one days, and 70 percent of detainees were detained for under a month, but there were many cases of much longer detentions (TRAC 2013; see also American Friends Service Committee 2010; ACLU 2011). Since then, the average time detained has only increased, as detention numbers swell and court backlogs grow (discussed below). To immigration officials within the detention and deportation system, detainees' varied trajectories from apprehension to deportation may be routine, even banal. To detainees themselves, and those outside the detention and deportation bureaucracy, it can be a murky, frustrating, unpredictable process.

Lost in Time and Space

In addition to uncertainty and confusion around how long they will be detained, many detainees are transferred multiple times between facilities. Migrants detained in the United States experience a high degree of forced mobility (Human Rights Watch 2009; TRAC 2009; ACLU 2011). Detainees are rarely held in only one detention center, and many are transferred numerous times before being deported. A 2009 report noted that as of 2008, the numbers of transfers that take place per year exceeded the number of detainees. Over 50 percent of detainees were transferred at least one time, and one in every four detainees was transferred multiple times (TRAC 2009). It has become more difficult to track individual transfers due to restrictions on the information DHS makes available, but it is clear that frequent transfers remain a staple of immigration detention today (TRAC 2016b). Together, the unpredictable durations of detention and multiple transfers can create a sense of vertigo for detainees and their supporters. The spatiotemporality of the chaotic geographies of detention came up constantly in my research, in my searches for detained Ecuadorians, and in interviewing deportees.

In my forty interviews with deportees in Ecuador, I asked them to name, in order, the places where they had been detained and how long they were detained, including the time at each location. The average number of places detained was 3.4. Ten interviewees were detained in more than four places. One was transferred eight times. The total time detained for my interviewees ranged from two and a half to twenty-eight weeks. Here, I first explore what this mobility looks like by mapping the transfer paths of six interviewees.[13] Then, I decipher transfer patterns together with detention durations to the extent possible. Finally, I consider the consequences of transfers for those outside the system, especially family members in Ecuador. In the next chapter I fully explore ramifications for detainees, though some will begin to emerge here.

The maps of transfer paths illustrate that while some transfer patterns appear logical—in that they move detainees closer to deportation departure sites—other transfers appear to defy geographical reason (see maps 2–7). Maps 2–4 illustrate the paths of migrants transferred four times. Eduardo (map 2) was initially detained near the U.S.-Mexico border in Arizona and was transferred progressively closer to the Louisiana facility that serves as a hub for ERO flights. Remigio (map 3), one of the four Santa Luisan men discussed in the previous section, passed through three facilities in the state of Pennsylvania, and then he was moved to Louisiana for an ERO flight. Hugo (map 4) was apprehended in New York City, then moved inland to Pennsylvania, then flown west two-thirds of the way across the country to New Mexico, and then back east to Louisiana for deportation.

Maps 5–7 depict the paths of migrants detained in more than four places, which was the experience of one quarter of my interviewees. Marcelo's path, shown in map 5, illustrates the geographical absurdity inherent to many transfers. Detained first in New Jersey, Marcelo zigzagged and looped through space as he passed through a total of six facilities before being deported. Some transfer paths were so complicated as to make mapping them a challenge. The route of Oscar (map 6), apprehended in Queens, New York, involved seven stops, and one of his transfers moved him back to a facility where he had been previously. Diego (map 7), like numerous other interviewees, did not know the

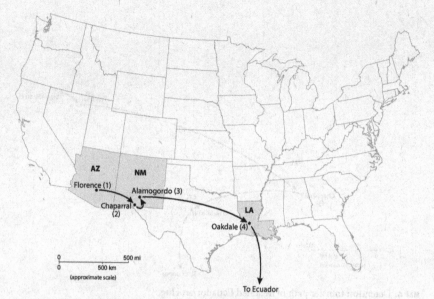

MAP 2. Detention transfer path of detained Ecuadorian Eduardo

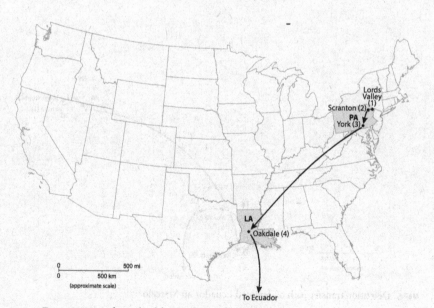

MAP 3. Detention transfer path of detained Ecuadorian Remigio

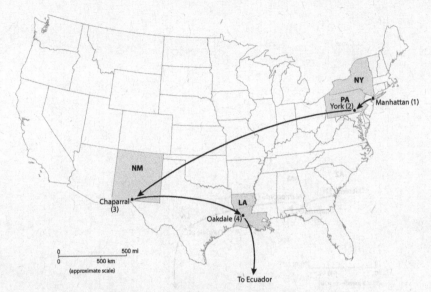

MAP 4. Detention transfer path of detained Ecuadorian Hugo

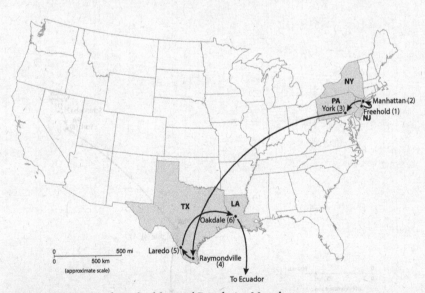

MAP 5. Detention transfer path of detained Ecuadorian Marcelo

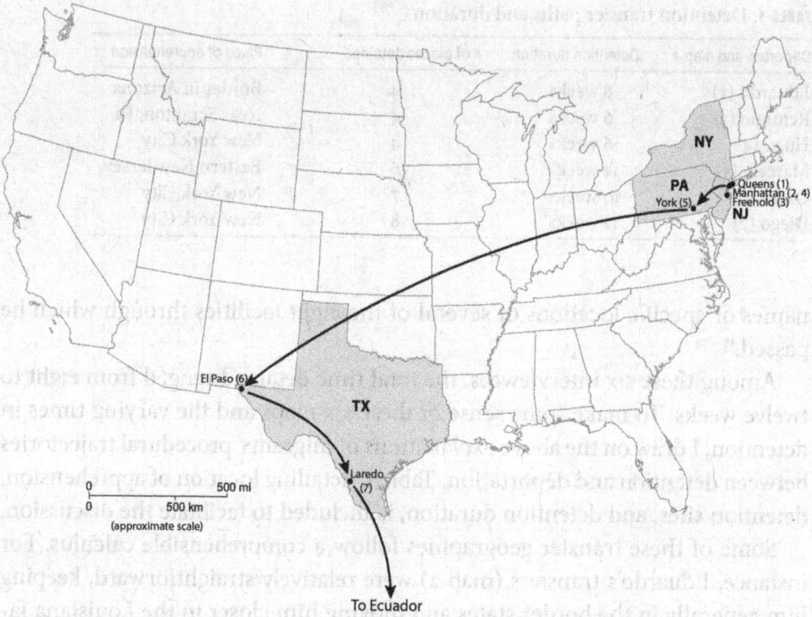

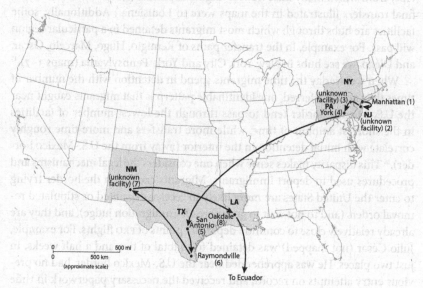

MAP 6. Detention transfer path of detained Ecuadorian Oscar

MAP 7. Detention transfer path of detained Ecuadorian Diego

TABLE 1. Detention transfer paths and duration

Deportee and map #	Detention duration	# of places detained	Place of apprehension
Eduardo (2)	8 weeks	4	Border in Arizona
Remigio (3)	6 weeks	4	Near Scranton, Pa.
Hugo (4)	6 weeks	4	New York City
Marcelo (5)	12 weeks	6	Eastern New Jersey
Oscar (6)	10 weeks	7	New York City
Diego (7)	12 weeks	8	New York City

names or specific locations of several of the eight facilities through which he passed.[14]

Among these six interviewees, the total time detained ranged from eight to twelve weeks. To make some sense of these six maps and the varying times in detention, I draw on the above explanations of migrants' procedural trajectories between detention and deportation. Table 1, detailing location of apprehension, detention sites, and detention duration, is included to facilitate the discussion.

Some of these transfer geographies follow a comprehensible calculus. For instance, Eduardo's transfers (map 2) were relatively straightforward, keeping him generally in the border states and moving him closer to the Louisiana facility from which many interviewees' flights departed. (Note that five of the six final transfers illustrated in the maps were to Louisiana.) Additionally, some facilities are hubs through which most migrants detained in a particular region will pass. For example, in the transfer paths of Remigio, Hugo, Marcelo, Oscar, and Diego, we see hubs in New York City and York, Pennsylvania (maps 3–7).[15]

When we overlay the time migrants spend in detention with the number of times they are transferred, one identifiable pattern is that migrants caught near the U.S.-Mexico border tend to pass through the lowest number of facilities in the shortest amount of time, while more transfers and more time roughly correlate with initial detention in the interior (away from the U.S.-Mexico border).[16] This disparity makes sense when one considers the legal mechanisms and procedures used to deport immigrants. Migrants caught on the border trying to enter the United States are more likely to receive expedited or stipulated removal orders (and to not wait to go before an immigration judge), and they are already relatively close to common departure points of ERO flights. For example, Julio César (not mapped) was detained for a total of two and a half weeks, in just two places. He was apprehended near the U.S.-Mexico border, had no previous entry attempts on record, and received the necessary paperwork in time for the first available deportation flight to Ecuador. In contrast, those caught in the U.S. interior, with less chance of receiving a stipulated or expedited removal order, are more likely to see an immigration judge.[17] Due to mandatory detention laws and court backlogs, those migrants who are waiting to see a judge face extended detention times (Human Rights Watch 2009; ACLU 2011; TRAC

2013, 2015a, 2015b), particularly those seeking relief from removal (Welch 2002; Dow 2004; Fernandes 2007; American Friends Service Committee 2010; ACLU 2011; TRAC 2013).[18] A predictor of the longest detention durations, then, is tied to attempts to fight a removal decision, wherever someone was picked up. Saira (not mapped) was apprehended near the border and then detained for sixteen weeks while trying to obtain asylum. Sergio (not mapped) was picked up in the U.S. interior after living in the United States for eight years and detained for twenty-eight weeks while he fought a removal order. Both eventually gave up.

In a type of double jeopardy, transfers can contribute to extended detention durations, as pieces of information are lost and paperwork—such as travel documents—is rerouted (ACLU 2011). On numerous occasions in my work searching for migrants, I was told that the paper "file" had not arrived with a new transfer, meanwhile precluding advancement in her or his procedural trajectory. Also, a new set of personnel must become familiar enough with the migrant's case to take the appropriate procedural steps.

But the spatiotemporal geography of many interviewees' detention did not seem to follow any discernible pattern or logic. For example, despite the fact that Eduardo's (map 2) situation was similar to that of Julio César's (not mapped, detained two and a half weeks), Eduardo was detained for significantly longer (eight weeks) and transferred two more times. We can also compare Franklin (not mapped), who was in the same place for all sixteen weeks of his detention, with Clemente (not mapped), who passed through five detention places in just four weeks. What's more, transfers do not necessarily bring a migrant closer to a departure point for flights, such as Diego's (map 7) transfer from Texas to New Mexico before being transferred to and deported from Louisiana. Another example is that of Martín (not mapped), who was transferred from Massachusetts to Puerto Rico and then back to the continental United States before deportation to Ecuador. Others' paths show migrants being shuffled back and forth between the same facilities or geographically proximate facilities, as was Oscar's (map 6) experience. Different facilities have different procedures and average detention times (TRAC 2013). The case of two brothers who were traveling together, with identical migration histories, illustrates this point well. Andrés and Juan were both captured by ICE on the Texas border and detained in the Willacy Detention Center in Harlingen, Texas. Juan was transferred to the South Texas Detention Center in San Antonio, due to, as explained to me by an ICE official, lack of "bed space" in Harlingen. This move led to a much longer detention time for Juan; Andrés returned to Ecuador after three weeks, while Juan returned almost two months later.

How can these baffling variations be explained? One factor is the piecemeal way in which the detention and deportation apparatus was constructed, as described in chapter 3. The rapid expansion initiated in 1996 and accelerated in 2001 occasioned a mismatch of available facilities with places of capture. A

2009 report by the Transactional Records Access Clearinghouse at Syracuse University (TRAC 2009, n.p.) states, "As the number of detainees has grown, the agency—at least until recently—has not sought to balance where it located new detention beds with where the individuals were apprehended. Instead ICE has adopted a free-wheeling transfer policy to deal with the resulting imbalances. Under this policy, ICE transports detainees from their point of initial ICE detention to many different locations—often over long distances and frequently to remote locations." A lack of long-range planning and coordination—the ad hoc manner in which the detention system has been thrown together (Wadhia 2015)—is therefore a contributor to the high number of transfers.

The power and influence of the immigration industrial complex is also critically important in the shaping of this spatiotemporal chaos, beyond its role in propelling the growth of the detention and deportation system in general. The fact that a detention center makes money for every day it houses a migrant contributes to extended durations because managers are not motivated to facilitate a detainee's departure. That per-day fee also influences migrants' circuitous transfer paths, as different players wrangle to fill "beds" (Dow 2004; Barry 2010; Cervantes-Gautschi 2010; Wood 2011). Targeted lobbying efforts by private prison companies in the business of detention also contribute to the broad lack of government oversight of the unwieldy detention and deportation system (Flynn and Cannon 2009). How this lack of oversight impacts the material conditions of detention is discussed in the next chapter, but here I point to how it contributes to considerable unevenness in detention times and physical routes through the detention system.

While I have discerned some of the logics behind uneven detention durations and multiple transfers, for the most part all of these reasons remain illegible to family members in Ecuador, who do not have—nor likely would they want—maps to trace detainees' physical locations, charts of average detention times to help them gauge, or lists of possible reasons for variations in either of these. The confusing, disorienting spatiotemporality of detention simply adds to the sense that detainees are lost in time and space.

Conclusion

This chapter attempts to bring some order to the seeming chaos of the detention and deportation system's organization and operation, from a country of migrant origin. Family members of detained migrants come up against a formidable bureaucracy, composed of many diverse entities and actors, shifting and uneven policies and practices, and competing interests. First, migrants are detained in more than two hundred facilities. To "find" a detainee, one must piece together partial bits of information and negotiate varying sets of rules and procedures, as well as different degrees of cooperation and knowledge among employees. For most people outside the system, such navigations are impossible, effectively blocking them from entry. Then, for detained migrants, the legal paths between apprehension and deportation are not only complex, but they also can be significantly shaped by discretionary decisions at multiple points by numerous actors, ranging from intaking officers to immigration judges. Accidents of circumstance, too, can have important consequences, such as lack of "bed space" in one facility that leads to a transfer, a medical quarantine, or delayed paperwork. Finally, detention is characterized by an often perplexing spatiotemporality. Detainees can be jerked between facilities while simultaneously feeling suspended in time.

The collective effect is the projection of chaos at the heart of the detention and deportation system. It contributes to the construction of thick barriers protecting the system—literally and metaphorically—from view and scrutiny. Even the challenges of communicating, such as unanswered calls and uneven responses, provide revealing glimpses at the bureaucratic walls around U.S. migrant detention and deportation. My efforts to gather information also illustrate that government immigration policies are enacted by individuals, with their own opinions, beliefs, and personal stories (Mountz 2003, 2004, 2007, 2010; Hall 2012; Bosworth 2014), which can act as additional builders of unpredictability and insulation. It is tempting to link design to intentionality in ways that inadvertently limit our ability to understand the forces that constitute immigration control. In contrast, by recognizing how the detention and deportation system produces chaos exactly through a kind of unintentional design, we create cracks in the chaos and open opportunities for contesting it.

The next chapter focuses on detention and deportation's chaos from inside the system. That is, I further explore how the chaos is experienced by those inside the system and what exactly the chaos works to conceal—two questions that are tightly intertwined.

CHAPTER 5

The "Peculiar" Advantages of Chaos

Detainees' Experiences

The U.S detention and deportation system—made up of hundreds of facilities under varying models of ownership, pushing detainees through complex legal procedures, and full of uneven practices—projects a sense of chaos. This projected chaos has important effects, or Weizman's (2007, 8) "peculiar structural advantages," that serve the goals of the U.S. state. This chapter explores how particular, pervasive conditions of detention work to foreclose alternatives to deportation—the contention at the core of my naming of and attention to the U.S. detention and deportation "system." Detainees often experience what Welch calls the "Kafkaesque nature of detention" (Welch 2002, 109; see also Sutton and Vigneswaran 2011), in reference to a 1937 play by Franz Kafka that tells the story of a man trying to defend himself without knowing the charges and evidence against him or how long his imprisonment and trial will last. The chaos of detention functions in a similar manner, blocking detainees' access to support networks, obscuring alternatives to deportation, and dehumanizing and demoralizing detainees. For many detained migrants, these barriers and frustrations work collectively to gradually wear away at their resolve to fight deportation, and to accept deportation as inevitable and—after extended time in the grind of detention—even welcome (Coutin 2010a; Martin 2012; Fischer 2013; Hasselberg 2014).

This chapter also points to additional "peculiar" advantages of the detention and deportation system's chaos for the state. The most important of these is that the chaos cloaks the role of entrenched interests in maintaining and expanding the system, or what has been called the immigration industrial complex. Entities and individuals who benefit in some way from anti-immigrant rhetoric and policies—private companies, federal government agencies, local governments contracting "bed space," politicians, and the media—all come together in the hype around and promotion of detention and deportation (Golash-Boza 2009; Doty and Wheatley 2013; Hernández-León 2013; Menz 2013; Sørenson and Gammeltoft-Hansen 2013; Martin 2016). The system grows ever bigger, therefore, due to the convergence of revenue-generating strategies with the politically popular optics of being "tough" on immigrants racialized as un-American and therefore unwanted. This convergence profoundly shapes the experiences of detained migrants, as facilities adopt practices that increase profits but make life miserable for detainees.

Then, another "peculiar advantage" of the chaos is concealment of these rights, abuses, and system shortcomings. Any taking of responsibility is avoided through bureaucratic processes of contracting and the involvement of a wide network of entities and individuals (Bosworth 2014; Gill 2016; Martin 2016; Hiemstra and Conlon 2017). Inefficiencies and waste within the system go unchecked and unremarked. There is little notice, for example, of the needless costs of multiple, geographically illogical transfers of detainees or of extra days of detention for which the federal government pays—at an average of $124 per day—because a detainee's paperwork was lost. This chapter also considers, in the final section, another advantage for the state. The detention and deportation system does not just reflect a negative scripting of immigrants. Importantly, it also provides a crucial space for bolstering national identity and, with it, narratives of homeland security.

Systematizing Injustices, Funneling Deportation

Legally, detention and deportation are considered administrative procedures and not criminal punishments. This distinction is completely at odds with how detention and deportation are experienced by migrants (Golash-Boza 2010). All facilities that detain immigrants on behalf of ICE are required to follow ICE's Performance-Based National Detention Standards (PBNDS).[1] These standards, first implemented in 2000 and revised by the Obama administration in 2008 and again in 2011, provide guidelines for maintaining "a safe and secure detention environment for staff and detainees" (U.S. ICE, 2012, n.p.). Ideally, the PBNDS should guarantee that detainees receive appropriate care, in terms of access to legal resources, meeting daily needs, and protection from abuse. In practice, however, there is little federal oversight of detention facilities or enforcement of the PBNDS. Consequently, detainees' experiences are critically shaped by how the political goal of channeling migrants to deportation intertwines with revenue-generating strategies. In short, conditions of detention can be pocked with oppressions big and small. High levels of disorientation and uncertainty and innumerable everyday injustices are woven into detained migrants' experiences in ways that further intensify the chaos of detention. Seemingly mundane material characteristics of confinement are important for how they shape the conditions of detention, as well as how they work to further objectify and degrade detainees (Bosworth 2014; Gill 2016).

"UNDUE" PROCESSES

The structure and operation of the detention system contributes to stripping migrants of many of the due process rights theoretically guaranteed them by the U.S. Constitution (Miller 2003a; Kanstroom 2007a; D. M. Hernández 2008).[2] Instead, as D. M. Hernández (2008, 48) frames it, immigrant detainees are subject to a host of "undue processes," which curtail efforts and opportunities to contest deportation.

Being locked up in a carceral environment isolates detainees, and many detention facilities are located in faraway, hard-to-reach places, which further problematize detainees' access to resources and support systems (Bloch and Schuster 2005; Mountz and Loyd 2014). These conditions immediately complicate efforts to fight deportation, blocking access to personal networks, resources, and information. For example, it can be difficult to simply obtain documents necessary to support a legitimate immigration claim. One deportee I interviewed, Pato, could not get ahold of the documents needed for his application for relief from removal while in detention. He remarked, "You can't do anything there locked up."

Access to legal advice and representation is profoundly consequential to case outcomes, but most detained migrants do not obtain such counsel (TRAC 2006b; National Immigrant Justice Center 2010; ACLU 2011; Eagly and Shafer 2016). Detained migrants do have the right to legal counsel, but the sticking point is that—in contrast to the criminal justice system—they have to pay for it or find pro bono representation (D. M. Hernández 2008; Coleman 2009; Golash-Boza 2010). Detainees' ability to acquire counsel is complicated by cost, lack of information regarding pro bono possibilities, the remote location of many facilities, limited access to phone and rates charged for calls, and the practice of frequently transferring detainees.[3] Most detainees, therefore, do not have a lawyer; 84 percent of detained immigrants go unrepresented in immigration court proceedings, as compared with over half of all immigrants in proceedings (ACLU 2015; Eagly and Shafer 2016).

Without advice about the complicated legal framework of deportation, detainees often make uninformed decisions that ensure their deportation, and they are more susceptible to deception and coercion. For example, stipulated orders must be signed by the receiver. Thirteen of the forty Ecuadorian deportees I interviewed indicated that they signed stipulated orders because they did not realize what they were signing or were pressured to sign by immigration officials. Often the documents are not translated from English. Manuel said that "they made me sign things that I wouldn't have signed if I had known [what they were]." Detainees' signatures are also obtained by threat and bullying (Coutin 2010a). Armando recalled that "in the first detention place they made me sign papers. I told them that I didn't want to sign, that I wanted to see a lawyer. They told me that I didn't have the right to anything." Similarly, Tommy recalled,

"They told me that we aren't going to send you to a judge so [just] sign your deportation [papers] . . . they said to me that if you don't sign your deportation we are going to throw you in jail, throw you in jail for five years." Some of these Ecuadorians may have been able to present legitimate reasons to a judge for avoiding deportation (Koh 2008, 2013; American Immigration Council 2014).

Expedited removal can be applied to an undocumented migrant who has been in the country fewer than fourteen days and was caught within one hundred miles of any U.S. border. (In 2017, President Trump proposed making it applicable to undocumented immigrants caught anywhere in the country and present in the United States for up to two years.) Expedited removal does not require the migrant's consent or a hearing in an immigration court. Without access to counsel, most detainees do not know that expedited removal could be avoided by presenting evidence to prove that their length of residency is greater than two weeks. Furthermore, a lack of legal counsel contributes to missed opportunities to file for various forms of discretionary relief from removal. Unrepresented detainees are often not informed of possibilities to file for relief, are actively discouraged from doing so by facility and ICE personnel, and are not made aware of the strict time limits placed on filing (Miller 2003a; National Immigrant Justice Center 2010; ACLU 2011; Center for Latin American Studies 2013; Eagly and Shafer 2016). A lack of translation services or materials in languages other than English further prevents non-English speakers from understanding options available to them (Miller 2003a).

For those detainees who do maintain the right to appear in court, they face a backlogged and overworked system that some have likened to "kangaroo court" (De León 2015, 110). As of November 2017, there was a new high for pending cases in the Immigration Courts of 658,728 (TRAC 2018); in 2015, prior to this new high, the average wait time was already 599 days (calculation of days not available for 2017) (TRAC 2015a, 2015b).[4] The backlog is due partly to ICE's goal of raising deportation numbers (Preston 2011) as well as surging numbers of families and minors in the system. The backlog also stems from a failure to keep the courts adequately staffed (TRAC 2010, 2011, 2016a). Once migrants do appear in court, backlogs negatively influence their chances of a fair hearing. For example, judges are pressured to handle more cases with fewer resources at a faster pace (Becker and Cabrera 2009). In some detention facilities, migrants' or judges' appearances in court occur long distance, by videoconferencing, and studies have shown that such distance can be detrimental to case outcomes (Human Rights Watch 2009; Eagly and Shafer 2016). In addition, jaded and overworked judges are more likely to make decisions guided by personal opinion (TRAC 2006b; S. Hernandez 2010). Overall, chances for positive case outcomes are low. In 2014, for example, there were only 23,084 cases in which EOIR judges granted some form of relief (TRAC 2015c). Another important factor to consider pertains to the previous point about lack of legal counsel. Migrants without counsel are more likely to choose to advance claims with little chance of success. Counsel help determine if a claim is worth advancing and put forward claims with a higher probability of success. Under these circumstances, a migrant's "right" to present her or his case in court often turns into a fruitless extension of detention duration (D. M. Hernández 2008).

A recurring complaint of detained migrants is a serious lack of information regarding their situation (National Immigrant Justice Center 2010; ACLU 2011; Bosworth 2014). In direct violation of the PBNDS, the majority of the deportees I interviewed said that they did not receive sufficient information about what was happening to them, such as the status of their case and when they were to be deported (never mind their rights and possible alternatives to deportation). In the interviews I conducted with two of the four Santa Luisan men (discussed in the previous chapter), it was clear that neither ever had a clear idea of the details of their cases, including if and when they were to be deported. In fact, Iván said that he did not know that he was being charged with illegal reentry until several weeks after we knew at the House of the Migrant, and he did not know that he had been in a quarantine until I told him during our interview. It is remarkable that detainees' lack of information parallels that of their family members in Ecuador. Clearly, geographic distance is not the only barrier to information. Confusion, equivocation, and secrecy are embedded in the organization and operation of the detention and deportation system.

Here, as with personnel I spoke to via Skype, subjective decisions and uneven practices from facility to facility can significantly impact what detainees know, as well as the accuracy and consistency of information they are given. Carlos complained that he would receive one answer from one ICE official, but then another official would supply a different answer. Migrants' experiences also vary according to location. For example, in one facility Ana Lucía had no idea what was happening with her case. In a different place to which she was transferred, however, ICE officials came every Tuesday and Thursday to answer questions. Additionally, guards can exert a significant degree of control over detainees' access to information. José Carlos reported that guards decided which migrants were given the opportunity to speak with ICE officials when they visited. If the guards did not deem a detainee's request valid, then he or she was not granted a meeting. Carlos recounted, "Sometimes you put your name down to talk to a counselor to ask something, but were never called . . . It was because of the guards because they made up the list."

DISORIENTATION IN SPACE AND TIME

The spatiotemporalities of detention work to further isolate, disorient, and frustrate detainees. The unpredictability of how long they will be detained is one of the most difficult aspects of migrants' confinement (Conlon 2011; Bosworth

2014; Gill 2016). Most of my interviewees did not know when they would be deported until the moment of departure, and many expressed that they felt trapped in a purgatory of waiting. José Carlos stated, "Being locked up there you get desperate, because there was no way to communicate with anyone or know when you are going to be sent, nothing." Daniela, detained a total of two months, watched as a group of four Ecuadorians came in after her and stayed only three weeks; she was depressed and frustrated when she could get no explanation for her longer wait time from officials. Carlos also described feeling desperate when he could not obtain information, and said: "You suffocate because you don't know when they are going to get you out."

Extended and indefinite detention clearly influences detainees' decisions about contesting removal (ACLU 2011). Sergio had lived undocumented in the United States for eight years and had a U.S. citizen wife and child. Though Sergio believed he had a good chance at receiving relief from removal and had a lawyer paid by his U.S. employer, after twenty-eight weeks in detention he decided to give up his appeal because he was told the process would have meant at least another year in detention. David's decision to not apply for asylum provides another example. His experience of kidnapping and torture en route to the United States made him eligible to apply for asylum. I communicated with a paralegal working for the Florence Immigrant and Refugee Rights Project in Arizona who met with David; she emailed: "Although he said that initially he would like to fight his case, he is concerned by the amount of time it would take and the economic toll it would take on his family. This appears to be the main reason he intends to take a deportation order." Similarly, Saira, who applied for asylum based on claims of domestic abuse in Ecuador, said that after being detained three months she gave up. "I couldn't stand to be there any more time, locked up . . . there I was sick all the time, sometimes I could eat and sometimes I couldn't eat, and I couldn't stand to be shut in anymore, so I signed my deportation" (author's research journal, June 16, 2009).

The sense of being suspended in time intersects in painful ways with frequent mobility across space. Migrants often find the mobility between facilities disorienting and upsetting (Gill 2009a; Human Rights Watch 2009; ACLU 2011). ICE often treats transfers as guarded secrets. In a 2009 report, TRAC notes how its own efforts to compile information were complicated by ICE's and contracted facilities' reluctance and refusal to share even basic data regarding transfers. In my research, José Carlos explained how guards sustained a sense of secrecy throughout detainee movements: "They take you in a van . . . and they enter [detention facilities] by tunnels . . . you don't even know where you are." As already mentioned, some interviewees did not know names or locations of the facilities through which they passed. Most interviewees reported little to no advanced notice regarding when a transfer was to occur, to where, or why. Many reported being awoken during the night and made to leave immediately. Remigio recounted, "They just arrive at your cell saying 'you are going, get your things' and nothing else. They don't tell you ahead of time or don't let you call your family to let them know you are going to be transferred, none of that."

Detainee mobility is a tool for impeding due process to ensure deportation. Transfers can also be profoundly detrimental to case outcomes (Morawetz 2005; Human Rights Watch 2009; National Immigrant Justice Center 2010; ACLU 2011). For migrants detained while living in the U.S. interior, transfers away from their home area truncate access to familial and legal support networks that could assist efforts to avoid deportation (National Immigrant Justice Center 2010; ACLU 2011). Transfers interfere with established lawyer-client relationships, hinder detainees' right to select their own counsel, and change the set of laws applied to particular cases (Human Rights Watch 2009). To the DHS, difficulty of access is a plus when selecting detention sites (Martin 2012), and, therefore, as already stated, many detention facilities are located in remote, hard-to-reach areas far from urban areas (Human Rights Watch 2009; National Immigrant Justice Center 2010; ACLU 2011).

Some transfers are plainly orchestrated to ensure deportation. As Martin (2012, 329) writes, "Transferring detainees between facilities allows ICE to manipulate 'due process,' exploiting the U.S. Federal Court's uneven legal geography to attain its desired legal outcomes." Kanstroom (2007b) reported that immigrants apprehended during a 2007 raid in New Bedford, Massachusetts, were quickly transferred to detention facilities in Texas before they could inform family members and meet with lawyers. The rates of transfer to court districts known to be hostile to detainees' claims are notably higher than to those that are not (Morawetz 2005; Human Rights Watch 2009), and migrants are frequently transferred to places where few pro bono lawyers are available (Fernandes 2007; Human Rights Watch 2009; ACLU 2011). Transfers are also used to punish and control detainees (Gill 2009a). For example, detainees have been transferred in retribution for participating in protests regarding treatment and facility conditions (Bernstein 2010b), and known organizers have been moved to preempt continued organizing (Dow 2004).

Finally, high levels of mobility also work to maintain detainees on the path to deportation through the disciplinary effect that they have on both system employees and support groups potentially poised to assist them. As Gill (2009a, 2009b) found in the United Kingdom, frequent transfers undermine potentially helpful relationships in detention. He writes (2009a, 195), "The moral sensibilities of the manager cause him to respond to the mobility of detainees by reducing the level of support offered." Even if detainees (most of them asylum seekers in Gill's research) have a moving story, employees become numb to the relentless succession of crises. Support groups, too, are discouraged from providing aid when they know from experience that the time and energy they invest will be wasted in the event of a likely transfer (Gill 2009a, 2009b).

ISOLATION

Many detainees feel a disturbing sense of isolation, cut off from family and support networks. In addition to isolation negatively impacting their ability to contest deportation, it also fundamentally determines how they experience their confinement. Communicating with the world outside detention becomes a challenging, fraught endeavor for migrants immediately upon detention. Javier explained that while detained, "I lost contact with my family, I lost contact with everyone. That is, from the moment that Migration took me, I lost contact with, with everyone, and from there I couldn't make calls or tell anyone where they could find me."

Any cell phones are confiscated upon apprehension, making direct calls impossible and also resulting in the temporary loss of contact information stored in those phones. Most facilities do not permit incoming calls to a detainee. While communication by mail is possible, the process of sending and receiving letters, especially internationally, can be complicated and time consuming. Also, frequent transfers mean that a letter may arrive after the migrant has been moved from the facility. Email access, now becoming available in some facilities, is highly controlled, monitored, and not free. Consequently, with few exceptions, communication between a detainee and the outside world depends on the detainee initiating a call.

But the process of making a phone call is not straightforward or cheap, particularly for detainees attempting to communicate outside the United States. Migrants are technically entitled to one free domestic call upon arrival at a new place of detention. The experiences of several interviewees, however, suggest that this call is not always granted. Paúl reported, "When I was in [one facility], the official gave me a call, but I talked for only a minute, and no one answered the phone, but he marked it down on the paper as taken, so I never got a call." The free call may not include international calls (apparently depending on individual facilities' policies), complicating efforts to communicate with family members in countries of migrant origin. What's more, one free call falls far short of needs for communicating with family, legal counsel, and other support networks, especially for detainees held extended periods of time.

To communicate outside detention, therefore, detained migrants must purchase phone time, a process that can be plagued with challenges (National Immigrant Justice Center 2010; ACLU 2011; Conlon and Hiemstra 2014). Phone systems in detention facilities are contracted out to private, for-profit companies, and call rates tend to be grossly inflated. Even the procedure for obtaining a calling card may be challenging. For example, purchase requests for cards often take a week to fill. Calling cards are facility specific, so if transferred a detainee loses purchased cards. And, of course, if a migrant is not detained with money on her or his person, then the ability to buy a calling card depends on receiving money from family or friends (which can be a complicated process in itself) or earning money by working in the detention facility (discussed below).[5] While many ICE personnel informed me that detainees could make collect calls, the fact that few interviewees mentioned such a possibility suggests that they are not informed of it. To make matters worse, many phones in Ecuador are not able to receive collect calls.

In addition, there are often not enough phones available to meet demand, so detainees have to wait a long time to make a call, calls have to be short, and the "privilege" of making a call is determined according to a pecking order established by guards (National Immigrant Justice Center 2010; ACLU 2011). For example, Ecuadorian deportee Oscar reported that in one detention facility there was one phone for over twenty people; there was always a line, and you were not allowed to make multiple calls. José Carlos explained how inmates' success or failure in communicating outside the facility could depend on individual guards' attitudes. "It is up to [guards], if they feel like it they let you call but if they don't, no. There were a couple who were good, if you wanted to call you asked and they let you. On the other hand, when you told others you wanted to call, they said no, no, no, go away and don't bother me, it isn't allowed." Again, subjective decisions of facility personnel have important implications.

The fact that detainees are under constant surveillance (or believe that they are) also effectively restricts communication with family members, because detainees may fear that calls to undocumented family or friends could put them in danger. Many interviewees were informed that calls would be recorded, and others suspected or feared that would be the case. Some interviewees recalled that before making a call they had to state whom they were calling, their relationship to them, and record the phone number. Tulio explained that many of his family members in the United States were without papers, and he believed that immigration officials wanted him to call in order to obtain information about them. He said, "Migration asks you where your family lives, they know that I have grandchildren there . . . [they asked] 'Where do they live? Give me their phone number, call them.' You can never [call], and what's more all calls are intercepted, they are checked by the police and by Immigration, so you can never [call], and so I never communicated with anyone there."

Transfers between facilities further complicate communication efforts. Migrants, family members, and others in support networks often scramble to locate and reestablish communication after a transfer. Adding to this challenge is the fact that calling cards are specific to the facility in which they are purchased, which means that if a detainee is suddenly transferred the card becomes useless. José Carlos explained, "I had money, but the problem was that sometimes it took four or five days for them to give you the card. You fill out a request for the card and it comes after five days. They came to give me the card and that same day that the card arrived, that day they transferred me and that card was only good there, in the other one it was no good." Many interviewees reported that their account money, which is supposed to transfer with them, arrived at their new location weeks after they did (or in some cases, never arrived). Until that money arrived they could not purchase a calling card and were thus unable to inform people of their new location.

THE DAILY MATERIALITIES OF DETENTION

In addition to feelings of disorientation and isolation, many detainees contend with physical discomfort, even pain, and mental anguish stemming from the conditions of their confinement. In theory, the PBNDS should ensure that detainees do not suffer unduly physically or mentally while in detention. In practice, however, detention is rife with problems regarding the basic provision of care. My interviewees' accounts corroborate numerous reports on detention centers around the country, illustrating that these problems cannot be dismissed as specific to a few rogue facilities; they are system-wide.

Detainees often experience hunger due to both insufficient and inedible food (American Friends Service Committee 2010; ACLU 2011; Conlon and Hiemstra 2014). Certainly, the most common complaints among my interviewees had to do with food. Manuel, who said that he went from 220 to 175 pounds over the course of three months of detention, remarked, "It is a jail, and of course they cannot serve food made to order. But the food caused trauma!" Deportees complained, for example, of burned and spoiled food. Tommy explained, "They gave us food, but like you would give to a dog . . . No one liked it but from hunger one had to eat, even rotten, bad food. Some [people] got sick." In a separate research project that I conducted with Deirdre Conlon (Conlon and Hiemstra 2014; Hiemstra and Conlon 2016, 2017), we studied contracts between ICE and detention facilities. In the contracts we analyzed delineating detention in one county in New Jersey, it was specified that the detention facility had to supply a minimum number of calories per person per meal, but there was no mention of quality control. As long as detainees have access to food that could technically provide them with a target calorie count, ICE considers the terms of contracts met.

Some detainees also complained about the short times allotted for eating. Clemente lamented, "They gave us so little [food] that they should at least let us enjoy it for five minutes, but as soon as one sits down they are making you finish and leave," and, he added, you are not allowed to take any cafeteria food with you. The times at which detainees eat can also be unusually spaced throughout the day, with no snacks available in between meals (except for purchase, see below). Elsa, for example, reported that she ate at 4:00 a.m., 11:30 a.m., and 4:30 p.m. While such schedules may be set for bureaucratic reasons (perhaps to accommodate multiple shifts of detainees that must be fed), the effect may be cruel, forcing detainees to go for extended periods without food.

Inadequate medical care in detention is another common problem, as documented in a number of investigative reports (American Friends Service Committee 2010; Bernstein 2010a, 2010b; ACLU 2011, 2016; Human Rights Watch 2017). My interviewees expressed numerous grievances on this topic, in terms of both access to and the quality of care available. While some deportees said that they had received sufficient medical care in detention, others reported glaringly inadequate treatment. A top complaint was ignored or delayed requests to receive care. According to the detainees' accounts, in most facilities one must submit a written request and wait a minimum of three days to see a medical professional. Johnny, for example, said that "I got sick . . . but I had to fill out a form to submit, and after seven days I was seen, of course when I was already better!" Interviewees recalled being given aspirin and told to drink water for every malady. Detainees have also reported having a difficult time getting crucial prescription medicine (Human Rights Watch 2009, 2017; ACLU 2011).

Also, as documented in a number of reports (e.g., Bernstein 2010a, 2010b; ACLU 2016; Human Rights Watch 2017), detention personnel have repeatedly failed to respond appropriately to critical medical situations, suggesting an ingrained culture of doubting detainees' credibility. Carlos explained, "People can die [in detention]. There was a guy suffering from seizures, three months he was having seizures. They came and saw him, didn't do anything, they saw him a second time, the third time, because they thought it was more serious because the guy had started to bite his tongue until it bled. Only then did they take him to the doctor, because they saw it was a serious thing." The consequences of this neglect can be fatal. Just between May 2012 and June 2015, twenty-one people died in detention (Human Rights Watch 2017, 27; see also Dow 2004; Bernstein 2010a; ACLU 2011, 2016), and reports indicate that the number of deaths in detention is significantly increasing under the administration of Donald Trump (Glawe 2017). Additionally, the mental health care available appears minimal, which is particularly problematic for a detainee population dealing with the stress of radically altered lives and family separation, as well as the isolation and uncertainty of detention (Brabeck, Porterfield, and Loughry 2015). Several family members in Ecuador expressed that they were deeply concerned about the poor mental state of a detained migrant, and that no medical attention was being received for it.

Detainees regularly experience other forms of physical neglect. Transfers were frequently mentioned as a site of severe physical discomfort, during which detainees are routinely chained (Human Rights Watch 2009; ACLU 2011). While some interviewees were only mildly perturbed by this practice, others like Oscar found it traumatizing: "I want to forget that. One of the worst things in my life." Transfers typically entail lengthy processes for checking migrants out of one facility and into another. When large numbers of migrants arrive at the same time, detainees may have to wait for extended periods, still in chains. Interviewees told of waiting in crowded rooms without sufficient places to lie or sit, being provided with little food, and in exceedingly cold rooms. Julio recalled one miserable transfer experience: "Because we arrived at 8 p.m. it was too late to check us in, so we had to spend the night in a very cold room without food. Here I really suffered for the cold. It was a cement floor we had to sleep on with no beds or blankets." Many detainees report being held in such uncomfortably cold rooms—often called *hieleras*, or iceboxes—without sufficient clothing at some point during their detention (Welch 2002; ACLU 2011; Bruzzone 2016; SPLC 2016; Riva 2017). Ecuadorian interviewee Tulio recounted, "Something that is really hard . . . twenty-four hours a day it is like being in a restaurant freezer. It's something that is unbearable, and the majority of people get sick." The pervasiveness of *hieleras* across detention facilities, despite repeated complaints and reports, contradicts officials' explanations that instances of cold rooms and facilities are accidental (Riva 2017) and suggests an underlying intentionality, which can be extended to other immiserating conditions.

Former detainees also complained about poor sanitary conditions in facilities, as well as forced neglect of personal hygiene and care (SPLC 2016; American Friends Service Committee 2010; ACLU 2011). Ecuadorian deportees described filthy bathrooms, unwashed bedding and clothes, and not being allowed to bathe for extended periods. Carlos, for example, recounted "They would not wash the blankets for us . . . I was there three months and they never let me wash them. I went to leave them in the laundry, but they said no, that the chief has said that those can't be washed . . . Sometimes that caused allergies, imagine the dirt that they collect in three months!" Some interviewees reported that they had not been allowed to wash their one or two sets of issued clothes for two weeks or more, and some facilities only allowed sheet washing every three weeks. Others described how facility clothing issued to them was sometimes poorly laundered or in ragged condition from previous use. There are also complaints regarding the tight control over toiletries, like soap, shampoo, toothpaste, and sanitary pads, such that they must ask for more or try to purchase them (Barry 2009b; American Friends Service Committee 2010; Bernstein 2010b; ACLU 2011; SPLC 2016).

Finally, former detainees report struggling with the routines of daily life in detention, which can be characterized by surveillance, suspicion, and boredom. Truly in a carceral environment, every aspect of detainees' daily activities and spaces are controlled. Many facilities have video cameras in all rooms, and there are regular cell checks and head counts. Elsa recalled, "Frequently they came by, starting in the early morning, [and said] 'Count!' And you have to stand up so that they can count you." Ana Lucía was upset because guards did not let her close stall doors when using the bathroom. Detainees report being threatened with or actually placed in solitary confinement ("the hole") for actions such as complaining about conditions, refusing a guard request, or minor rule infractions (ACLU 2011). Some interviewees indicated that they felt like they were constantly suspected of wrongdoing. As Fernando said, "For everything, they cuff us feet, hands, and waist. They treat us like criminals." Rodrigo remarked that one facility was particularly nice because there were windows and you could look outside. "Except," he added, "if you looked for too long, the guards got mad and said you were thinking about escaping." Many interviewees said they tired of watching TV (especially when it was only in English), and recalled the difficulty of rarely or never being allowed outside or participating in any type of exercise. The constant surveillance and lack of ways to pass the time become more difficult to bear the longer migrants are detained.

Spending and Laboring in Detention

There are two additional components of detention discussed here: facility commissaries and voluntary work programs. Taken separately, they show how detainees' everyday routines are controlled and monetized to excruciating degrees. Taken together, they show how the chaos of detention contributes to the proliferation of strategies to commodify detainees. Understanding these commissaries and work programs, and how they interact, is critical to grasp the driving power of the immigration industrial complex. Deirdre Conlon and I have conducted research into how commissaries and in-facility work programs interact to generate additional revenue within and through the detention system (Conlon and Hiemstra 2014; Hiemstra and Conlon 2016, 2017). Here, I provide an abbreviated discussion to further fill out the picture of detainee experiences and to illustrate the critical role that privatization and contracting play in driving further detention expansion.

The material conditions of detention create demand for items such as food, medicine, clothing, and personal hygiene items. Commissaries, found in nearly every facility, offer a range of such things for purchase, and detainees are willing consumers. Saira explained that she had to purchase shampoo and toothpaste because the quantities issued were insufficient. Clemente reported that if you wanted to do anything other than watch television you could buy games, such as cards or dominoes. Commissaries typically do not sell these items cheaply; as the only option for detained migrants, they can charge inflated prices. Carlos asserted that one facility where he was detained charged triple what items normally cost, but the quality and quantity of the food provided still drove him to spend $400 to supplement it during the three months he was there.

Detainees purchase items from the commissary using personal funds kept in an account generated for them at each facility. Any money they had in their possession when detained goes into this account, and friends and relatives can add money to accounts via a complicated process of money orders or wire transfers (depending on the facility). But many people are detained with little to no money or do not have anyone who can deposit money for them. These individuals, therefore, cannot make purchases to ease the conditions of their confinement. Julio, who used the little money that he had with him when detained for phone calls, explained, "Those of us who were in jail there without money are those who suffer the most." Several interviewees told of kind fellow detainees who purchased items on their behalf and barter systems that sprang up among detainees in exchange for commissary purchases.

Here is where voluntary work programs come in, providing an option to earn money in detention. Many facilities throughout the detention system solicit detainees to perform low-skilled jobs necessary for daily operation, such as cleaning, food preparation, dishwashing, laundry, and maintenance (Wood 2011; Conlon and Hiemstra 2014; Urbina 2014; Hiemstra and Conlon 2016, 2017). In exchange for an eight-hour shift, detainees receive one dollar, which is roughly thirteen cents per hour. These so-called voluntary work programs and the pay rate were established by a 1950 law, and despite obvious changes in general wage rates since then, the work program rate has withstood challenges in court (Urbina 2014). In a revealing investigative article, Urbina (2014) reported that approximately 5,500 detainees (of the roughly 34,000 detained per day) participate in these programs. There is also evidence that some detainees labor in facilities that do not participate in voluntary work programs; instead of money, they are compensated with additional food or free time (Urbina 2014). Facilities in the detention system using detainees for internal labor save millions of dollars per year in labor costs (Urbina 2014; Hiemstra and Conlon 2016).

Despite the demeaning wage, many detainees were grateful, even desperate, for the opportunity to earn small amounts of money. Though José Carlos first laughed when speaking of the pay rate and said, "What can you even do with one dollar!" he continued, "But there, there when you are in need, when you do not even have money for a water, then one dollar is useful." Many deportees indicated that they wanted to work to be able to purchase calling cards or extra food. Ana Lucía said that she worked for fifteen days just to be able to call Ecuador once. Others want to work simply to break up the boredom of their incarceration (Urbina 2014; Sinha 2015). Indeed, interviewees indicated that there was not enough work to satisfy detainee demand. Some deportees recalled that facility guards had established systems for deciding who could work, or they claimed that one had to ingratiate oneself with the guards to get a work slot (Sinha 2015).

Regardless of the fact that immigration detention is technically administrative and not punitive, and despite the existence of the PBNDS, detention facilities are punitive, carceral environments, without even many of the safeguards in place for prisons. For detained migrants, space and time are unpredictable. Information and communication are controlled and curtailed. The everyday realities of detention, from isolation to material deprivation, spur detainees to buy from facility commissaries and perform essential labor in facilities at rock-bottom rates. Days are punctuated with injustices at multiple scales. The unintentional design of the detention and deportation system works to produce a chaos that is, for detainees, intimately experienced and deeply impactful.

Performing Security, Shoring Up National Identity

This final section discusses another "peculiar structural advantage" of the detention and deportation system for the U.S. state. The chaos of detention and deportation is critically connected to dominant narratives of national identity and plays an important role in the performance of discourses of (homeland) security. Detention facilities become sites where processes of immigrant securitization, racialization, and criminalization play out and are reinforced at the micro scale.

As I argue elsewhere with Alison Mountz (Mountz and Hiemstra 2014), states create and capitalize on crisis and chaos to rationalize exceptional actions and to maintain and build out power (see also Agamben 1998; Mountz 2004, 2010; Hiemstra 2013). By identifying particular groups of migrants as "deportable and unwanted" (Bosworth 2014, 109), detention draws (barbed-wire) lines between citizen and outsider, justifying and performing state power and actions (D. M. Hernández 2008; Martin 2012; Doty and Wheatley 2013; Hiemstra 2014). The incarceration and expulsion of immigrants reinforces public perceptions of them as outsiders and criminals by linking to exclusive notions of home and heightening non-immigrants' sense that national security is endangered (Chacón 2007; Coleman 2008; Nevins 2010; Mainwaring 2012). D. M. Hernández (2008, 49) writes that for noncitizens, detention can create an "illusion of security," and "in this sense, the noncitizen is an instrument and constitutive factor of our security state, legitimizing its expansion, and drawing support from voters and popular opinion."

It is no coincidence that the majority of detained migrants are racialized as nonwhite, thereby affirming racist ideas of who can be "American." D. M. Hernández (2008, 49) argues that by creating an illusion of security, "the detention of Latinos and other racialized immigrants helps constitute the normative white citizen and white nation. It, along with the government's expansive immigration control apparatus, serves a disciplinary function that consolidates the power of the state and formulates U.S. nationalism and sovereignty by constructing and controlling insiders and outsiders." The racist dimensions of immigration policing, however, are obscured in narratives of security (Golash-Boza 2015) and the chaos of detention and deportation. And the confusion and disorder projected by the system to non-immigrants build on racialized ideas of criminality embedded in securitized narratives of migration and come to play an important role in shoring up national identity itself, through determination of who can belong. Mountz et al. (2013, 531) write, "Spaces of detention, like borders, become important and productive locations for affixing categories of exclusion to migrants' bodies."

Broader narratives combine with how the chaotic detention system operates—in particular the bureaucracy—to dehumanize and distance detainees in employees' eyes (Mountz 2003, 2010; Hall 2010, 2012). Heyman, for example, studied how discourses about immigration come together with the bureaucratic immigration enforcement system to condition immigration officers to see migrants with potentially legitimate rights claims as "logistical problems," instead of as people deserving assistance (Heyman 1995, 269). Bosworth (2014, 208) pays special attention to the relationships between detainees and staff, arguing that "bureaucracy and paperwork offer an important bulwark against feelings." Likewise, Gill (2016) suggests that bureaucratic arrangements work to distance staff from detainees, leading to indifference and insensitivity to suffering even in personal encounters.

In addition, the sheer volume of migrants moving through the system turns them into numbers, objects, bodies. For example, when I spoke with one staff person during a search for a detainee, she explained the role of her facility: "we ship them, send them out to smaller centers, and then depending on where they are is where their cases are managed" (author's research journal, July 1, 2009). Migrants, then, are bodies "shipped out" and managed. One ICE officer's attempt at levity illustrates how employees become anesthetized to the never-ending volume of detainees. I wrote, "[He said,] 'The system is so slow today. But really, it's going through millions of names.' He looked for and found two different [Ecuadorian women named] Mercedes for me, and joked, 'I guess the Mercedes like to get caught!'" (author's research journal, January 22, 2009). The continuous pool of migrants being detained and deported becomes a source of humor for a courteous bureaucrat. Similarly, Gill found that transfers (in the UK detention system) represent asylum seekers as "transient and fleeing" (2009a, 187), in ways that negatively impact their interactions with staff, staff willingness to assist them, and therefore detention outcomes (2009a, 2009b).

Detention is also structured in such a way as to constantly reinforce the assumed criminality and difference of principally nonwhite immigrants. Detention facilities are not just run like prisons, with similar routines and management; in fact, many facilities are prisons, either repurposed from use in the criminal justice system, splitting their space between criminal justice system prisoners and immigration detainees, or merging prisoners and detainees. Often guards and other staff have previously worked in prisons. Aspects of migrants' appearance that express their individuality and personhood are removed, and the migrant becomes one body among many others. As soon as they are detained, migrants must surrender personal clothing and don facility uniforms, and they are identified by numbers instead of names. Jorge described the ID bracelet stamped with his A-Number, name, date of capture, home country, and a miniature photograph: "[It was] a plastic strip attached with two little metal pieces, very secure, you can't take it off, it can only be cut off with scissors." The common dearth in translation services may mean that personnel cannot communicate clearly with detainees.

Everyday procedures, such as constant surveillance, counting, and shackling for any kind of mobility, provide space for the reinscription of narratives of immigrants as dishonest, dangerous, and Other (Hall 2010, 2012; Gill 2016). Gill emphasizes ways in which UK asylum seekers are produced as "a separate and threatening category" (2009b, 225) to employees through aggressive "micro-spatial security measures" (226), such as separate queues and screens between asylum seekers and interviewers. The fact that staff control even the seemingly little details of life infantilizes the ways in which staff interact with and perceive the migrants (Gill 2016). The work programs can also have negative consequences for how staff view and treat detainees generally, from the tasks detainees perform to the absurdly low wage (Gill 2016). As deportee Pato complained, "In detention, I was nobody, just like everyone else. They treated me like a criminal, when all I ever did was work. With them, a dog is treated better than a migrant."

Finally, the carceral environment of detention gives staff tremendous power over detainees, and the scripting of migrants as criminal outsiders influences how this power is used and shapes detainees' experiences. Interactions are permeated with hierarchy, indifference, distrust, and sometimes disgust (Hall 2010, 2012). Deportee Tulio explained it through the metaphor of a chess game, "They have you in, as they say in chess, in check, they have you in check all the time." As discussed above, staff may limit access to medical care, force detainees to eat quickly, curtail access to laundry, maintain rooms at cold temperatures, and determine phone use. Tulio recounted forty hours in cuffs during one transfer and noted that personnel checking in new arrivals took leisurely breaks as waiting detainees sat and tried to sleep on bare cement floors. Carlos reported that guards only let detainees watch TV channels in English: "They said to us that we were stupid, that why would we come here if we don't know English." Fernando said that after the car he was in flipped over during the Border Patrol's effort to stop it, his eye was bloody and clearly injured. He recalled, "We were taken first to Migration, even though some of us were obviously hurt. Migration didn't pay attention to our injuries, saying 'It's your fault you're hurt.'"

Detention centers, and the actions of immigration system employees, can thus be understood as critical components of nation building (Heyman 1995; Mountz 2003, 2010; Hall 2010, 2012; Bosworth 2014). The detention and deportation system is both an outlet for particular negative narratives of immigrants and a space for the reinforcement of these narratives. As Hall (2010, 894) contends of immigration detention in the UK, "staff at the grassroots *matter* because the task falls to them to make meaningful (in mundane daily routines) the cultural, social and political distinctions between citizen and other that the UK immigration and detention system seeks to draw." Detention facilities thus become sites where "hegemonic geopolitical discourse is not only hierarchically translated into everyday life, but also (re)produced through banal, embodied experiences and practices" (Haldrup, Koefoed, and Simonsen 2008, 118). At the confluence of pervasive negative narratives of immigration and the chaotic operation of the detention system, employees' interactions with detainees allow for the repetitive performance of migrants as outsiders, for marking immigrants as prisoners and "excludable" (Bosworth 2014, 108; Hall 2012; Mountz et al. 2013; Hiemstra 2014; Golash-Boza 2015). The chaos of detention and deportation facilitates the conceptualization of immigrants as the opposite of the citizen, the Other against whom national belonging is defined and understood. Despite and because of its chaotic geographies, therefore, detention and deportation contribute to bringing a sense of order and reason to the often disordered, contradictory discourses of homeland security and nation.

The next chapter illuminates how this chaos reverberates to, and what it obscures in, countries of migrant origin. The realities and injustices of detention are certainly impressed upon detainees' bodies. However, a transnational ethnographic perspective reveals a profound mismatch between policy objectives— how these policies are presumed to work—and actual consequences in Ecuador.

CHAPTER 6

"You Don't Know How I Suffer, Waiting Every Day"

Reverberations of Detention in Ecuador

The underlying premise of U.S. immigration and border enforcement policies, however piecemeal and ad hoc in their assembly and realization, is that collectively they work to deter migration to the United States. Practices driven and justified by rationales of U.S. homeland security—including aggressive border patrolling, detention of even the most vulnerable populations, conditions of detention replicating or worse than those found in criminal incarceration, and deportation with little consideration of individual rights and claims—are intended to generate *in*security for migrants, in the United States and in countries of migrant origin. This goal has become increasingly central and explicit since the early days of Prevention Through Deterrence in the 1990s and is now openly stated in documents such as the Border Patrol's Consequence Delivery System plan (Slack et al. 2015; Meissner et al. 2013; Bruzzone 2016; Lowen 2016). Policymakers and those who implement policy therefore understand and even embrace the potential for U.S. actions to cause fear, danger, and uncertainty for migrants and their families, from fear of the migration process to heightened risk en route to uncertainty regarding the migration attempt outcome. Generating a broad range of personal insecurities for migrants and their families has in fact become linked to the broader project of protecting U.S. homeland security.

This chapter and the next explore how these insecurities reverberate to Ecuador—for detained migrants' families, for migrants during and after deportation, and for Ecuadorian communities more broadly. Through transnational ethnography, we see that U.S. policymakers' intentions of generating insecurity far beyond U.S. borders are indeed realized by injecting malaise into rhythms of everyday life during migrants' detention as well as after deportation. What also becomes clear, however, is that the insecurities generated do not necessarily bring about the intended outcome of deterrence. In practice, these policies have a number of additional outcomes, including those that may be, in the long term, contradictory to the goal of deterrence. Instead of executing clean breaks in links formed by transnational migration, detention and deportation solidify and extend these links, in the form of increased insecurity, the continuation of dependence and ties between Ecuador and the United States, and repeat and new migration.

This chapter considers how the chaotic structure and operation of the U.S. detention system generates economic, social, and ontological insecurities in Ecuador. Previous studies have explored the effects of detention and deportation on immigrants and families in the United States and the effects of deportation outside the United States (e.g., Kremer, Moccio, and Hammell 2009; NNIRR 2009; Coutin 2010a, 2010b, 2016; Hagan, Rodriguez, and Castro 2011; Kanstroom 2012; Zilberg 2011; Brabeck, Porterfield, and Loughry 2015; Dingeman-Cerda and Rumbaut 2015; Golash-Boza 2015; Lykes et al. 2015). The chapter focuses on what detention does outside of U.S. borders. It also explores the process of deportation as a transitional space bridging the experiences of migrants with their families in Ecuador. First, I discuss how migration has wrought profound shifts in Ecuador, such that daily life—especially for migrants' families—is tightly linked to the United States.

Entrenched Patterns

Ecuador has been fundamentally changed by—and become dependent on—international migration, with economic shifts at the forefront. At $2.6 billion in 2016 (Banco Central del Ecuador 2016), remittances are now the country's second source of national income, after oil (Acosta, López, and Villamar 2006; Jokisch 2014).[1] The United States is the source of 50 percent of these remittances (compared to 30 percent from Spain) (Maldonado and Hayem 2015, 31). Foreign-earned cash is central to many household livelihood strategies and local economies, inflating costs of goods, services, and properties particularly in areas of high emigration (Acosta, López, and Villamar 2004; Jokisch and Kyle 2006; Jokisch 2014). Businesses have developed around facilitating money transfers, communication, and shuttling goods back and forth (Jokisch and Pribilsky 2002). Furthermore, to some degree remittances have permanently taken the place of government expenditures on services and infrastructure (Acosta, López, and Villamar 2004). Ecuador's economy, like that of other migrant-sending countries, is strongly oriented to and influenced by the economies of countries to which Ecuadorians have migrated (Price and Breese 2016). In the Azuay and Cañar region, this means an especially tight relationship with the U.S. economy. For example, the United States' 2007–2008 Great Recession was reflected in local economic health in Cuenca and the surrounding areas in the form of reduced personal spending and business profits, as well as a temporary lull in emigration to the United States.

Ecuadorian cultural and social life has been permanently altered. Economic changes brought about by migration contribute to shifting social norms and expectations regarding the standard of living, acquisition of material goods, and services (Jokisch and Pribilsky 2002; Acosta, López, and Villamar 2006; Escobar 2008). International migration has also entailed significant shifts in cultural expectations and practices in regions of high migration. In many communities, migration has become culturally entrenched as an expected undertaking for young adults. This is often especially true for the children of migrants who grow up planning to join their parents in the United States (Jokisch and Pribilsky 2002; Escobar 2008; Herrera 2008). Family reunification drives a considerable portion of contemporary migration, and for those unable to reunite legally, undocumented migration is seen as the only alternative (Herrera 2008; Herrera, Moncayo, and Garcia 2012; Jokisch 2014). For those who stay behind, family composition can change, as grandparents or other relatives assume parental roles in the absence of migrant parents (Escobar 2008). Furthermore, migration of household members can lead to significant shifts in gender roles, for both women and men, when one parent migrates and the other remains behind (Pribilsky 2004; Camacho and Hernández 2005a; Boehm 2012).

Importantly, the everyday in Ecuador and the United States can become closely interwoven, not just economically but also in quotidian family happenings. International migration often leads to the development of transnational families (Menjívar 2000; Pribilsky 2004; Boehm 2012; Abrego 2014). Certainly there are distressing tales of family disintegration, in which the migrant distances herself or himself from family in Ecuador and in some cases may cut ties altogether, leading to situations of severe financial and emotional distress (Camacho and Hernández 2005a). More often, however, families physically separated by migration find ways to maintain connections despite the geographic distance (Herrera 2004; Pribilsky 2004; Jokisch and Kyle 2006). With modern technology, they typically communicate regularly—even, for some, multiple times a day—by phone, email, and videoconferencing. Although these families are not physically proximate, their daily lives may be intimately interdependent.

These profound transformations and interdependencies are not easily dismantled by U.S. immigration enforcement strategies. Detention and deportation, however, can immediately disturb and destabilize the rhythms of daily life, with significant implications for everyday (in)security.

Detention

After living in the United States for eight years, Paúl was pulled over and arrested for driving under the influence of alcohol. He was immediately imprisoned in a county jail in New Jersey, where he spent six months, and then he was taken into ICE custody and detained for two months before being deported to Ecuador.[2] I learned of Paúl when his elderly father came in to the House of the

Migrant asking for information about his son and inquiring if there was anything he and other family members could do to try to help Paúl get out more quickly. Over the next eight months, I followed Paúl's progression from arrest to deportation by periodically calling the county jail and then the appropriate ICE offices once he was in ICE custody. During this time, Paúl's father returned to the House of the Migrant roughly every two weeks, sometimes every week, to ask about his son's situation. The father lived in an indigenous agricultural area over an hour away by bus, and the round trip was time consuming as well as costly, especially given that Paúl's family was struggling financially because until his detention he supported his parents with regular remittances. On several occasions Paúl's mother also came in, often crying and expressing that she was very worried about Paúl, especially when they had not heard from him in a while. Concern for their detained son occupied a considerable portion of their daily lives until he was finally deported.

WAITING AND WORRYING

Legal and spatiotemporal indeterminacy is a "distinguishing characteristic" of detention (Martin and Mitchelson 2009, 465), with disturbing psychological consequences for family members in both the United States and in the migrant's country of origin (Lykes et al. 2015). As evident in the anecdote about Paúl's family, the detention system's unpredictability and opacity immediately change how a migrant's absence is experienced, becoming more disruptive and traumatic.

Family members' attempts to simply locate detainees and verify their situation often become a source of frustration and anxiety. Relatives want to know migrants' location, what is happening to them, and if and when they will be deported. But many family members cannot find and establish contact with a detainee, not to mention figure out how to comprehend the bureaucratic procedures a detainee must negotiate. Typically, due to facilities' policies, the complicated structure of detention facilities' for-profit phone systems, and prohibitive rates, it is nearly impossible for family members in Ecuador to initiate a call to a detainee. The burden of direct communication therefore lies with detainees, who contend with these same challenges, plus restricted phone access, surveillance, and frequent transfers. If detained migrants do manage to phone Ecuador, calls are usually limited to several minutes, and detainees often fail to communicate information that would enable family members to obtain more information, such as their facility name or their A-Number.

Other modes of communication are also complicated for family in Ecuador. Visits from relatives or friends in the United States who could share information may not be feasible due to the remote, dispersed locations of many facilities and limited visitation hours, as well as the practice of transferring detainees far from the site where they were captured. In addition, if potential visitors are undocumented, they are justifiably hesitant to risk contact with ICE. I recorded this interaction with family members: "[Detainee Marco's sister] said everyone they knew in the U.S. is without papers so can't go to see him. The mother, crying, asked if there was any way to talk to him. I said no, but perhaps they could send a letter" (author's research journal, June 15, 2009). To send a letter, however, family members must obtain an address for the detention center and often the detainee's A-Number. The frequency of unexpected transfers increases the possibility that the detainee will never receive the letter.

For many relatives in Ecuador, therefore, detained migrants disappear. This sudden absence from everyday life can cause distress. In another example from my notes on Marco: "Friends in New York told [Marco's sister and mother that] he was detained maybe a month ago; they haven't heard from him and are very worried . . . His mother cried several times and begged me to find him" (author's research journal, June 1, 2009). Similarly, the wife of detainee José Carlos said: "That is why I came to the House of the Migrant, because I was desperate. I didn't know if he was alive, okay, sick. I didn't know anything, nothing, there is no communication."

Often, faced with a lack of information, family members imagine spaces of detention through conjecture and fear, constructing images of detention by drawing on other accounts they have heard. Sometimes they envision detention as worse than it actually is. The following journal excerpt records an encounter with parents of two detained brothers (author's research journal, January 26, 2009): "I relayed the info . . . and comforted them about the probable conditions of the detention centers, that their sons were likely being fed and treated well, just waiting and waiting. That seemed to relieve the mother who was worried that they were in horrible places." This mother, like numerous other relatives, expressed fears that imprisoned migrants did not receive food or beds if no one paid the jail directly, as can be the case in transit countries such as Mexico and Guatemala. Intersections between the migrant detention system and the criminal punishment system add to relatives' fears. For example, I noted after a conversation at the House of the Migrant with Paúl's mother that she had been crying, and that "she has heard horrible stories about police abuse in U.S. jails and people being killed by guards" (author's research journal, April 6, 2009).

Like detainees, relatives in Ecuador may feel profoundly disoriented by the chaotic spatiotemporal characteristics of the detention system's operation, such as frequent transfers between facilities and extended detention durations. Patricia's family, for example, did not understand why she remained in detention a month after her capture on the border when she had already received a removal order: "The sister said, with tears in her eyes, that everyone in the family is so worried about Patricia, that her parents are consumed thinking about her, wondering if she is locked up so long because she is being hit and robbed" (author's research journal, June 15, 2009). Faustino's mother was perplexed and frightened by the lengthy detention time and the impossibility of speaking with him. She "wanted to know if they could pay his passage to get him home sooner . . . [She said] 'You don't know how I suffer, waiting every day, without knowing when he is coming and if he is okay'" (author's research journal, February 11, 2009). The fact that the migrant will almost certainly be deported regardless of the time detained is baffling. Also, the punishments for particular criminalized acts are markedly different in the United States and Ecuador. For example, offenses such as driving without a license or driving under the influence of a substance—"aggravated felonies" in the United States if committed by a migrant—are minor infractions in Ecuador (and in the United States if committed by a citizen), punishable with a ticket and fine. Therefore, in Ecuador, incarceration and expulsion are interpreted as vastly incommensurate with the severity of such actions.

The conditions of detention are another source of concern for relatives in Ecuador. Detainees who are able to communicate may relate troublesome details, as shown in this journal entry: "[Antonio's sister] said that her brother had called her father [also in the U.S.] to say that he didn't get three meals a day, sometimes just one" (author's research journal, July 29, 2009). Relatives also expressed fear that detainees were not receiving adequate medical care. Detainee Carlos called his family and "asked them to do anything they could to get him out, that he is sick. His left arm and side are numb, which has happened to him before when stressed" (author's research journal, June 26, 2009). Concerns regarding appropriate care for the psychological trauma induced by detention surfaced repeatedly as well: "[Marcelo's sister] asked if there was medical care in the facility, said Marcelo had called a family member in the U.S. crying, depressed, desperate without any information" (author's research journal, April 3, 2009). The next section explores how family members' worries and anxiety can be overwhelming and debilitating, leaching into many aspects of daily life.

EVERYDAY INSECURITY AND MOBILITY

Family members' daily realities are disrupted not only by concern for the detainee but also by the numerous insecurities detention generates in their own lives in Ecuador. Typically, the most pressing, cutting problem has to do with their own material well-being. The financial security of many households in Ecuador, particularly in the Azuay and Cañar region, is heavily dependent on remittances sent from migrants in the United States. The most immediate economic consequence of detention, therefore, is loss of income. While migrants are detained, they can do nothing to support relatives in Ecuador.

The following journal excerpt (author's research journal, June 25, 2009) records an encounter with detainee Carlos's mother, who was caring for Carlos's two daughters (her granddaughters) in his absence. Carlos's mother was entirely dependent on money sent by her son. "The mother of Carlos came in again. She teared up several times, saying they were desperate for him to get back, she and his kids are so anxious, that they didn't have any money left to buy food, that the kids were just eating once a day, and they didn't have money to pay school fees, that she didn't know what to do, and why can't they just send him, they've been waiting so long." In another instance, "the sister of Pedro came in [to the House of the Migrant] saying that they were desperate, that they needed Pedro to come back to help them financially, that they couldn't support the children" (author's research journal, February 10, 2009). As evident in these excerpts, dependent families may suddenly be unable to pay for a range of living expenses, such as food, housing, medical care, and school fees. Their daily lives become more insecure and precarious the longer a migrant is detained. Migration debts can add another layer to financial distress. If a migrant was caught attempting to migrate or was living in the United States but still in the process of repaying a migration debt, relatives may be unable to continue payments. The consequences for failing to pay may be severe. Detainee Paulino's sister reported that "her brother was desperate to get out, get back here, and work to pay the debt to the bank so they don't take his house" (author's research journal, August 3, 2009). Family members also mentioned recurring visits from lenders pressing them to pay.

Financial insecurity may also deepen through assisting a detainee in hiring a lawyer, either in Ecuador or the United States. This expense is usually assumed as additional debt. Marcía's detained husband asked her to send $3,000 to the United States to pay for a lawyer so he could fight his deportation. She agonized about what to do; she would have to take out a loan to send the money, thereby adding to her already difficult financial situation without her husband's remittances—particularly if he still was deported. It is true that legal counsel is very important for fighting deportation, and there are many honest lawyers who work tirelessly pro bono or at reduced rates to help detainees. However, there are also many who charge exorbitant amounts to take cases with virtually no chance of success or who do not have the legal expertise necessary to navigate the complexities of immigration law with success. Indeed, the maelstrom of the U.S. detention and deportation apparatus has created space for dishonesty and downright scams. For example, the $3,000 requested by Marcía's husband would likely have covered only the lawyer's fees for her husband's first court appearance. To pay a private lawyer in the United States to fight a deportation, a process that takes months or years, costs many times more. So, if Marcía's husband's case did proceed, many more thousands of dollars would have been requested to follow it through. In Ecuador, too, a market has developed for taking advantage of detainees' and their families' desperation. For instance, a relative of detained migrant Iván "had talked to a lawyer who said that the family should pay for him [the lawyer] to fly to Quito to talk to the Ministry of Foreign Relations or the U.S. Embassy to make a request that Iván be transferred to Ecuador to serve his time" (author's research journal, May 15, 2009). This proposal had no chance of helping Iván's case or getting him home more quickly. At that time, Iván was in an immigration detention facility, not a criminal jail, already with a removal order and simply awaiting a deportation flight to Ecuador, so the idea that he could "serve his time" in Ecuador was completely false. The lawyer who suggested it either had no knowledge of U.S. law or (more likely) wanted to charge the family for his time and obtain a free flight to Quito.

There are additional economic consequences. Studies regarding the U.S. criminal incarceration system have found that families' efforts to maintain contact with inmates can have considerable costs, largely pertaining to the time, effort, and money required to visit (Christian, Mellow, and Thomas 2006). This is certainly true for families in Ecuador of migrants detained in the United States. Though visits are obviously impossible, there are alternate expenses related to attempts to communicate or obtain information. The persistent efforts by the elderly father of detainee Paúl, presented earlier in this chapter, illustrate how relatives in Ecuador often expend significant money and energy in attempts to simply find out and understand what is happening to a detained migrant. Their efforts are complicated by factors in Ecuador, such as poverty, distance from urban centers, and weak public infrastructure, in addition to characteristics of the chaotic U.S. detention and deportation system, including its opacity, frequent transfers of detainees, and the difficulty and high price of communication.

The lengths to which families will go, and the bureaucratic barriers that they must get around, are exemplified in one family's attempts to send money to a detained migrant in order to facilitate a direct call. This can be an exceedingly complex process, involving verifying the detainee's location and A-Number and negotiating the specific money transfer system used by that detention center. Detainee David's family made multiple attempts over three weeks to transfer money to the Eloy, Arizona, detention facility so that David could call them. Because the facility was operated by the Corrections Corporation of America (CCA), and not locally, the money had to be sent to a CCA office in Tennessee, via Western Union, using a specific account code for David. I assisted them in making numerous phone calls to verify details of the procedure to be used. Then, the Western Union offices in Cuenca would not make the transfer without a specific person's name (not just a company name), which was outside of the procedure outlined by CCA. David's family ultimately transferred money to other relatives in the bigger capital city of Quito, where there was a Western Union willing to follow CCA's guidelines. The entire process—to transfer under $50—took approximately three weeks and required a considerable amount of time out of family members' daily lives.

For families in Ecuador, the chaos of detention can extend beyond the economic to the ontological, evoking a personal sense of disorientation, uncertainty, and insecurity. Daily activities and routines can be altered or disrupted through stress regarding a detainee's situation, the time-consuming efforts to obtain information about or assist detainees, and new financial limitations. Money struggles may also force extensive changes in social worlds, personal mobility, health, and outlook. Many relatives expressed a sense of anxiety and loss about their own material existence, including fear regarding the future. The sister of Marco, awaiting her brother's deportation, lamented, "What will we do now? We still have almost all his debt" (author's research journal, June 1, 2009). Some family members remarked that they did not like leaving the house anymore for fear of seeing people to whom they owed money or for not wanting to explain their family's situation. Family members may no longer be able to pay for educational and recreational activities and for routine or even emergency medical care. In the case of Carlos's mother and daughters, eating only once a day undoubtedly affects not just the rhythms of daily life but also general health and well-being. Furthermore, worries and fears regarding detention can be internalized in ways that have serious ramifications for mental and physical health. Many Ecuadorians who came into the House of the Migrant indicated high levels of psychological distress as they waited for information about or deportation of their family member and worried about the experience of the detained migrant as well as the situation of their family in Ecuador. I recorded the following impression when meeting with family members of one detainee: "The mother was the most upset, saying she can't sleep for worrying, and cried again" (author's research journal, July 2, 2009). Similarly, Daniela's mother, who said that she was already on hypertension medication, conveyed that the stress of her daughter's detention made it difficult to sleep, and her blood pressure was out of control.

The stress that U.S. detention causes for children in Ecuador merits additional discussion. Numerous studies have detailed ways in which detention and deportation can generate negative consequences for children in the United States (e.g., Amnesty International 2009; HURRICANE 2009; Kremer, Moccio, and Hammell 2009; Brabeck and Xu 2010; Brabeck, Porterfield, and Loughry 2015). Brabeck, Porterfield, and Loughry (2015, 174) draw on Dreby (2012) to explain that "unlike separations involved in voluntary migration decisions, which may hold the promise of economic benefits in spite of social/emotional costs, forced separations due to deportation incur social/emotional costs without the accompanying economic benefits." My research in Ecuador adds to a limited number of studies showing that these costs extend across territorial borders to countries of migrant origin, with critical consequences particularly for children, including anxiety, fear, and depression. For younger children, their understanding of and degree of comfort with a migrant's absence may be negatively transformed by adults' reactions or by the difficulty of communicating with detainees. It may also be difficult for adults to explain a migrant's absence when they themselves do not fully understand it or have no timeline for its duration. When I called detainee Saira's mother, for instance, to give her new information regarding her daughter's estimated return, "she said she was hoping Saira would return sooner because [Saira's son] is depressed waiting for her to come home" (author's research journal, February 9, 2009). Older children in Ecuador may assume the same worries and stresses that adult family members have regarding the detained family member and the family's financial situation in Ecuador. This reality was disturbingly clear in an emotional phone call at the House of the Migrant. Carlos was detained in a small county prison that, in an unusual move, allowed him to receive a phone call (which I made using Skype), and he spoke with his teenage daughter. Carlos was extremely upset and told his daughter that he should make himself a cadaver because that would bring him home faster. The daughter started to cry and said, "Papi, don't do anything to hurt yourself. We need you, we need you! Calm down, calm down" (author's research journal, July 2, 2009). Besides being painfully aware of her family's tenuous economic situation, the girl was thrust into an adult role when trying to comfort her father and, after the call, her grandmother (Carlos's mother). Minors, then, experience many of the same challenges and stresses regarding detention that adult family members do, but in ways that rip and scar childhood.

Finally, while the indeterminacy of detention ricochets through entire families, the consequences in Ecuador of detention are gendered in important ways. While historically more men than women migrated to the United States, during the late 1990s and early 2000s, the numbers of female and male migrants leaving Ecuador became roughly equal (Herrera 2008). Today, however, far more Ecuadorian men than women are deported. This is consistent with broad patterns of U.S. deportation, which pursues what Golash-Boza and Hondagneu-Sotelo (2013) call a "gendered racial removal program." As explained in chapter 3, this targeting of men for deportation occurs in the context of a U.S. economy with an excess of jobs typically performed by men, in industry and construction, but with a shortage of laborers for service jobs, such as cleaning and care work, typically filled by women. Important, too, is the post-9/11 conflation of primarily male immigrants with terrorists. The simultaneous racialization and criminalization of nonwhite immigrants has brought us to the present moment in which men are considerably more likely to be deported than women (Golash-Boza and Hondagneu-Sotelo 2013). In Ecuador, therefore, it is more often women who experience sustained periods of insecurity, waiting while male partners are detained. Certainly, both male and female family members sought help regarding a detainee at the House of the Migrant, but the majority were women, and as seen in the anecdotes throughout this section, distress about how detention was impacting daily realities was expressed more often by women—wives, mothers, children, and sisters maintaining households financially dependent on remittances. In Ecuador, as in most countries, the opportunities for women to find employment that can provide a livable income are more limited than for men, further proscribed by women's home-based roles as caretakers. When remittances dry up upon a migrant's detention, women in Ecuador are more likely to find themselves in an immediately tenuous economic position, aggravated by the uncertainty and fear that the black box of detention typically generates in families.

In the name of U.S. security, detention works within and across territorial borders to create a range of insecurities for migrants and for their families in countries of migrant origin. The previous two chapters explored how detainees' experiences are characterized by uncertainty, injustice, and spatiotemporal disorientation. This chapter has turned the lens on Ecuador, showing how the effects of detention stretch across space to disrupt and distort life in countries of migrant origin. During detention, the worlds of families in Ecuador can be profoundly, even violently, impacted. Economic and social realities are altered, health and well-being may decline, and everyday patterns, mobilities, and expectations shift. Detention, then, is both chaotic and chaos generating, with broad power to imprint and project disorder, uncertainty, and turmoil.

Deportation and Arrival

Most scholarship on detention and deportation tends to focus on the run-up to and experiences during detention, the laws and decisions regarding who and why people are deported, and migrants' experiences after they have been deported. Here, I concentrate on the transitional space between being a detainee and a deportee: detained migrants' actual deportation journey to Ecuador. Though brief, this period of mobility constitutes an important stage in migrants' detention to deportation trajectories. I follow Walters's (2016, 436) call for more attention to the deportation flight as integral to understanding "power struggles over mobility and control" and expand my inquiry to include the events immediately preceding and following the flight. As discussed in chapter 1, Drotbohm and Hasselberg (2015, 551) emphasize that deportation "crosses places and spaces, connects countries and nations." Deportation and arrival bring together, into the same place, the experiences of detainees and their families in Ecuador and represent a significant bridge to shared experiences after deportation—an important piece of what Drotbohm and Hasselberg (2015, 553) call the "deportation corridor."

The actual process of deportation does more than geographically dislocate the rejected migrant. It provides a final opportunity—in this particular migration journey, at least—to disorient and degrade migrants. In other words, it is a final space directly under U.S. control in which migrants are made to embody their exclusion and expulsion. While many migrants experience deportation as personally chaotic, there is a striking similarity across experiences that reveals the appearance of chaos to be something of a facade. That is, immigration officials seem to intend, to some degree, that deportation be an unpleasant experience, one that further contributes to their goals of deterrence. Indeed, Walters (2016, 446) notes how, in the United Kingdom, the chartered deportation flight is meant, in part, to act as a deterrent to future migration by showing that the government "will take strong measures to enforce asylum and removal decisions." In this sense, the deportation journey is threaded with disciplinary intentions, a spectacle aimed at deported migrants, as well as their families and broader communities as sources of potential future migrants. In addition, the behavior of detention and deportation system personnel during the process of deportation continues to illustrate the influence of broader sociopolitical narratives—of migrants as Othered, dangerous outsiders—on personnel, in terms of how they think about and interact with detained migrants.

Migrants' exit from detention is usually in keeping with their larger detention experience during which the reasons for and terms of confinement are shrouded in secrecy and uncertainty. Detainees often receive little or no advanced notice of when they are to be deported. While some interviewees reported that they knew several days ahead, the majority did not know until the moment they were told to leave their cell. Patricio recalled, "I had no idea. I was gone, from one minute to the next." Though most migrants are relieved to finally be exiting detention, this lack of prior notice often caused distress. As Bosworth (2014) found in the case of UK detention, not knowing a precise date elicited logistical concerns regarding arranging for someone to pick them up upon arrival. Some Ecuadorian migrants said that they did not believe they were really going at first, since they had been misled before when being transferred. Also, several interviewees were shocked because they had understood themselves to still be in a process of appealing their removal decision.

The physical conditions experienced by migrants being deported can be frustrating and humiliating. The act of "removal" often begins by being awoken in the night, being herded into a room with dozens of others, being held there for hours with no place to sleep, and being hungry. Some interviewees reported undergoing brief medical examinations during this time and having their belongings returned to them. Marcelo, for example, reported that he was taken from his cell at 9 p.m. and then kept in a cold room with forty-six other people, where they could sit on chairs or sleep on the floor. At 3 a.m. they were all chained up, loaded onto a bus, and driven approximately one and a half hours to the airport. Ana Lucía's experience was similar: she was taken out of her cell at 5 p.m. and held in a cold room (hers with beds and blankets) until 5 a.m.; she was told that the room was so cold to kill any germs the migrants might be carrying. The realization of deportation thus provides one more opportunity for migrants to experience the infamous *hieleras*, or iceboxes (Bruzzone 2016; Riva 2017), and to be Othered and represented as unhealthy and unclean (Falk 2010).

This final stage of detention also serves as an additional space for dehumanization. Rodrigo complained that his clothes, returned to him unwashed after over six weeks, were filthy and made him ill when he had to put them on. Iván said that while all of his belongings (on his person when detained) were returned to him, he heard others saying that some items were missing. Clemente explained that some men who had been detained thought they were about to be deported back to Ecuador, only to realize later that they were only being transferred to another facility. The move was done at night, and facility personnel told them that they could not get back possessions and money (taken from them upon detention) until morning, but if they waited they would miss that opportunity to leave detention. So the men signed forms giving up their money and possessions, only to find that they were just being moved to another location. These experiences are in keeping with recent investigative reports (Ewing and Cantor 2016). The specter of deportation, while brief in itself, haunts the detention experience.

The deportation flight was an additional, intense period of injustice for many. Walters writes (2016, 447), "The fact that [the plane] is mobile and extraterritorial does not make it any less real as a place of highly unequal power relations where the risk of violence lurks." Expelled migrants are deported on either commercial flights or through DHS's Enforcement and Removal Operations (ERO). Those flying on commercial airlines reported relatively smooth experiences. Accompanied by one or two ICE personnel for their journey, they were handcuffed between the detention facility and the airport, but most said that once on the plane they were uncuffed and treated as normal passengers. However, most of the deportees who arrived via ERO—thirty-one of my forty interviewees—reported abysmal experiences. The trips could be long, from roughly four to twelve hours, depending on the starting point for the trip and whether the plane stopped in Central America to drop off deportees before continuing to Ecuador. Numerous deportees recalled that they were provided only a small box lunch that was sorely insufficient for the long day.

Many also reported being treated as if they were dangerous criminals looking for any opportunity to escape, in an experience marked by shackling, armed guards, and barked orders. Some described their hands, feet, and waist being chained the entire flight, which caused severe discomfort, with few or no opportunities to leave their seats to use the bathroom. Fernando said on his flight passengers were not permitted to speak to each other, and the guards yelled and repeatedly threatened them with a return to detention if they "tried anything." Guards also warned migrants that they would be detained significantly longer if caught again, said Fernando, and "they tried to make us feel bad." Several interviewees observed that the guards were gruff and unpleasant until a short time before landing, when they removed migrants' chains and were suddenly nicer. Julio said that the guards stashed all of the chains in the bathroom, and he suggested that they did this so that Ecuadorian officials would not see how deportees had been treated.

Julio also recalled a final interaction with ICE personnel, which encapsulates the critical role of the immigration industrial complex in shaping and continuing the current approach to immigration enforcement: "When we were about to get off the airplane, one of the [guards] said to us, 'Well, boys, so long and don't come back,' and the boss who was there—they speak in English because a lot of the people don't understand so they think that no one understands, but I understood what they were saying—'so long and don't come back,' and the boss said, 'don't tell them that . . . if they don't come back, we won't have work.'" The continued emphasis on detention and deportation in U.S. policymaking is linked to the influence of multiple stakeholders, such as private companies, public entities like county jails, and individual employees who have become financially dependent on detention and deportation. Even the last moments of Julio's deportation were punctuated by the economic relationships sustained through his confinement and removal.

According to interviewees, some migrants whooped in celebration upon landing in Ecuador. But deportees must immediately confront challenges dealing with physical well-being and safety. All who arrive must pass through Ecuadorian Migration. Several people I interviewed who worked with nongovernmental organizations reported that in years past deportees were imprisoned upon arrival, until—depending on the account—their noncriminal status could be verified or until family members paid a bribe. This practice of temporary incarceration, however, appeared to no longer be a threat to deportees during the period in which I conducted my fieldwork, 2008–2009. Those who arrive on commercial flights are released by the agents who accompanied them upon exiting the plane. Those who arrive on ERO flights are bussed to the Ecuadorian Migration office near the airport and processed there. Often, if available, government representatives are also present (as they were at the arrival I witnessed, described at the beginning of chapter 1) to hand out bags of personal care items, a sandwich and drink, and pamphlets from various government agencies.[3]

Depending on the clothes that they were wearing when apprehended in the United States, deportees may suddenly find themselves inappropriately attired. ERO flights usually arrive at the city of Guayaquil, while commercial flights arrive at Guayaquil or Quito. Guayaquil has a coastal, tropical climate, and Quito has an equatorial highland climate with temperatures often dropping to fifty degrees Fahrenheit (ten degrees Celsius) at night. The temperature in the highlands around Cuenca where many of my interviewees were from (and other regions along the Ecuadorian Andes) may drop lower than that and be accompanied by bitter rain and even snow. An Ecuadorian Migration official at the Quito airport deplored the conditions of arrival for many of the migrants he saw coming in on commercial flights: "They arrive with nothing, only a T-shirt, at one in the morning, without money."

As most deportees are unable to inform family prior to their arrival, they must find a way to reach their homes with little or no money. Their destinations can be hours away; for example, from Quito to Cuenca is roughly ten hours by bus. When ERO flights come in, a federal government agency may provide a bus to transport deportees from Guayaquil to Cuenca, about four hours away (such as the one I rode, described in chapter 1). As the majority of Ecuadorians in the United States are from the greater Cuenca region, this service is of great use to many deportees, though they still must find a way to get from the Cuenca bus terminal to their home towns. Interviewees who arrived on commercial flights, however, told of begging and borrowing money to call family members or to pay for public transportation. Christian, for example, said that he begged ten dollars from someone in the detention center and another ten dollars from another deportee on his commercial flight, and then he asked other people for help along the way during his trip from Quito to Cuenca. The official at the Quito airport said that sometimes the Migration office lets deportees use their phone to call families, or employees give them a couple of dollars or a ride to the bus terminal, and sometimes bus drivers give deportees free trips.

For those in Ecuador awaiting deportees, fear regarding such circumstances of arrival is an additional source of anxiety. At the House of the Migrant in Cuenca, family members expressed concern regarding the physical conditions of deportation. For example, detainee Diego's sister told me "she was worried about how he would be treated during the deportation. From other acquaintances who had been deported she had heard that they come shackled hands and feet, in prison clothes" (author's research journal, April 7, 2009). Many family members are also aware of the fact that detainees frequently arrive without money, and they are concerned about how migrants will make the journey home. Relatives who came to the House of the Migrant were often preoccupied with learning exactly when the migrant would arrive, with the explicit aim of meeting the migrant at the airport. Obtaining arrival information, however, can be nearly impossible. Obviously, if detainees do not know when they will be deported, they cannot inform relatives. Other potential sources of this information are similarly problematic. When migrants are deported on commercial flights, the ERO does not routinely notify the Ecuadorian government that deportees are on board until the plane lands, so family members are not informed. For ERO flights, ICE officials usually issue a passenger list to the Ecuadorian Ministry of Foreign Relations one to five days prior to the flight. Only family members who have sought assistance at organizations such as the House of the Migrant, however, can be contacted, and the majority of relatives do not seek such help. For instance, the House usually had family contact information for no more than 5 deportees on a typical list of 70 to 120 names. Furthermore, there were numerous instances in which some of the migrants on the list did not arrive, which caused additional distress for relatives: "The mother of Bolívar and mother-in-law of Jorge came in, distraught. They did not arrive on the Friday plane, despite being on the ERO list that was received last Thursday. She and some other family members had gone to Guayaquil in the rain and gotten soaked and then waited and waited and others got off the plane but they never did!" (author's research journal, February 9, 2009). Such anxiety and misinformation is yet another frustrating component of detention's indeterminacy.

Though brief, these experiences between detention and deportation—the ending of detention, the deportation flight, and the circumstances of arrival in Ecuador—are important. More than just condensed episodes of often physical discomfort for deportees and anxiety for both deportees and family members in Ecuador, they must be recognized as critical spaces, heavy with disciplinary intentions. These experiences are geographical extensions of exclusion from the United States, meant to mark the minds of migrants and potential migrants in ways that disrupt migration patterns. But, instead of signaling a terminal break in migratory dreams, networks, and journeys, these experiences and spaces of deportation—what are collectively intense periods of insecurity—become part of the enduring bridge connecting Ecuador and the United States.

This chapter's exploration of reverberations of detention in Ecuador and the process itself of deportation pulls attention to experiences of fear and insecurity outside of those referenced in dominant Western narratives of homeland security. It also shows that because of the thick webs of connections between Ecuador and the United States that have been woven by migration, the traumas of detention and the injustices of deportation experienced by family members and deportees may cause intense stress and a lasting sense of injustice. The next chapter focuses on everyday realities after deportation for deportees, family members, and communities. Contrary to the rationale underlying dominant approaches to immigration enforcement, while these webs may be stretched and altered, they are not easily broken. What's more, these webs work against policymakers' expectations that the insecurities produced by deportation and detention effectively deter migration.

CHAPTER 7

"There Is No Other Way"

Postdeportation Insecurities
and Continued Migration

Tired after years of struggling to make ends meet, Saira had borrowed money to pay a smuggler, left her eight-year-old son with her mother, and departed for the United States. Saira described her migration trip as a horrible, life-changing experience. She was forced to ride in cargo trucks with no ventilation in which she felt like she was suffocating, saw bodies of dead children floating in rivers she was crossing, and felt like a criminal running from the U.S. immigration officials who finally cornered her under a bridge. She said she knew she had been unusually lucky not to be raped during her journey, as she had learned that this happened to most female migrants. Saira described her four months in U.S. detention as miserable, full of feelings of frustration, despair, and intense boredom. When I interviewed her six weeks after her deportation, she was working at a small restaurant near Cuenca's city center, putting in ten to twelve hours per day. Saira resolutely stated that she did not want to risk another migration attempt: "When I arrived here [after deportation], I felt a little bad because I hadn't reached my dream but I was also happy because I am here with my son . . . because when I was there I realized that I shouldn't have left him. Being jailed made me think about a lot of things. I thank God that I am here in my country with my son and my family, in good health."

I next saw Saira three months later, when she came into the House of the Migrant selling pirated CDs. The restaurant in which she had been working had closed, and she was desperate for ways to make money. Though her coyote had actually returned half of her migration money (a rare occurrence!), she said she was drowning in debt and unable to pay for her son's most basic needs. Saira told me that she was planning on leaving for the United States again soon, explaining, "My debts are crushing me, I have no choice" (author's research journal, July 20, 2009).

Despite the U.S. government's investment in policies intended to broadcast transnational messages to stay away, there is little attention to what actually happens after deportation. My transnational ethnography from Ecuador illustrates that while deportation and detention certainly do generate insecurity for migrants far beyond the United States, as policymakers intend, they do not, for the most part, work effectively as deterrents. These insecurities are important, but not because they bring the expected consequences. They are important for the ways in which they maintain and forge links between the United States and countries of migrant origin.

My research adds to a small but growing body of journalistic and academic work supporting this point through research in countries of migrant origin. Kanstroom (2012) provides an overview of deportees in countries such as Cambodia, the Dominican Republic, El Salvador, Haiti, and Jamaica. Wheatley (2011) worked with voluntary and involuntary return migrants in Mexico. Brotherton and Barrios (2011) conducted detailed ethnographic research with deportees in the Dominican Republic. Precil (1999) researched teens deported to Haiti. Peutz (2006, 2010) studied Somalis deported to Somaliland. Coutin (2007, 2010a, 2010b, 2011, 2016); Hagan, Eschbach, and Rodriguez (2008); and Zilberg (2004, 2006, 2011) worked with deportees in El Salvador. Golash-Boza (2014, 2015) conducted research in Jamaica, Guatemala, Dominican Republic, and Brazil with forced returnees. Headley, Gordon, and MacIntosh (2005) also looked at deportees in Jamaica. Lykes at al. (2015) considered experiences in Guatemala, and Dingeman-Cerda and Rumbaut (2015) looked at returnees in El Salvador. Drotbohm (2015) examines postdeportation realities in Cape Verde. A number of recent journalistic accounts show that deportation to Central America can effectively be a death sentence (e.g., Brodzinsky and Pilkington 2015). There are also many important studies regarding deportation from countries other than the United States (e.g., Ellerman 2008; Collyer 2012; Schuster and Majidi 2013, 2015). All of these scholars emphasize deportees' experiences of poverty, family separation, ostracism, incarceration, torture, even death, and—often—renewed mobility.

Ecuador is, in many ways, important for its unremarkableness as a deportee destination in comparison to Mexico and Central American countries. It does not share the same context of extreme violence found to drive migration out of Central America. It does not receive the massive numbers of deportees that countries with larger populations and closer proximity to the United States do. Geographically, it is relatively far. For these reasons, studying the postdeportation realities in a country like Ecuador can deepen understanding of the creeping everydayness of consequences of U.S. detention and deportation. In addition, this research expands attention beyond the deportees themselves to include their households, wider networks, and communities. In doing so, it broadens knowledge about the scales at which these insecurities are experienced and fosters additional consideration of potential future consequences. It also supports Drotbohm and Hasselberg's (2015, 553) reframing of deportation, pushing scholars to move away from thinking of deportation as a finite, disconnected end to migration and instead understanding that there exists a "deportation corridor" that involves multiple actors, times, and spaces.

This chapter explores postdeportation realities in Ecuador in order to, first, identify common experiences for deportees, their families, and communities; and, second, assess concrete policy outcomes against assumed policy outcomes. The chapter also delves further into the perverse relationship, introduced in chapter 2, between harsh immigration enforcement policies, human smuggling, debt, and the entrenchment of international migration patterns.

Haunting Everyday Life

For some deportees and their families, forced return to Ecuador was not necessarily a negative migration outcome. Deportation brings an end to the indeterminate waiting and stress related to detention for family members and deportees and offers opportunities to reconnect in families and communities. Relatives often expressed great relief and joy after their loved one had arrived. On many occasions, people whom I had met at the House of the Migrant asking for help regarding a detainee came in after deportation, often with the recent deportee, happy to introduce me personally and recount the pleasure of reunification. Deportees, too, shared similar feelings during interviews. For example, Marcelo said that after eight years in the United States, "You can't imagine how it is, like a dream." He continued that while he had not planned on returning, perhaps things happen for a reason because his family needed him, and he was meant to be back with them. Anderson, deported after five years in the United States, said that coming back felt "very good because this is my country, and I believe I just feel better, because there if you don't have papers you can't really do anything."

For many Ecuadorians, however, deportation was met with mixed feelings or viewed as wholly negative. The sense of persistent connections to and longing for the United States haunts not just the deportees but also their family members. Detention and deportation are indelibly imprinted on individuals—both deported migrants and those who have never migrated—in ways that critically impact daily family life as well as wider social networks in Ecuador.

ECONOMIC INSECURITIES

The most obvious repercussions of forced return are economic. A primary reason for migration is to improve household financial standing and well-being, and most migrants aim to send money from the United States to Ecuador. For Ecuadorians who had established lives in the United States, deportation often signified the severing of a critical economic source for their families in Ecuador. When asked how it felt to see his family upon arrival, Jorge, who had been deported after trying to enter the United States after a previous period of working and then deportation, replied, "I was content to see my family, but at the same time frustrated, with no job . . . It is the same problem as before, so for me the happiest thing would have been to arrive [in the United States] . . . to be there working and sending home money like I did before."

Deportees return to the same economic situation that pushed them to migrate months or years earlier: wages incommensurate with the cost of living, limited government support, and a saturated job market (Carriere 2001; Jokisch 2001; Acosta, López, and Villamar 2004). In the Azuay and Cañar region, this includes increasing labor competition from in-migrants from Colombia and Peru (Jokisch and Kyle 2006; Bowditch 2009a).[1] Not only are jobs generally sparse, but the wages may seem trivial in comparison to what migrants earn in the United States. For instance, while Geovanny found employment shortly after his return to Ecuador, he remarked, "Being in the United States affects us psychologically, all of us who were deported back, because you just don't earn here like you do there." As deportee Luis put it, "Working here—it just isn't enough!" Studies of deportees in other countries report similar and, in some cases, even more serious challenges in finding viable employment, which may be more severe the longer the deportees have been out of their country of origin (see, for example, Golash-Boza 2014, 2015; Buckinx and Filindra 2015).

The abrupt, violent way in which detention and deportation are often carried out can imprint deportees' experiences of return with a profound sense of material loss. Migrants are typically taken into ICE custody in surprise actions with no warning and are uniformly treated as high-risk criminals regardless of whether they were apprehended attempting to enter the United States or after living there for years. Not permitted to exit detention (either due to mandatory detention policies or the setting of impossibly high bonds), migrants who do not have family or friends to assist them are unable to attend to personal responsibilities and belongings. Juan Pablo told of begging ICE officials, "When the police were deporting me, I said, please, just let me be, I've got part of my life made here, I have to get out to see what happened to all my things." Interviewees had stories of cars left on the street and savings accounts rendered inaccessible because of lost account information. Geovanny said while a cousin still in the United States sold his car and sent him the money, he lost half of a house he had bought with a friend. Such losses could feel particularly acute in comparison to deportees' situation back in Ecuador. Tommy lamented that "I left everything, everything that I'd done, all the money I had invested into things there, here I have nothing." Other interviewees expressed deep regret about paying lawyers for unsuccessful attempts to fight deportation.

Debt is an additional, serious financial challenge for many deportees and their families (Stoll 2010, 2013; Schuster and Majidi 2013; Lykes et al. 2015). The burden of personal and family debt—tied to persistent poverty—influences the initial decisions of many Ecuadorians to migrate. Then, most Ecuadorians initiating illicit migration journeys take out loans to pay for all or part of the smuggling fee, typically $12,000 to $15,000, with the assumption that they will repay the loan by working in the United States. But while migration attempts may fail, the smuggling debt remains and may continue to grow due to high interest rates. Indebtedness may be particularly severe for migrants apprehended at the border or detained after a short period of time in the United States because they did not have the opportunity to pay any portion of the amount owed. Seventeen of my forty interviewees stated that debt was a significant problem for them, in ways that muted or negated possible happiness at returning to Ecuador. Rodrigo said that arriving in Ecuador, he felt "good, on one hand, to finally be free. On the other hand, I was suffering due to my debts. Because of the debts I was sad when I arrived." Manuel explained, "In those three months [of detention], you forget it all, but when you get out you can't any more. As soon as I arrived in Ecuador, there came my debts—boom, boom, boom—everything at once."

Many families, viewing the migration of one family member as a household strategy to get ahead, invest shared resources in the migration effort. Failed migration journeys, then, can impact extended families' everyday economic reality. For example, after Daniela's deportation, her mother explained that finances for the entire family were constrained because their house had been mortgaged to pay for Daniela's migration. Manuel went into more detail that gives a granular sense of the extent to which poverty and debt pervaded his everyday life after deportation. Since his deportation back to Ecuador, he and his family had moved in with his mother-in-law because they could no longer pay their own rent. Manuel, a metalworker by trade, had reopened a small workshop. "And that's what I'm doing now, I am fighting, but my debts are always right behind me . . . I owe money to a number of *chulqueros*, and I think I'm about to pay one off, but another will take five, maybe six years, and there are others, I am so in debt." For most deportees and their families, it is nearly unfathomable to repay the smuggling debt solely through wages earned in Ecuador.

CRISES OF BELONGING

Additional repercussions, entangled with economic conditions, are social and ontological; deportees may have to contend with an injured sense of belonging and purpose and a destabilized worldview. Those who had lived in the United States for an extended period of time may feel that they do not belong in their "home" country (Peutz 2006; Wheatley 2011; Coutin 2010a). As Coutin (2010a, 205) found in El Salvador, "For deportees who spent a significant portion of their lives in the United States . . . *presence within* their country of origin is simultaneously *absence from* the United States, and is therefore akin to exile." While deportees are physically present in Ecuador, many remain intimately connected to the United States through emotional relationships (Golash-Boza 2014, 2015; Coutin 2010a, 2016).

Family separation is a particularly painful outcome (Hagan, Eschbach, and Rodriguez 2008; Coutin 2010a, 2016; Wessler 2011; Golash-Boza 2014; Cardoso et al. 2014; Lykes et al. 2015; Dingeman-Cerda and Rumbaut 2015). Tommy, for instance, explained, "They grabbed me on a Wednesday, and I was getting married on Friday. Only two days before my wedding!" One-fourth of U.S deportees are parents of U.S. citizen children (Cardoso et al. 2014), leaving children with just one remaining parent, or in some cases sending children left behind into the U.S. foster care system (Wessler 2011; Wessler and Hing 2012). Five of the forty Ecuadorian deportees I interviewed were separated from children in the United States, generating tremendous anguish. Ronaldo had been torn from his wife and two young children in the United States. He said that he called home every day, but his children did not understand his absence, and his wife was struggling to pay for housing on her own. Forced removal can also lead to the geographical unmooring of lives beyond those of the deportees. Many deportees face the decision of whether to bring family with them from the United States after deportation (O'Neill 2012; Ybarra and Peña 2016). Sergio came into the House of the Migrant seeking information on how to acquire legal residency in Ecuador for his U.S. citizen wife and young son, neither of whom spoke Spanish or had been to Ecuador before. While their move to Ecuador would bring their family back together, innumerable challenges of adjustment awaited them.

While deportation brings joyful reunions and the resumption or rebuilding of relationships in Ecuador for some migrants, others return to a different social and familial landscape in Ecuador than that which they left. Coutin (2010a, 205) writes of Salvadoran deportees that their "prior history—the normalcy that they established in the United States and that was erased through detention and deportation—continues to differentiate them from other Salvadorans, placing them apart, and . . . creating internal spatial boundaries." Migrants who had contributed to their family primarily through the sending of remittance money may find themselves uncertain of their family role (Dreby 2012; Drotbohm 2015). Some deportees have been away from their country of origin so long that they face significantly altered family situations and in some cases few family ties (Wheatley 2011). Spouses may have found new partners. Children may have developed relationships with other family members to substitute for an absent parent (Escobar 2008).

Additionally, deportation may be associated with a stigma of failure and wrongdoing in ways that mark returned migrants (Peutz 2006; Ellerman 2008; Brotherton and Barrios 2009; Wessler and Hing 2012; Wheatley 2011; Golash-Boza 2014, 2015; Schuster and Majidi 2013, 2015; Buckinx and Filindra 2015; Drotbohm 2015). Patrons at the House of the Migrant indicated that deportation could be a source of shame and embarrassment. One interviewee, Javier, explained, "When people know that you have come back in that situation, they say, 'that person was deported,' in a way that makes you feel kind of bad." While my interviewees did not indicate the degree of stigma, discrimination, and criminalization directed at deportees in some other places of research, like the Dominican Republic, Jamaica, and El Salvador (Golash-Boza 2015; Dingeman-Cerda and Rumbaut 2015), and Cape Verde (Drotbohm 2015), Ecuadorians' experiences correspond with feelings of disconnection and exile found by other researchers of post-deportation.

The disorder of deportation can extend to all family members. Family reunification may not necessarily be welcome if the deportee comes home with no way to contribute financially (Hagan, Eschbach, and Rodriguez 2008; Golash-Boza 2014; Drotbohm 2015). Without the continued contribution of U.S. earnings or constrained by the migration debt, family members may have to significantly adjust their standard of living, daily activities, and aspirations (Wheatley 2011). The truncation of life plans may lead to profound experiences of personal emotional insecurity, regarding belonging and purpose. When deportee Edison, apprehended during his first migration attempt and heavily indebted, came to the House of the Migrant with his son for an interview, I wrote in my research journal (August 4, 2009), "It was depressing—he clearly seems desperate, not sure how to proceed with his life, very sad." The mother of another deportee, Joaquín, called the House of the Migrant soon after her son's arrival, reporting that he was not acclimating to life in Ecuador and wanted to return to the United States as soon as possible. The situation of Esteban, deported after living in the United States for sixteen years, was more extreme. Seven weeks after Esteban's arrival in Ecuador, his adult son told me, "It is very sad. He is sixty-four, and he can't get work. About three or four years ago he had given up drinking. With all this he entered into an emotional shock, and started to drink again. And I tell you that he already tried to commit suicide two weeks ago . . . So as his son, I am very excited, and content to have my father back after so many years but I am sad to see, to see him as a person totally broken, lost, totally destroyed." These examples illustrate deportees' sense of being out of place. They also show that it is not just the deportees who struggle in the aftermath of deportation. These ruptures in place can impact family relationships in critical ways. As experienced by Edison's son, Joaquín's mother, and Esteban's son, the pleasures of reunion may be tainted by transnational links—whether economic, emotional, or existential—that endure beyond the deportee's physical separation from the United States.

Additionally, the detention and deportation experience may continue to be tangibly embodied in the physical and mental health of deportees and their families after deportation. Permanently reduced family income can negatively impact health through reduced medical care and nutrition (Antón 2010). For some participants in Ecuador, these hauntings can be traced directly to the stresses of detention. In several cases during my fieldwork, migrants returned with serious medical issues that required treatment. For example, the mother of deportee Efraín "said he was sick in the detention center, and they had given him an IV and were going to do some other treatment but because he was coming back to Ecuador soon they didn't. She said they are working on getting him healthy here" (author's research journal, February 10, 2009). The scars from detention can also be psychological. When I called deportee Patricia's sister to inquire about the possibility of an interview with Patricia, she "said that Patricia hasn't been talking much because she is depressed about what happened to her there" (author's research journal, August 4, 2009). Health crises may persist for relatives of deportees as well. When I saw Daniela's father months after her return, he told me that he was "still suffering, receiving some kind of treatment for his nerves that started while she was gone" (author's research journal, May 23, 2009). These examples starkly illustrate how the insecurities produced by the chaos of deportation and detention become materially embodied across transnational space.

COMMUNITY INSECURITIES

Deportation from the United States to Ecuador reverberates beyond deportees and their families. Ecuador is unprepared for substantial return migration (Jokisch 2014), particularly of migrants forcibly returned and in precarious situations. Ecuadorian economists worry that a surge in deportation could add significantly to the country's economic woes, putting additional strain on labor markets (Bowditch 2008, 2009a; Jokisch 2014). Additionally, many sectors of Ecuador's economy are interwoven with international migration. Remittances sent back to Ecuador sustain many families and communities, contributing to the expenses of daily life, such as food, housing, health care, and education. Local economies depend on these expenditures, as well as the businesses that have sprung up to facilitate the transfer of money and goods between Ecuador and abroad. Detention and deportation also create social insecurity and deficits more generally at the local scale. This pertains to family members who expend time and energy worrying about their personal challenges related to detention and deportation, and they are therefore less able to contribute to their communities. It also relates to the creation of broader social problems. I spoke with numerous Ecuadorians working with issues of migration who expressed concern regarding the impacts that deportation has had and will have on the general public. For instance, one official attributed the formation of Ecuadorian branches of U.S. gangs to the forced return of migrants. While this has not occurred to the extent it has in Central America (Wolf 2010; Zilberg 2011; Gonzales 2014), it is a concern in Ecuador.

There are few public resources available to deportees and their families to help them negotiate these many challenges. While the Ecuadorian government under Rafael Correa forged a number of initiatives to maintain political and economic ties with Ecuadorian migrants abroad (Price and Breese 2016; Délano Alonso 2018), the limited attention to migrants returning to Ecuador has focused on those returning voluntarily. One program, called Bienvenidos@Casa, allows returning migrants to bring belongings back to Ecuador duty-free. Another, called Plan Cucayo, provides matching funds for new businesses to return migrants, through a competitive application process (Herrera, Moncayo, and Garcia 2012; Price and Breese 2016). However, while there has been a notable trend in voluntary return migration to Ecuador from Spain (supported by a number of Spanish programs offering incentives), voluntary return from the United States has been more limited (Jokisch 2014).[2] Even for these intentional returnees, who were making a deliberate decision to leave the United States, with time to plan as well as resources to reestablish themselves in Ecuador, reintegration in Ecuador can be difficult. In fact, Jokisch (2014, n.p.) found that "many return migrants to southern Ecuador re-migrated to the United States after their economic enterprises failed or when they could not earn what they were accustomed to in the United States."

Deportees, in contrast to those returning voluntarily, typically arrive in a state of precarity: with significant debts from the failed migration journey, stripped of material capital accrued while in the United States through the violence of apprehension or hefty legal fees, or unable to sufficiently support family in the United States or Ecuador. Many deportees expressed frustration at the lack of concrete assistance the government offered. Santiago, discussing the crippling debts hanging over him and his family, showed me the symbolic "Universal Passport" among the information pamphlets that he was given upon disembarking his deportation flight: a heavyweight piece of folded paper, the size of a passport, symbolizing the Correa administration's affirmation of the universal right to international human mobility. "What is that good for?" he said, exasperated. Government-sponsored and nongovernmental organizations generally do not have the resources to offer the type of services that would significantly benefit deportees and their families. While Cuenca's House of the Migrant where I volunteered did offer some services such as legal advice and limited mental health counseling, for the most part there are few government resources available to help families cope with traumas associated with detention and deportation, such as issues related to social adjustment or family separation (El Universo 2008). Very few organizations were able to offer other highly requested assistance, such as education scholarships or loans and employment placement. No organizations offered what was most asked for: programs for personal debt relief. Instead, members of the growing population of deportees are left to deal on their own with the most serious problems in the aftermath of deportation.

Finally, knowledge of detention and deportation seeps into community consciousness, as Lykes et al. (2015) found in Guatemala. Headlines announcing the arrival of deported migrants frequently punctuate local and national news media in Ecuador, and most Ecuadorians know or have at least heard of someone being deported. This awareness can alter daily realities in ways that increase fear and insecurity even for Ecuadorians who have not personally come into contact with these enforcement practices. For example, while riding a bus on a day trip with my family, I sat next to a woman wearing a baseball cap emblazoned with the words "New York." Though I had not spoken with her about the work that I was doing at the House of the Migrant, after I casually mentioned that I was from New York, she told me her youngest son had gone to New York a year ago, arriving on his second migration attempt. Starting to cry, she said she worried about him constantly, because she had heard of people being caught and deported. The woman's awareness demonstrates that even the potential for detention and deportation has the power to shape collective feelings of insecurity.

The Reality of Repeat Migration

With few tools available to overcome the many postdeportation challenges except their own resourcefulness, the majority of Ecuadorian deportees decide to try to return to the United States again, like Saira, with whose story this chapter began. Of the forty deportees I interviewed, twenty-one indicated that another attempt to migrate to the United States was certain or likely. It is also highly probable that some interviewees who told me that they would not return did not feel sufficiently comfortable with this question from a U.S. interviewer to answer candidly. Indeed, an Ecuadorian newspaper reported that 80 percent of arriving deportees said that they were going to attempt to return (*El Tiempo* 2009). Additional metrics from my research show that repeated migration attempts are common. Nine interviewees had been deported two or more times. One interviewee said that a man on his deportation flight had been deported six times. Also, there were numerous deportees I tried to contact within just weeks of their deportation whose relatives said they were already *viajando* (traveling) or had even arrived in the United States. Paúl's father, in the anecdote at the beginning of the previous chapter, told me that of the three people he knew who had been deported (another son, a nephew, and a neighbor), all had immediately gone back to the United States; two of them arrived successfully, and one was (at that time) in jail for reentry (author's research journal, April 27, 2009).

While the assumption that deportation and detention are necessary and effective deterrents to immigration pervades policymaking initiatives, there is a substantial body of academic and journalistic accounts that offer evidence to the contrary. The two groups that policymakers hope to dissuade are already-deported migrants and potential first-time migrants. In Ecuador, neither of these groups is categorically discouraged. The high likelihood of repeat migration found among Ecuadorian deportees is in line with findings in other studies of detention and deportation (e.g., Black et al. 2006; Collyer 2007; Cornelius and Salehyan 2007; Hagan, Eschbach, and Rodriguez 2008; D. M. Hernandez 2008; Wheatley 2011; Schuster and Majidi 2013; Stoll 2013; Cardoso et al. 2014; Dingeman-Cerda and Rumbaut 2015; Slack et al. 2015; Wong 2015). Summarizing existing scholarship, Schuster and Majidi (2013, 224) state that "the majority of those who are deported want to, will attempt to, and often do leave again." In addition, the frequency with which new border-apprehension detention cases came into the House of the Migrant indicates that there is still significant first-time migration to the United States.

A review of the immediate challenges and insecurities faced by deportees and their families serves as an initial catalog of reasons deportation and detention are not effective deterrents. Financial pressures are at the top of the list. Migrants return to the same economic situation that they left—a tight labor market and poor wages in Ecuador—or perhaps worse. As evidenced in Saira's story, debt, and a lack of options for repaying debt in their home country, is a primary driving force in deportees' decisions to remigrate (El Universo 2008; Stoll 2010, 2013; Schuster and Majidi 2013). As Schuster and Majidi (2013, 228) argue, entire families may invest in the migrant's journey, and "when they return empty handed, it is the entire family that bears the indebtedness and economic losses." In our interview, Manuel B still wrestled with whether he should try to migrate again, as he thought about the years and years it would take to pay off his debts. He explained, "I am worried, sometimes I think I should try [to migrate] again . . . sometimes you want to do something for your kids so that some day they have a way to get ahead, but there are no opportunities here, and everything gets more expensive." He went on, "But I am better off here, well, not right away—because of my debts, but better because I am with my kids, though it's hard because of the debts . . . Can you imagine, it has been three, four years that I've given nothing to my kids for Christmas. These things make me so sad." Manuel B wrestled painfully with the competing desires to provide material goods and better opportunities for his children and be part of his children's daily lives.

Migrants who are deported before they can repay their migration debt typically feel that they have no option but to migrate again (Stoll 2010). While smugglers usually will not return money if a migrant is deported, they do include multiple attempts in their price (Schuster and Majidi 2013). Here, I return to Santiago, whose story begins chapter 2. Both Santiago and his wife were desperate for alternatives to him attempting to migrate for a third time. He had felt his life was in danger numerous times on his previous journeys, he had been caught both times near the U.S.-Mexico border, and he suffered from a serious hernia and other health issues. But the coyote was not responding to their inquiries about getting their money back, and the *chulquero* was stopping by with more and more frequency to ask for payment. To fund Santiago's migration, they had mortgaged their property—land that they farmed for a key source of income, and on which their house sat. Their family would become homeless and destitute without the land. "I don't want to go again . . . But if I can't get the money back," Santiago said sadly, "there is no other way—I have to try again." Furthermore, as Stoll (2010) found in Guatemala, not only does debt exert significant pressure on deportees to attempt repeat migration, but additional family members may migrate in order to help relieve existing debt burdens.

Social and familial ties are another primary driver of repeat migration. For migrants deported after significant time in the United States, the country called their "home" by the U.S. government may no longer fit that label. A twenty-four-year-old deportee said he will just keep trying to return to the United States until he makes it, because "my life is there." Family separation significantly elevates the likelihood that deportees will attempt to migrate again. Parents forcefully separated from children are a particularly resolute group (Hagan, Eschbach, and Rodriguez 2008; Schuster and Majidi 2013; Cardoso et al. 2014; Brabeck, Porterfield, and Loughry 2015). One deportee with whom I spoke had a five-year-old son who remained in the United States. She said that "she is going to try to cross again and she'll do whatever it takes to see him, even if it means more time in U.S. detention. She has already spent several months detained and she was told the next time she is caught it could be a year" (author's research journal, January 21, 2009). Ronaldo, the deportee mentioned above who had been separated from his two children, came in to the House of the Migrant to inquire about possibilities for legal migration after his deportation. Upon our confirming that it was unlikely, he declared that, regardless, he would find a way to return to his family.

There is also the fact that Ecuadorian cultural and social life has been fundamentally changed by international migration. International mobility is regarded as a normal, even routine part of life. In many communities, migration has come to be an expected undertaking for young adults. This is especially true for the children of migrants who grow up planning to join parents in their destination country (Jokisch and Pribilsky 2002; Escobar 2008; Herrera 2008). In contrast to U.S. policymakers' view of migration as a source of instability and precarity, in countries of migrant origin migration is a rational, responsible choice to confront economic precarity and household instabilities. This is reflected in the comments of one deportee on the bus I rode from Guayaquil to Cuenca, when he said, "What is there for me here? Nothing. I have to go back. I have to do it for my family." In addition, new migration may be undertaken to mitigate the everyday economic and social insecurities spread throughout families and communities (Kyle and Siracusa 2005; Collyer 2007; Stoll 2010, 2013). Migrants often understand migration as a human right, not as illegal or morally wrong (Kyle and Siracusa 2005; Collyer 2007). Human mobility, then, is rooted in interpretations of security that are markedly different from the meaning embedded in narratives of homeland security (Staeheli and Nagel 2008). Kyle and Siracusa (2005, 157) suggest, "Illegal migrants often view themselves as a type of economic citizen of the political economic empire Western states and transnational corporations have created." Indeed, I frequently heard relatives protest that "she was only trying to work!" when reacting to information about a migrant's detention. Migrants' ideas of security and experiences of insecurity stand in opposition to U.S. policymakers' idea of security; migrants' framing of security justifies international migration, while policymakers' framing justifies detention and deportation.

Some potential migrants surely are deterred by deportation and detention. But many are not dissuaded (Wong 2015). The possible rewards can make migration appear as the most logical choice, regardless of the risks. Lykes et al. (2015, 219) found in Guatemala, "despite knowledge of workplace raids, violence on the journey north, and indebtedness for those who chose to leave home, youth report dreams of traveling north or being resigned that the only option for realizing their goals is through crossing the border without authorization." Ecuadorian deportee Elsa said she had seen some terrible things on her first journey to the United States and spent almost twelve weeks in U.S. detention facilities.[3] When I interviewed her three days after her deportation, Elsa explained her thought process as she decided whether to make another migration attempt: "I don't know, I have to think . . . because here the economic situation is very difficult. I know that [in the United States] it isn't easy either, but at least you earn more. But I also have to think about if I die in the desert, and after [my family] comes here crying to ask you to bring my body back." When I talked to Elsa just ten days later, she had decided to try again. Additionally, for deportees, to abandon migration goals would be perceived as a waste of time, money, and suffering already invested (Collyer 2007; Schuster and Majidi 2013). They may feel, as Collyer (2007, 686) found, that "migration owes them something."

Finally, it is important to return to the relationship between heightened border and immigration enforcement, human smuggling, and continued migration, discussed in chapter 2. As numerous scholars have argued, policies that make migration more difficult nurture the development of smuggling networks, because migrants must depend on smugglers to facilitate their illicit journeys (e.g., Spener 2004; Andreas 2000; Nevins 2010; Schuster and Majidi 2013). Many Ecuadorians did not regard smugglers as nefarious criminals, but as necessary facilitators. This was never more evident than when I attended the rare trial—and even rarer conviction—of a *coyote* in Cuenca. It was clear that the smuggler was not on trial for engaging in human smuggling; he was on trial for being a bad smuggler—for taking people's money without pure intentions to help them reach their migration destinations and therefore breaking the relationship of trust between migrants and smugglers. More restrictive and punitive policies directly lead to increased smuggling operations, as well as increased smuggling fees and, therefore, more debt assumed by migrants and their families. What's more, developing smuggling industries become interested in their own survival and growth and work to actively recruit new migrants, thus taking a role in the perpetuation of migration. Initiatives like the Border Patrol's Consequence Delivery System, together with deportation and detention—both anchored in rationales of deterrence—contribute to the development of illicit industries, increase risk and debt for migrants, and ensure that undocumented migration to the United States continues.

Conclusion

The discussion of reverberations of U.S. detention and deportation in Ecuador presented in this and the previous chapter compares assumed policy outcomes with how these policies actually work. The multiple and overlapping insecurities generated outside U.S. borders, in everyday, mundane realities, contribute to the repeat migration of a majority of Ecuadorian deportees, as well as new migration, presenting a stark contrast to the assumed deterrent effect of these policies. As evidenced in the fact that so many deportees return illicitly to the United States, deportation cannot be thought of as the termination of a migration journey. Rather, it is often experienced as an unwelcome detour, one among many challenges that must be overcome in pursuit of their migration goal. Hagan, Eschbach, and Rodriguez (2008, 85) surmise that deportation "does not end the migration of unauthorized or criminal migrants; it simply raises the human costs for migrants and their families." Migration continues, therefore, despite and because of the possibility of detention and deportation. Instead of definitively ending a particular migration journey and discouraging future migration, detention and deportation become central to migration cycles (Hagan, Eschbach, and Rodriguez 2008; Schuster and Majidi 2013; Mainwaring and Silverman 2017).

This is not to say that detention and deportation do not discourage some people from attempting to migrate to the United States; they most definitely do. It is important to remember, however, the displacement effect that can also occur (Wong 2015). That is, potential migrants make alternate choices that will have their own set of consequences. Expanding on Drotbohm and Hasselberg's (2015) concept of a "deportation corridor," Coutin (2015, 675), writes that "deportations involve and generate movements in multiple directions." Some potential migrants choose migration, while others make different decisions that reverberate both locally and transnationally. While we cannot predict these specific decisions or their consequences, global interconnectedness together with extreme inequalities suggests that reverberations will not be isolated to countries of migrant origin.

These findings regarding the real transnational consequences of deportation stand in obvious disagreement with dominant assumptions driving the detention and deportation "turn," but they are hardly surprising to migrants or those who work in or study migration and border enforcement. Migration will continue as long as there are pressures pushing migrants. Wong (2015, 144–145) succinctly explains, "because increased restrictiveness does not fundamentally change the underlying motives of migrants, more restrictive immigration control efforts are unlikely to result in less unwanted immigration." This glaring paradox, and the apparent failure of policymakers to recognize it and shift policies accordingly, raise the question, eloquently stated by Coutin (2015, 677): "Why, if deportation is so counterproductive, does it occur, and on a massive scale?"

One clear driving force is the immigration industrial complex, and the commodification of detainees by a wide range of public and private entities that make money off of detention and deportation, as well as politicians and media entities who benefit through public support and attention, as discussed in previous chapters. This collection of interests supports the writing and passage of immigration laws that punish and criminalize immigrants in ways that make disproportionate treatment seem justified and even necessary, and that conveniently ignore U.S. responsibility for international migration patterns.

Some scholars, however, find many explanations for the increased reliance on deportation, including those focusing exclusively on economic reasons, overly simple. For example, Coutin suggests (2015, 677–678), "Instead, if deportation is irrational, then perhaps explanations need to examine the fantasies that are made possible through deportation. What investments, whether material or psychological, require stigmatised others in order to persist? How do non-migrants' senses of self depend on the foil of the criminalised alien? How do deportations reinvigorate such irrationalities over time?" Mainwaring and Silverman (2017) present the concept of "detention-as-spectacle" to argue that detention is more about displaying sovereign power and control than effectively controlling migration.

These provocations bring us back to our earlier tracing of the development of the contemporary immigration enforcement approach in the United States. Critical factors in the construction of the detention and deportation apparatus include the long-standing connections between race, otherness, and national identity. From the founding of the United States, racialized hierarchies have been woven into its social, political, and economic fabrics, and immigration laws have reflected, shaped, and reinforced these hierarchies. In the last four decades, the perceived rise of terrorism and national security fears, together with sustained economic downturns, have led to hegemonic imaginings of immigration as a profound threat to not just national identity but also national security. Policies like detention and deportation simultaneously target people of color in ways that reinforce racialized ideas of national identity and animate narratives of homeland security that justify and expand state power. Today's turn to detention and deportation lies at the confluence of these forces of identity making, narratives of security, and relationships of interdependence.

CHAPTER 8

Ordering Chaos, Opening Space

Around the world, immigrant incarceration and expulsion are being normalized to such a degree that they no longer seem exceptional actions for isolated moments of crisis. Instead, these policies are made to seem the duty and right of legitimate governments and rational responses in ordinary times. There is a remarkable momentum behind the development of divisive, dehumanizing immigration enforcement apparatuses in more and more places. The massive detention and deportation system at the heart of the U.S. enforcement regime has roughly doubled in size since I began the research for this book ten years ago. While the overt hostility and vitriol of the current president has brought discussion of these practices to the forefront of national debates, it is important to not allow the Trump spectacle to obscure the many influences that built the U.S. system over the last forty years. Its foundations are xenophobia, racist ideas of national identity, and an enduring economic dependence on cheap labor. The system has evolved to its contemporary form in the context of globalized neo-liberal capitalism, drastic inequalities, and the commodification of immigrant bodies. It is propelled by racialized imaginaries of security and belonging and political, legal mechanisms for dehumanizing nonwhite immigrants, and it is further enabled by willful ignorance of how policies reverberate in space and time, irrespective of state borders.

This book explores the chaos projected by the U.S. detention and deportation system. I argue that this chaos serves important functions, masking both the drivers and consequences of the system itself. By thwarting scrutiny, chaos allows the state to set the narratives around immigration. Deportation and detention are firmly rooted in imaginaries of national borders as territorially fixed, natural, and controllable and are justified as policies that protect national security and deter future migration. The system's chaos distracts from the mismatch between these policy objectives and actual outcomes, in the United States, as well as in countries of migrant origin and transit. For non-immigrants, the perceived maelstrom of deportation and detention obscures the racist nature of immigration enforcement and reinforces larger processes and discourses criminalizing migrants and securitizing migration. The disordered, uneven operation of the detention and deportation system also distracts from the power of the immigration industrial complex, inefficiency and waste within the system, and deplorable conditions of detention. Finally, the chaotic spatial and temporal geographies of migrants' detention experiences work to block detainees' access to support networks, hide alternatives to deportation, and contribute to disciplining immigrant laborers to behave passively. In detention and deportation, chaos is both a central characteristic and a very effective barrier, creating a black box that blurs views of what happens inside the system as well as what these policies do outside it.

Detain and Deport is grounded in the conviction that chaos should not be allowed to work as a determinant of what can be seen. If we yield to the perceived impenetrability of chaos, we inadvertently accept state narratives about why these policies are necessary and what they accomplish, and we more easily default to rigid ideas of borders. Even critical scholars can unintentionally bolster states' discourses, simply by letting them stand unchallenged. Instead, scholarship and activism must aim to order the chaos of detention and deportation. Focusing on chaos—and the seeming impenetrability projected by chaos—can contribute to opening the black box of these systems to better understand what happens inside detention, after deportation, and how those two spaces are linked. Through making the drivers, operation, and consequences of the system more visible, we can offer a counterforce to the momentum of detention and deportation.

This book has employed a transnational, ethnographic approach to order the chaos of detention and deportation policies. Instead of accepting the chaos as a characteristic of immigration, this approach interrogates the chaos, questioning what it hides and what it allows. Transnational ethnography of immigration enforcement policy endeavors to get around physical and bureaucratic barriers by identifying and assessing U.S. immigration enforcement practices through research conducted in and from a country of migrant origin. This approach brings attention to the "doing" of both detention and deportation, centering everyday, embodied consequences of policy. It concentrates on the more mundane processes, those that are often overlooked but are important precisely because it is in the more banal operations that detention and deportation are normalized, made to seem routine, and then are accepted as automatic responses to perceived immigration crises. And by beginning the research with those who experience policy, instead of with those who make it, this approach facilitates a better understanding of the actual effects of policy, circumventing a lens defined by the state's intended outcomes and framing.

Transnational ethnography opens space for shifting the powerful narratives, assumptions, and influences surrounding the system by creating cracks in the conceptual pillars—and chaos—shielding the U.S. detention and deportation system from scrutiny. As both a conceptual and methodological approach, transnational ethnography promotes supra-border thinking in a way that destabilizes the assumptions and principles on which detention and deportation systems rest. With its attention to a range of spaces and times, a transnational ethnographic lens works to shift assumptions and narratives purporting that detention and deportation strengthen territorial borders and protect national security. By tracing the people detained and deported, transnational ethnography simultaneously relies on the webs woven by these immigration enforcement policies in action and shows that the existence of these webs contradicts national border logics of defined and confined space.

In recognizing that these policies actually forge—rather than break—links across national borders and time, transnational ethnography counters ideas that these approaches could ever bring an "end" to migration, thereby contradicting the rationale of deterrence. I come back to Saira's decision to try to migrate again, recounted at the beginning of the previous chapter. When Saira was deported to Ecuador, she expressed relief at being back with her son and emotional injury from her harrowing journey and time in U.S. detention. Three months later, however, despairing about her financial situation, she decided to try to get to the United States again. For most Ecuadorians who leave, migration is a bid to escape crushing poverty. In contrast, in some of the top source countries of migrants to the United States, such as the Northern Triangle countries of Central America and parts of Mexico, migration is literally a matter of life and death, due to crime, corruption, and gang violence. If someone like Saira—in debt but not facing immediate physical violence, knowing how bad the journey can be, and having previously been detained in the United States—is not deterred, people choosing mobility as a last-ditch effort to escape death will certainly not be dissuaded. One significant outcome, then, is the persistent expansion of human smuggling operations, increased violence for migrants, and more criminal activity. Instead of cutting down on illegal activities and increasing security at and within U.S. borders, politically popular strategies do the opposite, without regard to (and because of) territorial borders.

A transnational ethnographic approach to policy also forces a more complex, multiscalar view of why people migrate as well as the reverberations of policies, a view that explodes—instead of maintaining—the tunnel vision of a state-centric and fixed-border lens. Employing a transnational lens in policy analysis goes beyond just looking at the consequences of immigration policies. For example, the history of Ecuadorian migration to the United States shows that migration decisions and patterns are influenced by many types of policies and relationships: immigration and border enforcement, foreign policy and diplomatic, military, economic, and business policies and relationships. And continued migration is tied to the paradoxical relationship between national-scale security and micro-scale (family, home, individual) insecurity. Deportation and detention make daily life in Ecuador more precarious in ways that produce more everyday insecurities, and it is everyday insecurities that push people to migrate. So the logics at the heart of detention and deportation work to compound, rather than solve, the factors driving migration in the first place. We see how processes of securitization can generate an extraterritoriality for policymaking states, a reality that is the polar opposite of what policies anchored in a security rationale are supposed to do. It becomes evident that forced territorial removal has consequences that reverberate across national borders. And not only are these policies ineffective at deterring migration and enforcing territorial breaks, but they can also work to stretch ties through time and space.

A transnational ethnographic lens thus pushes policymakers, scholars, and the broader public to spatiotemporally extend their thinking when they consider broader consequences of these policies. For example, in the last years of the Obama administration and the first years of the Trump administration, government officials have touted lower border apprehension numbers to claim that illicit migration to the United States has dropped precipitously, with many nods being given to the efficacy of deterrence policies. But there is intentional ignorance of the fact that detention and deportation in Mexico and Central America are simultaneously on the rise. The broader lens employed in this book facilitates recognition of this reality and opens up consideration of consequences of "deterrence" beyond U.S. borders: When migrants are deterred from the United States, what happens instead? How will tougher enforcement impact migration journeys, in terms of risk, danger, routes, and cost? What violences, dislocations, and disruptions develop? Will migration to other countries increase instability, and/or strengthen their economies, and how will those consequences reverberate to the United States? A spatiotemporally expansive lens can illustrate that the deterrence frame curtails understanding of the effects of these policies. Detention and deportation can therefore be understood to contribute to the production of the United States as a territory with an elastic geography extending well beyond its perimeter as conventionally understood, and the linking of migrant destination and origin countries across borders.

The more detention and deportation are institutionalized as normal, necessary immigration enforcement strategies, the more difficult they are to contest. As more entities—government agencies, private companies, and individuals—become dependent on detention and deportation systems, they also become invested in discourses, laws, and other processes that racialize and criminalize particular immigrant groups to create targetable "Others." Therefore, at the same time as efforts are focused on counteracting the easily identifiable violences of overtly hostile approaches, we must also address the bureaucratic entrenchment of detention and deportation systems and the economic relationships greasing the wheels of this entrenchment. Through its border-defiant methodology, transnational ethnography forces a transparency that contributes to destabilizing the bureaucratic and economic foundations on which the system rests. We can expose what happens inside detention facilities: the abysmal, often abusive conditions of detention and the injustices woven into the system. While some publics will not be alarmed, others will be morally outraged and demand change. Similarly, revealing how dehumanizing detainee experiences are rooted in profit making can work against the commodification of immigrants and decrease the involvement of profit incentives in detention and deportation. For example, if contracted companies are compelled to feed detainees appropriately, they make less money. If detainees who labor in detention facilities are paid at least minimum wage, facility operation costs will be significantly higher, and detention will become less lucrative. Transnational ethnography can therefore contribute to showing how those profiting from detention and deportation are driving system growth.

Far-reaching, durable transformations to immigration enforcement practices and approaches will not be achieved without a profound shift regarding the place of migration in national imaginaries of security, borders, and belonging. Nationalistic discourses of homeland security racialize, criminalize, and dehumanize immigrants as foreign bodies out of place. Powerful players who profit from punitive immigration enforcement promote political will and legal mechanisms to turn immigrants into fodder for detention and deportation systems. Intentionally ignoring how policies reverberate in space and time, irrespective of political borders, enables continued investment in policies that work in contradictory ways. Then, the chaos of immigration enforcement systems strips migrants of their histories, prevaricates motivations, and facilitates the conceptualization of immigrants as the opposite of citizens—the Other against whom national belonging is understood. We must fundamentally rework understandings of security to incorporate a range of scales and spaces in addition to the state. In pointing to contrasting experiences and understandings of insecurity, transnational ethnographies of policy can bring some sense of order and reason to the often disordered, contradictory discourses of homeland security and nation behind violent policies and make space for alternate narratives and approaches.

APPENDIX A

Interviewed Functionaries

	Location	Position	Type of organization
1	Quito	Director	National NGO
2	Small town near Cuenca	Pastor	Catholic church
3	Cuenca	Lawyer, program director	Federal government agency, regional branch
4	Quito	Official	U.S. Embassy
5	Cuenca	Case worker	NGO
6	Cuenca	Lawyer	Law office
7	Small city near Cuenca	Pastor & advisory board	Catholic organization (4 people attended interview)
8	Quito	Unit director	Federal government ministry
9	Quito	Unit director	Regional government agency
10	Quito	Lawyer, program director	National NGO
11	Quito	Lawyer	Federal government agency
12	Quito	Unit director	Federal government agency
13	Quito	Director	Regional government agency
14	Cuenca	President	Local association
15	Cuenca	Lawyer	Law office
16	Cuenca	Lawyer	Federal government agency, regional branch
17	Cuenca	Lawyer, unit director	Federal government agency, regional branch
18	Cuenca	Lawyer	Law office
19	Quito	Director	Federal government agency, regional branch
20	Quito	Administrator	Federal government agency
21	Quito	Program director	Federal government agency
22	Quito	Employee	Federal government agency
23	Quito	Director	Federal government ministry
24	Guayaquil	Lawyer, administrator	Federal government agency, regional branch
25	Cuenca	Director	NGO

Interviewed Deportees, Basic Data

	Pseudonym	Gender (F or M)	Age	Caught border or interior	If interior, time in U.S.	Where lived in U.S.	Weeks detained	No. places detained
1	Jorge	M	38	border			12	3
2	Juan	M	29	interior	2 years	New York City	8	3
3	José Carlos	M	47	interior	8 years	New York City	8	6
4	Faustino	M	24	interior	5 years	Chicago	8	2
5	Anderson	M	20	interior	5 years	Chicago & Minneapolis	12	1
6	Pato	M	28	interior	11 years	Philadelphia	18	4
7	Saira	F	23	border			16	2
8	Patricio	M	40	interior	8 years	Newark, N.J.	20	4
9	Oscar	M	40	interior	8 years	New York City	10	7
10	Javier	M	26	interior	6 years	New York City	8	4
11	Daniela	F	24	border			8	1
12	Johnny	M	25	border			8	3
13	Clemente	M	41	interior	11 years	New York City	4	5
14	Julio	M	33	border			2.5	2
15	Santiago	M	38	border			5	4
16	Eduardo	M	24	border			8	4
17	Juan Carlos	M	31	border			2.5	2
18	Fernando	M	26	border			18	5
19	Tulio	M	47	interior	10 years	New York City	8	7
20	Joaquín	M	22	interior	4 years	New York City	8	4
21	Tommy	M	24	interior	7 years	Chicago & St. Louis	8	1
22	Rodrigo	M	28	border			7	4
23	Remigio	M	21	interior	4.5 years	Danbury, Conn.	6	4
24	Manuel	M	35	border			4	2
25	Armando	M	34	border			3.5	3
26	Franklin	M	23	border			16	1
27	Juan Pablo	M	29	interior	7 years	Indianapolis, Chicago, & New Jersey	20	5
28	Diego	M	30	interior	10 years	New York City	12	8
29	Sergio	M	25	interior	8 years	Columbus, Ohio	28	1
30	Marcelo	M	32	interior	8 years	Westchester County, N.Y.	12	6

/	Pseudonym	Gender (F or M)	Age	Caught border or interior	If interior, time in U.S.	Where lived in U.S.	Weeks detained	No. places detained
31	Christian	M	24	border			13	3
32	Luis	M	20	border			8	4
33	Geovanny	M	32	interior	9 years	New York City	5.5	4
34	Elsa	F	29	border			11	2
35	Paúl	M	34	interior	9 years	New Jersey	7	3
36	Carlos	M	37	interior	8 years	Connecticut	12	3
37	Hugo	M	38	interior	10 years	New York City	6	4
38	Iván	M	25	interior	3 years	Danbury, Conn.	17	3
39	Edison	M	42	border			14	3
40	Ana Lucía	F	29	border			22	3

NOTES: If the interviewee had made previous migration journeys to the United States, the data here is for the most recent journey. The time detained does not include any time the detainee may have spent incarcerated prior to ICE custody.

Deportee Interview Question Guide

Preguntas—Entrevistas de deportados

Seudónimo: _____

DATOS BÁSICOS

- edad
- de dónde en Ecuador? Barrio?
- educación? Trabajo en Ecuador?
- casado/a?
- qué era su estatus legal en los EEUU?
- hijos? Dónde están? Son ciudadanos estadounidenses?
- p/q decidió viajar a EEUU?
- cuántos viajes a EEUU?
- viaje a los EEUU: indocumentado? Con coyote? Deuda acumulada? Ruta? Tiempo del viaje?
- antes de viajar a EEUU, sabía de las prácticas de detención y deportación en EEUU?
- cuánto tiempo vivió en los EEUU?
- en qué trabajaba en EEUU?
- con qué frecuencia se comunicó con familiares en Ecuador?
- envió dinero?

CIRCUNSTANCIAS DE CAPTURA

- dónde: calle, trabajo, auto, transporte?
- p/q? por ser indocumentado? cargos especiales? En redada?
- por quién? Policía local, de estado, federal? De ICE?
- tratamiento por policía?
- en un cárcel normal antes de pasar a Migración?

EXPERIENCIA DE DETENCIÓN

- dónde detenido primero?
- qúe información recibió?
- representación legal? Experiencia en corte?
- pagó fianza? Se lo devolvieron la fianza?
- transferido a diferentes cárceles? Centros de detención? Transporte para transferencias?
- comunicación con otras personas? Familiares?
- duración de detención?
- cuidado médico?
- alimentación?
- que hizo mientras detenido? Ejercicio? Trabajo?
- tratamiento por guardias, etc. en la cárcel? algún maltrato? Frustraciones?

PROCESO DE DEPORTACIÓN

- información recibido?
- con qué anticipación sabía de la deportación?
- en un vuelo comercial? Del gobierno?
- experiencia del vuelo: tratamiento, en cadenas, tiempo?

AL LLEGAR EN ECUADOR

- cómo era la recepción? Trámites en el aeropuerto? Tenía que hablar con SENAMI, Fiscalía, MMRREE, ICE?
- familiares esperando para Ud? Para otros deportados?
- adónde iban otros deportados? Qué iban a hacer al salir del aeropuerto?
- al llegar, qué hizo Ud?
- cómo se sentía al llegar en Ecuador?
- qué hace ahora? Trabaja?
- piensa en regresar a los EEUU? p/q?

PARA TERMINAR

- dejó dinero u otras cosas en EEUU? Intentando recuperar?
- pensamientos sobre la experiencia de detención, deportación?
- Qué piensa ahora de los EEUU? Del ICE?

- en el proceso de detención, deportación, llegada al Ecuador, se sintió apoyado por el gobierno ecuatoriano? Piensa que hay más que el gobierno ecuatoriano debía haber hecho?
- conocen a otras personas deportados varias veces? Otros casos particulares de los cuales quieres hablar?

NOTES

Chapter 1. A Transnational Ethnography of U.S. Detention and Deportation

1. I avoid the term *multisited ethnography* because I intentionally eschew the notion of distinct geographic sites of research (Hage 2005), emphasizing instead the ways in which immigration enforcement policy creates connections through time and space.

2. I explore ethical issues and methodological challenges related to this research in depth in two articles: Hiemstra 2017 and the coauthored Billo and Hiemstra 2013.

3. Ecuador's annual numbers of deportees are consistent in recent years. Ecuador was basically tied with Brazil for sixth place until the 2017 fiscal year, when the Trump administration's targeting of Haitians for deportation vaulted Haiti from fifteenth to sixth place (DHS 2017).

4. I started research activities in January 2007, when I began reviewing local Ecuadorian newspapers online, and in July 2007 I made a month-long trip to Ecuador to conduct preliminary fieldwork.

5. The Casa offers, among other things, legal advice, counseling services, free internet and videoconferencing, and small capital project guidance, and it hosts events and workshops.

6. To protect the identity of family members discussed in this document, I either assign them a pseudonym or refer to them by their family role (i.e., mother, brother-in-law, etc.). If the participant is a family member of an interviewed deportee, then I refer to her or him in relation to that interviewee and use the interviewee's pseudonym (explained in note 11).

7. The identity of system personnel was largely protected simply by virtue of the inherent anonymity of a phone call. Employees with whom I spoke typically provided only the name of the facility or office, and rarely a personal name or title.

8. In-person interviews were audio-recorded with participant consent. For all interviews, including recorded ones, I took detailed handwritten notes, which I later typed up. I then translated from Spanish to English any quotes included in English publications.

9. These interviews were conducted in July 2007 and between November 2008 and August 2009. To protect the identity of these interviewees, I refer to them with a general explanation of the type of work that they do, for example, "official at the federal level" or "employee of a Cuenca-based religious organization." See Appendix A: Interviewed Functionaries.

10. See Appendix B: Interviewed Deportees, Basic Data. The average age of deportees interviewed was thirty; the youngest was twenty, and the oldest forty-seven. Of the forty people who consented to an interview, four were women and thirty-six were men. The

percentage of women among my participants, therefore, is lower than overall deportation numbers, of which roughly 20 percent at that time were women. Eighteen of the forty interviewees were caught near the U.S.-Mexico border attempting to migrate. Twenty-two were apprehended in the country's interior, reflecting the contemporary rise in interior immigration policing. Of those apprehended in the interior, the average number of years living in the United States was 7.3. I also interviewed one adult son of a deportee (not included in Appendix B).

11. At the beginning of each interview of a deportee, I asked the participant to choose a pseudonym. See Appendix C: Deportee Interview Question Guide.

12. The papers are *El Tiempo*, *El Universo*, and *El Mercurio*.

Chapter 2. Ecuadorian Migration, U.S. Policy, and Human Smuggling

1. While the United States was overwhelmingly the destination of Ecuadorian emigrants during this phase, Ecuadorians also ventured to Australia, Canada, Israel, and Venezuela (Borrero and Vega 1995).

2. Drawing on the 2000 U.S. census, Gratton (2006) reported that Ecuadorian men in the United States typically worked in building trades, food service industries, and, to a lesser degree, managerial and professional employment. Ecuadorian women were employed in factory work, domestic work, white- and pink-collar (traditionally female-oriented) jobs, managerial positions, and food service.

3. For example, the percentages of population abroad for the *cantón* (county) of Biblián within the province of Cañar is 9.1 percent, and for the Azuay *cantón* of San Fernando it is 7.9 percent (Herrera, Moncayo, and Garcia 2012). Migration rates can be even higher in certain areas at the household level; for example, in the *cantón* of Cañar in Cañar province, 41 percent of households have one or more members abroad (Escobar 2008).

4. Until a 2003 change in policy, those headed to Spain took advantage of a 1963 agreement between Spain and Ecuador that allowed Ecuadorians to travel to Spain as tourists without a visa (Jokisch and Pribilsky 2002; Cornelius 2004). Also, the European Union's Schengen Area (in which internal border checks are largely removed) facilitated migration by allowing Ecuadorians to enter Europe via another signatory country (such as the Netherlands) without a visa and then travel to their country of choice (Jokisch and Pribilsky 2002; FLACSO 2008). Growing antimigrant sentiment in the European Union eventually led to tightened entry requirements (Herrera 2008), as well as increasing migrant legal irregularity (Ciriano 2004; Cornelius 2004; Calavita 2005) and repatriation programs, including deportation initiatives (FLACSO 2008). Today, with the exception of family reunification provisions, it is difficult for Ecuadorians to gain legal entry (with the intent to remain) to European countries (Herrera, Moncayo, and Garcia 2012).

5. The near impossibility of legally sanctioned family reunification has also had other effects, such as the normalization of transnational families who maintain relationships despite distance (Pribilsky 2004; Herrera 2008) and the development of nontraditional family forms (Escobar 2008; Herrera 2008).

6. Between 1961 and 1995 more than 185,000 Ecuadorians received legal permanent resident status (16,292 by virtue of the 1986 legislation) (Jokisch 2007). These Ecuador-

ians and the limited others who have received legal residency or citizenship since then were (and still are) able to extend residency to additional family members in Ecuador (Jokisch 2007; Ramírez and Álvarez 2009).

7. These bases' leases technically limited U.S. activities on and from the bases to those related to combating narcotics trafficking, but there was significant evidence of "mission creep" into migrant interception at sea (Flynn 2005, 25).

8. Ecuador was one of six countries specifically mentioned in a U.S. Coast Guard table recording interdictions (U.S. Coast Guard 2015); the table was taken offline after the Trump administration took office. The first Ecuadorians interdicted at sea were reported in 1999, totaling 298. Totals peaked in 2004 at 1,189 and then steadily dropped to near zero.

9. De León (2015, 321) suggests that the 2014 price was down to $12,000.

10. During my fieldwork, the economic recession also decreased migrants' opportunities for employment in the United States, thereby increasing difficulties with maintaining loan payments.

11. Anecdotal evidence during my fieldwork suggested that some smugglers promised up to five attempts.

12. Sources of deteriorating relations include Correa's 2011 expulsion of the U.S. ambassador after Wikileaks released cables in which she spoke unfavorably about Correa, the sheltering of Wikileaks founder Julian Assange in Ecuador's London embassy, Correa's offer to take in Edward Snowden, Ecuador leaving the Andean Trade Promotion and Drug Eradication pact with the United States in 2013, Correa's attacks on the Ecuadorian press, and the forging of trade and diplomatic agreements with Iran, China, and Russia. Relations may be improving recently. For example, the "Security Cooperation" Office at the U.S. Embassy, closed in 2014, reopened in 2018.

13. The recession coincided with Correa's government developing programs to encourage return and the Spanish government offering incentives for migrants to leave (both initiatives, however, produced limited results) (Jokisch 2014).

14. Dollarization has also attracted a small but notable number of Chinese migrants to Ecuador (Jokisch 2007; Jokisch and Kyle 2008).

15. U.S. Southern Command reports to Congress in 2015 and 2016 stated that the Western Hemisphere is under threat from international criminal networks, Iranian influence (statements specifically mention relationships between Iran and Ecuador, Cuba, and Nicaragua), Hezbollah, and growing Chinese and Russian influence and contacts (Kelly 2015; Tidd 2016).

16. A long-standing Cold War–era U.S. policy automatically admitted Cubans arriving by land (not water) to the United States, so Cubans flew to Ecuador and then traveled north. (This was established by the Cuban Adjustment Act of 1966 granting amnesty to all Cubans, amended in 1995 to admit only those entering by land; Cubans arriving by sea were returned to Cuba.) In 2015 and 2016, Cubans fearing a change in this policy with the normalization of U.S.-Cuba relations sought to take advantage of it while they could. The Correan government, however, took strong steps to stop this flow of Cubans into Ecuador. In July 2016, they detained 150 Cubans and deported at least 47. President Obama did indeed end special immigrant status for Cubans in January 2017.

Chapter 3. The Making of a Massive System

1. To racialize is to differentiate groups or individuals on the basis of perceived racial characteristics, a process that is typically littered with stereotypes, fear, and misinformation. Ways in which a particular group is racialized can change throughout time. For example, in the nineteenth century the Irish—today firmly ensconced as "white" citizens—were racialized as nonwhite, immoral, and unclean (Takaki 2008).

2. For more comprehensive, detailed histories of deportation, see, for example, Kanstroom 2007a; Moloney 2012; on detention, see, for example, D. M. Hernández 2008; Silverman 2010; Wilsher 2012.

3. These policies included the institution of formal immigration procedures, a literacy test, entry taxes at the border, and the regulation of the U.S.-Mexico border.

4. Many of these deportations entailed the denaturalization of U.S. citizens (Kanstroom 2007a). Such a precedent is particularly interesting in the context of current political proposals to eliminate birthright citizenship and invalidate naturalized citizenship if any parts of the application are proven incorrect.

5. Approximately the same number of Mexicans "voluntarily" left as the result of scare campaigns by nativist groups.

6. For detailed histories of 1980s expansion of detention, see Kahn 1996; Welch 2002; Dow 2004; Silverman 2010.

7. The term *prison industrial complex* builds on the *military industrial complex*, a term coined in 1961 by President Eisenhower to warn of the danger of growing relationships between the military, businesses, and legislators.

8. Reagan supported the right-wing military governments of El Salvador and Guatemala despite their widespread human rights abuses, including the use of paramilitary "death squads." As part of his support of these governments, Salvadoran and Guatemalan refugees were almost summarily denied asylum in the United States and subjected to detention and deportation (Kahn 1996). In contrast, Reagan did not support the left-leaning Sandinista government of Nicaragua, instead supporting the anti-Sandinista guerrilla movement called the Contras. As a way to discredit the Sandinista government, Nicaraguan refugees were typically exempted from mandatory detention and granted asylum.

9. The Arizona facility had also housed interned Japanese Americans during the Second World War.

10. For example, by setting up huge tents on prison grounds, the Port Isabel immigrant detention center's capacity instantly increased from 425 to 10,000 (Kahn 1996).

11. Cervantes-Gautschi (2010) observed, "From 2005 through 2009, for every dollar that GEO spent lobbying the government, the company received a $662 return in taxpayer-funded contracts, for a total of $996.7 million. CCA received a $34 return in taxpayer-funded contracts for every dollar spent on lobbying the federal government, for a total of $330.4 million."

12. While wording could be interpreted to mean that 34,000 beds be *available* at all times, it has generally been interpreted as 34,000 beds must be *filled* at all times.

13. In 2014, the Obama administration replaced Secure Communities with the Priority Enforcement Program, which appeared to take a considerably less aggressive approach to forcing cooperation. However, in the first days of his presidency, Donald Trump reactivated Secure Communities.

Chapter 4. Ordering Chaos

1. This officer appeared to be of high rank and had considerable experience. He also commented that he had tried to train others how to search in that way, but most people still did not know how.

2. To address this problem, I eventually compiled a key of common mis/pronunciations to leave at the House of the Migrant for those conducting searches after I left.

3. This is not the real name of the town.

4. Many local, government-run facilities contracted by ICE to hold immigrant detainees were originally built as prisons and continue to operate as prisons. Usually ICE detainees and prison inmates are housed in separate areas of the facility.

5. For more comprehensive and technical explanations, see, for example, Kanstroom 2007a; Wadhia 2015; Kocher 2017.

6. Reasons include, for example, the migrant is not at the address on file; the court misfiled the address; the migrant filed a change of address, but the court delayed in updating the address in their records; the migrant's attorney does not pass along the notice; or the postal service misdelivers or loses the NTA. Other issues related to sending NTAS by mail include the receiver not being able to translate from English, or the court rescheduling the hearing to a different date or location without giving adequate notice (Kocher 2017).

7. There are other forms of relief available in general, such as Cancellation of Removal, Adjustment of Status, Convention Against Torture, Withholding of Removal, Temporary Protective Status, NACARA, and 212c. The detained Ecuadorians on whose cases I worked were typically not eligible for most of these forms for a variety of reasons.

8. The legal logic of this is that the migrant leaves before the removal order becomes a final removal order, meaning that the appeals period has passed.

9. It is a three-year bar if in the United States between 180 and 365 days, ten-year bar if in the United States more than 365 days.

10. If a migrant initiated a clandestine trip to the United States with an Ecuadorian passport, he or she likely discarded it or a smuggler took it en route so that the migrant could claim nationality from another country if caught (see note 11). Also, several migrants who did have an Ecuadorian passport at their home in the United States did not want to contact other occupants (because they were undocumented) to ask them to send the passport for fear of putting them at risk.

11. Smugglers frequently coach Ecuadorian migrants to give false names and claim that they are from Mexico or Guatemala, in hope that they will be deported to a country closer to the U.S.-Mexico border and thus be poised to more easily make another border-crossing attempt. However, while successful in the past, after the shift to mandatory detention of "Other Than Mexicans" and identification verification before deportation, this ruse rarely works.

12. In contrast, in other instances I encountered of repeat entry after deportation, the migrant's previous removal order was simply reinstated.

13. Cartography is by Joseph Stoll, Syracuse University Department of Geography.

14. The fact that some interviewees could not remember (or never knew) specific facility names or locations required creative mapping techniques. To represent the unknown points on this map, I chose proximate points representing known sites of detention.

15. Since this research was conducted in 2008 and 2009, the Manhattan facility (on Varick Street, in New York City) has shifted to be used mainly for short-term detention and processing of recently apprehended migrants. Now migrants apprehended in New York City are usually detained initially in one of several New Jersey facilities.

16. As shown in the maps, for Ecuadorians the "interior" often references the East Coast, due to historic settlement patterns.

17. In February 2017, the Trump administration proposed new DHS guidelines that would allow expedited removal to be applied anywhere in the United States, a change that could dramatically impact this pattern.

18. Though detention after a positive credible fear decision is discretionary, many asylum seekers remain detained during their entire wait to see a judge (which can last months and even years), either due to officials' refusal to release them or inability to pay the bond set.

Chapter 5. The "Peculiar" Advantages of Chaos

1. In 2017, President Trump proposed that only ICE-run facilities must comply with the PBNDS, along with additional proposals to remove human rights protections for detainees.

2. "Due process of law" is an important tenet of the American legal system, one not constitutionally limited to U.S. citizens. It is defined as "a fundamental, constitutional guarantee that all legal proceedings will be fair and that one will be given notice of the proceedings and an opportunity to be heard before the government acts to take away one's life, liberty, or property" as well as "a constitutional guarantee that a law shall not be unreasonable, arbitrary, or capricious" (*Free Dictionary* 2015).

3. Although the PBNDS state that facilities are required to provide information regarding resources for counsel, many facilities do not follow guidelines, do not provide accurate up-to-date information, or do not explain the importance of obtaining counsel.

4. In recent years, the Departments of Homeland Security and of Justice have had to orchestrate legal changes to make longer detention durations possible to accommodate wait time.

5. One interviewee said that if you did not have money to make a call, you could fill out a request for a free call. If this policy was applied beyond the place in which this particular migrant was detained, the fact that he was the only interviewee aware of such an option suggests little publication of this option.

Chapter 6. "You Don't Know How I Suffer, Waiting Every Day"

1. While remittances dropped sharply in 2008 with the global recession, they are gradually rebounding (Jokisch 2014; Maldonado and Hayem 2015; Banco Central del Ecuador 2016).

2. Paúl's lengthy imprisonment had to do partly with the private immigration lawyer he contracted to represent him; because Paúl and relatives in the United States were unable to pay the full lawyer's fee, his case took longer to move through the courts than it needed to because the lawyer would not act until paid.

3. During my fieldwork period, this service was provided by SENAMI (Secretaría Nacional del Migrante, or National Secretariat of Migrants), a government agency formed

by President Correa to specifically deal with issues related to migration. SENAMI was eventually merged with the Ministry of Exterior Relations due principally to overlaps in responsibilities.

Chapter 7. "There Is No Other Way"

1. While exact numbers are difficult to ascertain, estimates suggest that approximately 320,000 Peruvians and 600,000 Colombians have migrated to Ecuador in recent years (Herrera, Moncayo, and Garcia 2012).

2. The 2005 Ecuadorian census found that approximately 16,000 Ecuadorians had previously lived in the United States, and a 2013 report indicated that rates of return to Ecuador (from all migrant destination countries) were on the rise (Jokisch 2014).

3. For the first eight weeks, Elsa was being detained in order to have her testify in the trial of a smuggler (whose case did not ultimately go to court).

BIBLIOGRAPHY

Abraham, I., and W. van Schendel. 2005. Introduction: The making of illicitness. In *Illicit flows and criminal things: States, borders, and the other side of globalization*, ed. W. V. Schendel and I. Abraham, 1–37. Bloomington: Indiana University Press.

Abrego, L. J. 2014. *Sacrificing families: Navigating laws, labor, and love across borders*. Stanford: Stanford University Press.

ACLU. 2011. Outsourcing responsibility: The human cost of privatized immigration detention in Otero County. https://www.aclu-nm.org/sites/default/files/wysiwyg /ocpc_report.pdf (last accessed 1 June 2017).

———. 2015. Deportation and due process. https://www.aclu.org/issues/immigrants -rights/deportation-and-due-process (last accessed 1 June 2017).

———. 2016. Fatal neglect: How ICE ignores deaths in detention. https://www.aclu.org /report/fatal-neglect-how-ice-ignores-death-detention (last accessed 1 June 2017).

Acosta, A., S. López, and D. Villamar. 2004. Ecuador: Oportunidades y amenazas económicas de la emigración. In *Migraciones: Un juego con cartas marcadas*, ed. F. Hidalgo, 259–301. Quito: Ediciones Abya-Yala.

———. 2006. Las remesas y su aporte para la economía ecuatoriana. In *La migración ecuatoriana: Transnacionalismo, redes e identidades*, ed. G. Herrera, M. C. Carrillo, and A. Torres, 227–252. Quito: FLACSO.

Actis, W. 2006. Ecuatorianos y ecuatorianas en España: Inserción(es) en un mercado de trabajo fuertemente precarizado. In *La migración ecuatoriana: Transnacionalismo, redes e identidades*, ed. G. Herrera, M. C. Carrillo, and A. Torres, 169–201. Quito: FLACSO.

AFP. 2010. Inician en México autopsias e identificación de 72 emigrantes asesinados. *El Universo*, 26 August.

Agamben, G. 1998. *Homo sacer: Sovereign power and bare life*. Stanford: Stanford University Press.

———. 2005. *State of exception*. Chicago: University of Chicago Press.

American Friends Service Committee. 2010. Locked up but not forgotten. http://afsc .org/sites/afsc.civicactions.net/files/documents/LockedUpFINAL.pdf (last accessed 1 June 2017).

American Immigration Council. 2014. Removal without recourse: The growth of summary deportations from the United States. *Immigration Policy Center*, 28 April. http://www.immigrationpolicy.org/just-facts/removal-without-recourse-growth -summary-deportations-united-states (last accessed 1 June 2017).

Amnesty International. 2009. *Jailed without justice: Immigrant detention in the USA*. Washington, D.C.: Amnesty International USA.

Andreas, P. 2000. *Border games: Policing the U.S.-Mexico divide*. Ithaca: Cornell University Press.

———. 2001. The transformation of migrant smuggling across the U.S.-Mexican border. In *Global human smuggling: Comparative perspectives*, ed. D. Kyle and R. Koslowski, 107–125. Baltimore: Johns Hopkins University Press.

Andrijasevic, R. 2010. From exception to excess: Detention and deportations across the Mediterranean space. In De Genova and Peutz, *Deportation regime*, 147–165.

Antón, J.-I. 2010. The impact of remittances on nutritional status of children in Ecuador. *International Migration Review* 44 (2): 269–299.

Archibold, R. C. 2010. Grief across Latin America for migrant killings. *New York Times*, 1 September. http://www.nytimes.com/2010/09/02/world/americas/02migrants.html (last accessed 1 June 2017).

Bacon, D. 2004. *The children of NAFTA: Labor wars on the U.S./Mexico border*. Berkeley: University of California Press.

Banco Central del Ecuador. 2016. Evolucion de las remesas anual. https://contenido.bce .fin.ec/documentos/Estadisticas/SectorExterno/BalanzaPagos/Remesas/ere201605 .pdf (last accessed 10 February 2018).

Barahona, F. 2016. Migration is not a crime. *NACLA*, 4 January. https://nacla.org/news /2016/01/03/migration-not-crime (last accessed 1 June 2017).

Barry, T. 2009a. A death in Texas: Profits, poverty, and immigration converge. *CIP Americas*, 26 October. http://www.cipamericas.org/archives/1894).

———. 2009b. National security business on the border. *CIP Americas*, posted September 27: http://www.cipamericas.org/archives/1858 (no longer available).

———. 2010. The shadow prison industry and its government enablers. *CIP Americas*, 29 January. http://www.ciponline.org/images/uploads/publications/Barry_The _Shadow_Prison_Industry_01-10.pdf (last accessed 1 June 2017).

Bauder, H. 2006. *Labor movement: How migration regulates labor markets*. New York: Oxford University Press.

Becker, A., and H. Cabrera. 2009. America's ICE backwards approach to immigration. *Truthdig: Drilling beneath the headlines*, 30 June. http://www.truthdig.com/report /item/20090629_americas_approach_to_immigration_is_ice_backwards/ (last accessed 1 June 2017).

Belcher, O., and L. L. Martin. 2013. Ethnographies of closed doors: Conceptualising openness and closure in U.S. immigration and military institutions. *Area* 45 (4): 403–410.

Benton-Cohen, K. 2011. *Borderline Americans: Racial division and labor war in the Arizona borderlands*. Cambridge, Mass.: Harvard University Press.

Bernstein, N. 2010a. Officials hid truth of immigrant deaths in jail. *New York Times*, 9 April. http://www.nytimes.com/2010/01/10/us/10detain.html?_r=1&ref= incustodydeaths (last accessed 1 June 2017).

———. 2010b. Volunteers report on treatment of immigrant detainees. *New York Times*, 29 April. http://www.nytimes.com/2010/04/29/nyregion/29visitors.html?_r=1&sq =Volunteers%20Report%20on%20Treatment%20of%20Immigrant%20Detainees (last accessed 28 September 2015).

Bialasiewicz, L., D. Campbell, S. Elden, S. Graham, A. Jeffrey, and A. J. Williams. 2007. Performing security: The imaginative geographies of current U.S. strategy. *Political Geography* 26: 405–422.

Bigo, D. 2000. When two become one: Internal and external securitizations in Europe. In *International relations theory and the politics of European integration*, ed. M. Kelstrup and M. Williams, 171–204. New York: Routledge.

———. 2001. The Möbius ribbon of internal and external security(ies). In *Identities, borders, orders: Rethinking international relations theory*, ed. M. Albert, D. Jacobson, and Y. Lapid, 91–116. Minneapolis: University of Minnesota Press.

———. 2002. Security and immigration: Toward a critique of the governmentality of unease. *Alternatives* 27: 63–92.

———. 2007. Detention of foreigners, states of exception, and the social practices of control of the Banopticon. In *Borderscapes: Hidden geographies and politics at territory's edge*, ed. P. K. Rajaram and C. Grundy-Warr, 3–33. Minneapolis: University of Minneapolis Press.

Billo, E., and N. Hiemstra. 2012. Mediating messiness: Expanding ideas of flexibility, reflexivity, and embodiment in fieldwork. *Gender, Place & Culture* 20: 313–328.

Billo, E., and A. Mountz. 2015. For institutional ethnography: Geographical approaches to institutions and the everyday. *Progress in Human Geography* 40 (2). DOI: 10.1177/0309132515572269. (last accessed 1 June 2017).

Black, R., M. Collyer, R. Skeldon, and C. Waddington. 2006. Routes to illegal residence: A case study of immigration detainees in the United Kingdom. *Geoforum* 37: 552–564.

Bloch, A., and L. Schuster. 2005. At the extremes of exclusion: Deportation, detention and dispersal. *Ethnic and Racial Studies* 28 (3): 491–512.

Bloom, L. R. 1998. *Under the sign of hope: Feminist methodology and narrative interpretation*. Albany: State University of New York Press.

Boehm, D. A. 2012. *Intimate migrations: Gender, family, and illegality among transnational Mexicans*. New York: New York University Press.

Borrero, A., and S. Vega, eds. 1995. *Mujer y migración: Alcances de un fenómeno nacional y regional*. Cayambe, Ecuador: Abya-Yala.

Bosworth, M. 2008. Border control and the limits of the sovereign state. *Social and Legal Studies* 17 (2): 199–215.

———. 2014. *Inside immigration detention*. New York: Oxford University Press.

Bowditch, S. 2008. Ecuador feels loss of money from abroad. National Public Radio, 20 December. http://www.npr.org/templates/story/story.php?storyId=98562892 (last accessed 1 June 2017).

———. 2009a. Ecuadorians return home, unemployment swells. National Public Radio, 9 May. http://www.npr.org/templates/story/story.php?storyId=103974656 (last accessed 1 June 2017).

———. 2009b. Smuggling route goes through Ecuador to U.S. National Public Radio, 28 February. http://www.npr.org/templates/story/story.php?storyId=101305866 (last accessed 1 June 2017).

Brabeck, K. M., K. Porterfield, and M. Loughry. 2015. Immigrants facing detention and deportation: Psychosocial and mental health issues, assessment, and intervention for individuals and families. In *The new deportations delirium: Interdisciplinary responses*, ed. D. Kanstroom and M. B. Lykes, 167–191. New York: New York University Press.

Brabeck, K., and Q. Xu. 2010. The impact of detention and deportation on Latino immigrant children and families: A quantitative exploration. *Hispanic Journal of Behavioral Sciences* 32 (3): 341–361.

Brodzinsky, S., and E. Pilkington. 2015. U.S. government deporting Central American migrants to their deaths. *Guardian*, 12 October. https://www.theguardian.com/us-news/2015/oct/12/obama-immigration-deportations-central-america (last accessed 1 June 2017).

Brotherton, D. C., and L. Barrios. 2009. Displacement and stigma: The social-psychological crisis of the deportee. *Crime, Media, Culture* 5 (1): 29–55.

———. 2011. *Banished to the homeland: Dominican deportees and their stories of exile.* New York: Columbia University Press.

Bruzzone, M. 2016. On exterior and interior detention regimes: Governing, bordering and economy in transit migration across Mexico. In *Intimate economies of immigration detention: Critical perspectives*, ed. D. Conlon and N. Hiemstra, 105–120. London: Routledge.

Buckinx, B., and A. Filindra. 2015. The case against removal: *Jus noci* and harm in deportation practice. *Migration Studies* 3 (3): 393–416.

Burnett, J. 2016. Central American families fear deportation as raids begin. National Public Radio, January 5. http://www.npr.org/2016/01/05/462057211/u-s-begins-to-deport-central-americans (last accessed 1 June 2017).

Butler, J. 1997. *Excitable speech: A politics of the performative.* New York: Routledge.

Buzan, B., O. Waever, and J. D. Wilde. 1998. *Security: A new framework for analysis.* Boulder, Colo.: Lynne Rienner.

Calavita, K. 1992. *Inside the state: The Bracero program, immigration, and the I.N.S.* New York: Routledge.

———. 2005. *Immigrants at the margins: Law, race, and exclusion in Southern Europe.* Cambridge: Cambridge University Press.

Camacho, G. 2004. Feminización de las migraciones en Ecuador. In *Migraciones: Un juego con cartas marcadas*, ed. F. Hidalgo, 303–325. Quito: Ediciones Abya-Yala.

Camacho, G., and K. Hernández. 2005a. *Cambió mi vida: Migración femenina, percepciones e impactos.* Quito: UNIFEM.

———. 2005b. La migración irregular y la problemática que enfrentan los migrantes sin papeles. In *Tendencias y efectos de la emigración en el Ecuador*, ed. G. Solfrini, 9–108. Quito: IMPREFEPP.

Cardoso, J. B., E. R. Hamilton, N. Rodriguez, K. Eschbach, and J. Hagan. 2014. Deporting fathers: Involuntary transnational families and intent to remigrate among Salvadoran deportees. *International Migration Review* 50 (1). DOI: 10.1111/imre.12106 (last accessed 1 June 2017).

Carriére, J. 2001. Neoliberalism, economic crisis and popular mobilization in Ecuador. In *Miraculous metamorphoses: The neoliberalization of Latin American populism*, ed. J. Demmers, A. E. Fernández Jilberto, and B. Hogenboom, 132–149. New York: Zed Books.

Carson, B., and E. Diaz. 2015. Payoff: How Congress ensures private prison profit with an immigrant detention quota. Grassroots Leadership, April. http://grassrootsleadership.org/reports/payoff-how-congress-ensures-private-prison-profit-immigrant-detention-quota (last accessed 1 June 2017).

Castles, S., and M. J. Miller. 2003. *The age of migration: International population movements in the modern world.* 3rd ed. New York: Guilford Press.

Center for Latin American Studies, University of Arizona. 2013. In the shadow of the wall: Family separation, immigration enforcement and security. http://las.arizona .edu/sites/las.arizona.edu/files/UA_Immigration_Report2013web.pdf (last accessed 1 June 2017).

Cervantes-Gautschi, P. 2010. Wall Street and the criminalization of immigrants. *Counterpunch*, 15 October. https://www.counterpunch.org/2010/10/15/wall-street -and-the-criminalization-of-immigrants/ (last accessed 22 February 2018).

Chacón, J. 2007. Unsecured borders: Immigration restrictions, crime control and national security. *Connecticut Law Review* 39 (5): 1827–1891.

Chavez, L. R. 2008. *The Latino threat: Constructing immigrants, citizens, and the nation*. Stanford: Stanford University Press.

Chebel d'Appollonia, A. 2012. *Frontiers of fear: Immigration and insecurity in the United States and Europe*. Ithaca: Cornell University Press.

Chin, K.-L. 1999. *Smuggled Chinese: Clandestine immigration to the United States*. Philadelphia: Temple University Press.

Christian, J., J. Mellow, and S. Thomas. 2006. Social and economic implications of family connections to prisoners. *Journal of Criminal Justice* 34: 443–452.

Ciriano, E. J. G. 2004. La política migratoria de España y de la Unión Europea a través de sus instrumentos legislativos. In *Migraciones: Un juego con cartas marcadas*, ed. F. Hidalgo, 171–189. Quito: Ediciones Abya-Yala.

Coleman, M. 2007a. A geopolitics of engagement: Neoliberalism, the war on terrorism, and the reconfiguration of U.S. immigration enforcement. *Geopolitics* 12: 607–634.

———. 2007b. Immigration geopolitics beyond the Mexico-U.S. border. *Antipode* 39 (1): 54–76.

———. 2008. U.S. immigration law and its geographies of social control: Lessons of homosexual exclusion during the Cold War. *Environment and Planning D: Society and Space* 26: 1096–1114.

———. 2009. What counts as the politics and practice of security, and where? Devolution and immigrant insecurity after 9/11. *Annals of the Association of American Geographers* 99 (5): 904–913.

———. 2012. Immigrant Il-Legality: Geopolitical and legal borders in the U.S., 1882–present. *Geopolitics* 17 (2): 402–422.

Coleman, M., and A. Kocher. 2011. Detention, deportation, devolution and immigrant incapacitation in the U.S., post 9/11. *Geographical Journal* 177 (3): 228–237.

Coleman, M., and A. Stuesse. 2016. The disappearing state and the quasi-event of immigration control. *Antipode* 48: 524–543.

Collyer, M. 2007. In-between places: Trans-Saharan transit migrants in Morocco and the fragmented journey to Europe. *Antipode* 39 (4): 668–690.

———. 2012. Deportation and the micropolitics of exclusion: The rise of removals from the UK to Sri Lanka. *Geopolitics* 17 (2): 276–292.

Conlon, D. 2010. Ties that bind: Governmentality, the state, and asylum in contemporary Ireland. *Environment and Planning D: Society and Space* 28: 95–111.

———. 2011. Waiting: Feminist perspectives on the spacings/timings of migrant (im) mobility. *Gender, Place & Culture* 18 (3): 353–360.

Conlon, D., and N. Hiemstra. 2014. Examining the everyday micro-economies of immigrant detention in the United States. *Geographica Helvetica* 69: 335–344.

Cornelius, W., and I. Salehyan. 2007. Does border enforcement deter unauthorized immigration? The case of Mexican migration to the United States. *Regulation & Governance* 1 (1): 139–153.

Cornelius, W. A. 2004. Spain: The uneasy transition from labor exporter to labor importer. In *Controlling immigration: A global perspective*, ed. W. A. Cornelius, T. Tsuda, P. L. Martin, and J. F. Hollifield, 387–429. Stanford: Stanford University Press.

Cornelius, W. A., and J. M. Lewis, eds. 2005. *Impacts of U.S. immigration control policies on Mexican migration: The view from sending communities*. La Jolla, Calif.: Center for Comparative Immigration Studies.

Coutin, S. B. 2005. Being en route. *American Anthropologist* 107 (2): 195–206.

———. 2007. *Nation of emigrants: Shifting boundaries of citizenship in El Salvador and the United States*. Ithaca: Cornell University Press.

———. 2010a. Confined within: National territories as zones of confinement. *Political Geography* 29: 200–208.

———. 2010b. Exiled by law: Deportation and the inviability of life. In De Genova and Peutz, *Deportation regime*, 351–370.

———. 2011. Legal exclusion and dislocated subjectivities: The deportation of Salvadoran youth from the United States. In *The contested politics of mobility: Borderzones and irregularity*, ed. V. J. Squire, 169–183. London: Routledge.

———. 2015. Deportation studies: Origins, themes and directions. *Journal of Ethnic and Migration Studies* 41 (4): 671–681.

———. 2016. *Exiled home: Salvadoran transnational youth in the aftermath of violence*. Durham, N.C.: Duke University Press.

Cowen, D., and E. Gilbert. 2008. Fear and the familial in the U.S. war on terror. In *Fear: Critical geopolitics and everyday life*, ed. R. Pain and S. J. Smith, 49–58. Hampshire, U.K.: Ashgate.

Davis, A. Y. 2003. *Are prisons obsolete?* New York: Seven Stories Press.

De Genova, N. 2004. The legal production of Mexican/migrant "illegality." *Latino Studies* 2 (2): 160–185.

———. 2005. *Working the boundaries: Race, space, and "illegality" in Mexican Chicago*. Durham, N.C.: Duke University Press.

———. 2009. The production of culprits: From deportability to detainability in the aftermath of "Homeland Security." In *Securitizations of citizenship*, ed. P. Nyers, 157–188. London: Routledge.

———. 2010. The deportation regime: Sovereignty, space, and the freedom of movement. In De Genova and Peutz, *Deportation regime*, 33–65.

De Genova, N., and N. Peutz, eds. 2010. *The deportation regime: Sovereignty, space, and the freedom of movement*. Durham, N.C.: Duke University Press.

Délano Alonso, A. 2018. *From here and there: Diaspora policies, integration, and social rights beyond borders*. New York: Oxford University Press.

De León, J. 2015. *The land of open graves: Living and dying on the migrant trail*. Berkeley: University of California Press.

Detention Watch Network. 2017. Immigration detention 101. *Detention Watch Network*. https://www.detentionwatchnetwork.org/issues/detention-101 (last accessed 1 June 2017).

Dingeman-Cerda, K., and R. G. Rumbault. 2015. Unwelcome returns: The alienation of the new American diaspora in Salvadoran society. In *The new deportations delirium: Interdisciplinary perspectives*, ed. D. Kanstroom and M. B. Lykes, 227–250. New York: New York University Press.

Dodds, K. 2001. Political geography III: Critical geopolitics after ten years. *Progress in Human Geography* 25 (3): 469–484.

Doomernik, J., and D. Kyle. 2004. Introduction. *Journal of International Migration and Integration* 5 (3): 265–272.

Doty, R. L. 1998. Immigration and the politics of security. *Security Studies* 8 (2–3): 71–93.

Doty, R. L., and E. S. Wheatley. 2013. Private detention and the immigration industrial complex. *International Political Sociology* 7: 426–443.

Dow, M. 2004. *American gulag: Inside U.S. immigration prisons*. Berkeley: University of California Press.

Dowler, L., and J. Sharp. 2001. A feminist geopolitics? *Space and Polity* 5 (3): 165–176.

Dowling, J. A., and J. X. Inda eds. 2013. *Governing immigration through crime: A reader*. Stanford: Stanford University Press.

Dreby, J. 2012. The burden of deportation on children in Mexican immigrant families. *Journal of Marriage and Family* 74: 829–845.

Drotbohm, H. 2015. The reversal of migratory family lives: A Cape Verdean perspective on gender and sociality pre- and post-deportation. *Journal of Ethnic and Migration Studies* 41 (4): 653–670.

Drotbohm, H., and I. Hasselberg. 2015. Introduction: Deportation, anxiety, justice: New ethnographic perspectives. *Journal of Ethnic and Migration Studies* 41 (4): 551–562.

Dunn, K. 2000. Interviewing. In *Qualitative research methods in human geography*, ed. I. Hay, 50–82. New York: Oxford University Press.

Dyck, I. 1993. Ethnography: A feminist method? *Canadian Geographer* 37 (1): 52–57.
———. 2011. Embodied life. In *A companion to social geography*, ed. V. J. Del Casino, M. E. Thomas, P. Cloke, and R. Panelli, 346–61. Malden, Mass.: Blackwell.

Eagly, I., and S. Shafer. 2016. Access to counsel in immigration court. American Immigration Council, September. https://www.americanimmigrationcouncil.org/sites/default/files/research/access_to_counsel_in_immigration_court.pdf (last accessed 1 June 2017).

Edkins, J. 2003. *Trauma and the memory of politics*. Cambridge: Cambridge University Press.

Ellerman, A. 2008. The limits of unilateral migration control: Deportation and inter-state cooperation. *Government and Opposition* 43 (2): 168–189.

El Tiempo. 2008. Repatrian a los ecuatorianos capturados en alta mar por guardacostas de EEUU, 10 September. https://www.eltiempo.com.ec/noticias/ecuador/4/repatrian-a-los-ecuatorianos-capturados-en-alta-mar-por-guardacostas-de-eeuu (last accessed 29 May 2018).

———. 2009. La deportación los obliga a volver a su país, 22 December. http://www
.eltiempo.com.ec/noticias-cuenca/30260-la-deportacia-n-los-obliga-a-volver-a-su
-paa-s/ (last accessed 1 June 2017).

El Universo. 2008. En 20 meses, casi 2.000 migrantes deportados, 8 September. http://
www.eluniverso.com/2008/09/08/0001/626/3F303581F2D64BA8A06713F7A4156670
.html (last accessed 1 June 2017).

———. 2009. Correa expulsó a agregado de la embajada de EE.UU, 7 February. http://
eluniverso.com/2009/02/07/1/1355/47B1BBE3E07E442CAC6C5C57C9BC68E1.html
(last accessed 1 June 2017).

Escobar, A. 2008. Tras las huellas de las familias migrantes del cantón Cañar. In
América Latina migrante: Estado, familia, identidades, ed. G. Herrera and J.
Ramírez, 243–258. Quito: FLACSO, Sede Ecuador.

Ewing, W., and G. Cantor. 2016. Deported with no possessions: The mishandling of
migrants' personal belongings by CBP and ICE. American Immigration Council, December. https://www.americanimmigrationcouncil.org/sites/default/files/research
/deported_with_no_possessions.pdf (last accessed 1 June 2017).

Falconí, F., and C. Ordoñez. 2005. Las mujeres migrantes irregulares del cantón Cuenca.
In *Tendencias y efectos de la emigración en el Ecuador*, ed. G. Solfrini, 109–193. Quito:
IMPREFEPP.

Falk, 2010. Invasion, infection, invisibility: An iconology of illegalized immigration.
In *Images of illegalized immigration*, ed. C. Bischoff, F. Falk, and S. Kafehsy, 83–99.
London: Transcript.

Fang, L. 2017. Trump's new immigration crackdown has private prison investors
salivating. *Intercept*, 22 February. https://theintercept.com/2017/02/22/geo-group
-trump (last accessed 1 June 2017).

Farah, D. 2011. Hezbollah in Latin America: Implications for U.S. security. Hearing
before the Subcommittee on Counterterrorism and Intelligence of the Committee
on Homeland Security, House of Representatives, before the 112th Congress, 7 July.
https://www.gpo.gov/fdsys/pkg/CHRG-112hhrg72255/pdf/CHRG-112hhrg72255.pdf
(last accessed 13 October 2018).

Farah, D., and G. Simpson. 2009. Ecuador at risk: Drugs, thugs, guerrillas and the
Citizens' Revolution. International Assessment and Strategy Center. http://www
.strategycenter.net/docLib/20101214_EcuadorFINAL.pdf (last accessed 28 September 2015; no longer available).

Fernandes, D. 2007. *Targeted: Homeland Security and the business of immigration*. New
York: Seven Stories Press.

Finley, B. 2004. U.S. takes border war on the road. *Denver Post*, 19 December: A-01.

Fischer, N. 2013. Negotiating deportations: An ethnography of the legal challenge of
deportation orders in a French immigration detention centre. In *The social, political
and historical contours of deportation*, ed. B. Anderson, M. J. Gibney, and E. Paoletti,
123–142. Oxford: Springer.

———. 2015. The management of anxiety: An ethnographical outlook on self-
mutilations in a French immigration detention centre. *Journal of Ethnic and Migration Studies* 41 (4): 599–616.

FLACSO. 2008. *Ecuador: La migración internactional en cifras*. Quito: United Nations
Population Fund and FLACSO.

Flynn, M. 2002. Dónde está la frontera? *Bulletin of the Atomic Scientists* July–August: 24–35.

———. 2005. What's the deal at Manta? *Bulletin of the Atomic Scientists* 61 (1): 23–29.

———. 2014. There and back again: On the diffusion of immigration detention. *Journal on Migration and Human Security* 2 (3):165–197.

———. 2016. Detained beyond the sovereign: Concepualising non-state actor involvement in immigration detention. In *Intimate economies of immigration detention: Critical perspectives*, ed. D. Conlon and N. Hiemstra, 15–31. London: Routledge.

Flynn, M., and C. Cannon. 2009. The privatization of immigration detention: Towards a global view. Geneva: Global Detention Project.

Foucault, M. 1979. *Discipline and punish: The birth of the prison*. New York: Vintage Books.

———. 1991. Governmentality. In *The Foucault effect: Studies in governmentality*, ed. G. Burchell, C. Gordon, and P. Miller, 87–104. Chicago: University of Chicago Press.

———. 2007. *Security, territory, population*. New York: Palgrave Macmillan.

The free dictionary. 2015. Due process of law. http://legal-dictionary.thefreedictionary .com/Due+Process+of+Law (last accessed 1 June 2017).

Gambino, L. 2010. Program prosecutes illegal immigrants before deporting them. *ASU News* 21. http://asu.news21.com/2010/prosecuting-illegal-immigrants/ (last accessed 1 June 2017).

Gammeltoft-Hansen, T., and N. N. Sørensen, eds. 2013. *The migration industry and the commercialization of international migration*. New York: Routledge.

Garcés, I. 2005. Reseña histórica de la migración ecuatoriana hacia Estados Unidos. In *Emigración y política exterior en Ecuador*, ed. J. Ponce Leiva, 95–122. Quito: Abya-yala.

George, S. 1988. *A fate worse than debt*. London: Penguin.

Gerlach, A. 2003. *Indians, oil, and politics: A recent history of Ecuador*. Wilmington, Del.: Scholarly Resources.

Gill, N. 2009a. Governmental mobility: The power effects of the movement of detained asylum seekers around Britain's detention estate. *Political Geography* 28: 186–196.

———. 2009b. Presentational state power: Temporal and spatial influences over asylum sector decisionmakers. *Transactions of the Institute of British Geographers* 34: 215–233.

———. 2016. *Nothing personal? Geographies of governing and activism in the British asylum system*. Chichester, UK: Wiley-Blackwell.

Glawe, J. 2017. Immigrant deaths in private prisons explode under Trump. *Daily Beast*, 30 May. https://www.thedailybeast.com/immigrant-deaths-in-private-prisons -explode-under-trump (last accessed 23 February 2018).

Golash-Boza, T. 2009. The immigration industrial complex: Why we enforce immigration policies destined to fail. *Sociology Compass* 3 (2): 295–309.

———. 2010. The criminalization of undocumented migrants: Legalities and realities. *Societies without Borders* 5 (1): 81–90.

———. 2012. *Immigration nation: Raids, detentions, and deportations in post-9/11 America*. Boulder, Colo.: Paradigm.

———. 2014. Forced transnationalism: Transnational coping strategies and gendered stigma among Jamaican deportees. *Global Networks* 14 (1): 63–79.

———. 2015. *Deported: Policing immigrants, disposable labor, and global capitalism*. New York: NYU Press.

Golash-Boza, T., and O. Hondagneu-Sotelo. 2013. Latino immigrant men and the deportation crisis: A gendered racial removal program. *Latino Studies* 11 (3): 271–292.

Gonzales, A. 2014. *Reform without justice: Latino migrant politics and the Homeland Security state.* New York: Oxford University Press.

Gratton, B. 2006. Ecuador en la historia de la migración internacional: ¿Modelo o aberración? In *La migración ecuatoriana: Transnacionalismo, redes e identidades*, ed. G. Herrera, M. C. Carrillo, and A. Torres, 31–55. Quito: FLACSO.

Grindle, M. S. 1985. *State and countryside: Development policy and agrarian politics in Latin America.* Baltimore: Johns Hopkins University Press.

Gupta, A. 1995. Blurred boundaries: The discourse of corruption, the culture of politics, and the imagined state. *American Ethnologist* 22 (2): 375–402.

Haddal, C. C., and A. Siskin. 2010. Immigration-related detention: Current legislative issues. Congressional Research Service, 27 January (7–5700; RL32369). http://digitalcommons.ilr.cornell.edu/key_workplace/707/ (last accessed 1 June 2017).

Hagan, J., K. Eschbach, and N. Rodriguez. 2008. U.S. deportation policy, family separation, and circular migration. *International Migration Review* 42 (1): 64–88.

Hagan, J. M., N. Rodriguez, and B. Castro. 2011. Social effects of mass deportation by the United States Government, 2000–10. *Ethnic and Racial Studies* 34 (8): 1374–1391.

Hage, G. 2005. A not so multi-sited ethnography of a not so imagined community. *Anthropological Theory* 5 (4): 463–475.

Haldrup, M., L. Koefoed, and K. Simonsen. 2008. Practicing fear: Encountering O/other bodies. In *Fear: Critical geopolitics and everyday life*, ed. R. Pain and S. J. Smith, 117–127. Aldershot, UK: Ashgate.

Hall, A. 2010. "These people could be anyone": Fear, contempt (and empathy) in a British immigration removal centre. *Journal of Ethnic and Migration Studies* 36 (6): 881–898.

———. 2012. *Border watch: Cultures of immigration, detention and control.* London: Pluto Press.

Hansen, T. B., and F. Stepputat. 2001. States of imagination. In *States of imagination: Ethnographic explorations of the postcolonial state*, ed. T. B. Hansen and F. Stepputat, 1–38. Durham, N.C.: Duke University Press.

Harper, R. K., and A. G. Cuzán. 2001. The economies of Latin America. In *Understanding contemporary Latin America*, ed. R. S. Hillman, 135–168. Boulder, Colo.: Lynne Rienner.

Hasselberg, I. 2014. Whose security? The deportation of foreign-national offenders from the UK. In *The anthropology of security: Perspectives from the frontline of policing, counter-terrorism and border control*, ed. M. Maguire, N. Zurawski and C. Frois, 139–157. London: Pluto Press.

Headley, B., M. D. Gordon, and A. MacIntosh. 2005. *Deported: Entry and exit findings; Jamaicans returned home from the U.S. between 1997 and 2003.* Kingston: Stephenson Litho Press.

Herbert, S. 2000. For ethnography. *Progress in Human Geography* 24 (4): 550–568.

Hernández, C. C. G. 2015. Naturalizing immigration imprisonment. *California Law Review* 103 (6): 1449–1514.

Hernández, D. M. 2008. Pursuant to deportation: Latinos and immigrant detention. *Latino Studies* 6: 35–63.

Hernández, K. L. 2010. *Migra! A history of the U.S. Border Patrol*. Berkeley: University of California Press.

Hernández, S. 2010. Complaint targets immigration judge. *LA Daily Journal*, 8 March.

Hernández-León, R. 2013. Conceptualizing the migration industry. In Gammeltoft-Hansen and Sørensen, *Migration industry*, 24–44.

Herrera, G. 2004. Elementos para una comprensión de las familias transnacionales desde la experiencia migratoria del sur del Ecuador. In *Migraciones: Un juego con cartas marcadas*, ed. F. Hidalgo, 215–231. Quito: Ediciones Abya-Yala.

———. 2006. Mujeres ecuatorianas en las cadenas globales del cuidado. In *La migración ecuatoriana: Transnacionalismo, redes e identidades*, ed. G. Herrera, M. C. Carrillo, and A. Torres, 281–303. Quito: FLACSO.

———. 2008. Políticas migratorias y familias transnacionales: Migración ecuatoriana en España y Estados Unidos. In *América Latina migrante: Estado, familia, identidades*, ed. G. Herrera and J. Ramírez, 71–86. Quito: FLACSO.

Herrera, G., M. I. Moncayo, and A. E. Garcia. 2012. *Perfil Migratoria del Ecuador 2011*. International Organization for Migration. http://www.iom.int/files/live /sites/iom/files/pbn/docs/Migration-Profile-Ecuador-2011.pdf (last accessed 1 June 2017).

Heyman, J. M. 1995. Putting power into the anthropology of bureaucracy: The Immigration and Naturalization Service at the Mexico–United States border. *Current Anthropology* 36 (2): 261–287.

Heyman, J. M., and A. Smart. 1999. States and illegal practices: An overview. In *States and illegal practices*, ed. J. M. Heyman, 1–24. Oxford: Berg.

Hiemstra, N. 2010. Immigrant "illegality" as neoliberal governmentality in Leadville, Colorado. *Antipode* 42 (1): 74–102.

———. 2012. U.S. and Ecuador: Is intervention on the table? *NACLA Report on the Americas* 45 (4): 20–24.

———. 2013. "You don't even know where you are": Chaotic geographies of U.S. migrant detention and deportation. In *Carceral spaces: Mobility and agency in imprisonment and migrant detention*, ed. D. Moran, N. Gill, and D. Conlon, 57–75. Farnham Surrey: Ashgate.

———. 2014. Performing homeland (in)security: Employee-detainee relationships within the immigrant detention center. *Environment and Planning D: Society and Space* 32: 571–588.

———. 2017. Periscoping as a feminist methodological approach for researching the seemingly hidden. *Professional Geographer* 69: 329–336.

Hiemstra, N., and D. Conlon. 2016. Captive consumers and coerced labourers: Intimate economies and the expanding U.S. detention regime. In *Intimate economies of immigration detention: Critical perspectives*, ed. D. Conlon and N. Hiemstra, 123–139. London: Routledge.

———. 2017. Beyond privatization: Bureaucratization and the spatialities of immigration detention expansion. *Territory, Politics, Governance* 5 (3): 252–268.

Hillman, R. S., ed. 2001. *Understanding contemporary Latin America*. Boulder, Colo.: Lynne Rienner.

Hodai, B. 2010. Ties that bind: Arizona politicians and the private prison industry. *In These Times*, June 21. http://www.inthesetimes.com/article/6085/ties_that_bind _arizona_politicians_and_the_private_prison_industry/ (last accessed 1 June 2017).

Honig, B. 1998. Immigrant America? How foreignness "solves" democracy's problems. *Social Text* 16 (3): 1–27.

Human Rights Watch. 2009. Locked up far away: The transfer of immigrants to remote detention centers in the United States. http://www.hrw.org/en/node/86789 (last accessed 1 June 2017).

———. 2017. Systemic indifference: Dangerous and substandard medical care in U.S. immigration detention. https://www.hrw.org/report/2017/05/08/systemic -indifference/dangerous-substandard-medical-care-us-immigration-detention (last accessed 1 June 2017).

Hyndman, J. 2004a. The (geo)politics of mobility. In *Mapping women, making politics: Feminist perspectives on political geography*, ed. L. A. Staeheli, E. Kofman, and L. J. Peake, 169–184. New York: Routledge.

———. 2004b. Mind the gap: Bridging feminist and political geography through geo-politics. *Political Geography* 23 (3): 307–322.

———. 2007a. Conflict, citizenship, and human security: Geographies of protection. In *War, citizenship, territory*, ed. D. Cohen and E. Gilbert, 241–257. New York: Routledge.

———. 2007b. The securitization of fear in post-tsunami Sri Lanka. *Annals of the Association of American Geographers* 97 (2): 361–372.

Hyndman, J., and A. Mountz. 2008. Another brick in the wall? Neo-refoulement and the externalization of asylum in Australia and Europe. *Government and Opposition* 43 (2): 249–269.

Igielnik, R., and J. M. Krogstad. 2017. Where refugees to the U.S. come from. Fact Tank: News in the Numbers, Pew Research Center, 3 February. http://www.pewresearch .org/fact-tank/2017/2002/2003/where-refugees-to-the-u-s-come-from/ (last accessed 19 January 2018.

Jokisch, B. D. 1997. From labor circulation to international migration: The case of south-central Ecuador. *Yearbook, Conference of Latin Americanist Geographers* 23: 64–75.

———. 2001. Desde Nueva York a Madrid: Tendencias en la migración ecuatoriana. *Ecuador Debate* 54: 59–83.

———. 2007. Ecuador: Diversity in migration. *Migration Information Source*, 1 February. http://www.migrationinformation.org/Profiles/display.cfm?ID=575 (last accessed 1 June 2017).

———. 2014. Ecuador: From mass emigration to return migration? *Migration Information Source*, 24 November. http://www.migrationpolicy.org/article/ecuador-mass -emigration-return-migration (last accessed 1 June 2017).

Jokisch, B., and D. Kyle. 2006. Las transformaciones de la migración transnacional del Ecuador, 1993–2003. In *La migración ecuatoriana: transnacionalismo, redes e identidades*, ed. G. Herrera, M. C. Carrillo, and A. Torres, 57–69. Quito: FLACSO.

———. 2008. Ecuadorian international migration. In *The Ecuador reader*, ed. C. de la Torre and S. Striffler, 350–358. Durham, N.C.: Duke University Press.

Jokisch, B., and J. Pribilsky. 2002. The panic to leave: Economic crisis and the "new emigration" from Ecuador. *International Migration* 40 (4): 75–101.

Kahn, R. S. 1996. *Other people's blood: U.S. immigration prisons in the Reagan decade.* Boulder, Colo.: Westview Press.

Kanstroom, D. 2007a. *Deportation nation: Outsiders in American history.* Cambridge, Mass.: Harvard University Press.

———. 2007b. Reaping the harvest: The long, complicated, crucial rhetorical struggle over deportation. *Connecticut Law Review* 39 (5): 1911–1922.

———. 2012. *Aftermath: Deportation law and the new American diaspora.* New York: Oxford University Press.

Kaplan, A. 2003. Homeland insecurities: Reflections on language and space. *Radical History Review* 85: 82–93.

Katz, C. 1996. The expeditions of conjurers: Ethnography, power, and pretense. In *Feminist dilemmas in fieldwork*, ed. D. L. Wolf, 170–184. Boulder, Colo.: Westview Press.

Kearns, R. A. 2000. Being there: Research through observing and participating. In *Qualitative research methods in human geography*, ed. I. Hay, 103–121. New York: Oxford University Press.

Kelly, J. F. 2015. Posture statement of General John F. Kelly, U.S. Marine Corps Commander, U.S. Southern Command, before the 114th Congress Senate Armed Forces Committee, 12 March. https://www.armed-services.senate.gov/imo/media/doc/Kelly_03-12-15.pdf (last accessed 1 June 2017).

Khosravi, S. 2009. Sweden: Detention and deportation of asylum seekers. *Race and Class* 50 (4): 38–56.

King, R. D., M. Massoglia, and C. Uggen. 2012. Employment and exile: U.S. criminal deportations, 1908–2005. *American Journal of Sociology* 117 (6): 1786–1825.

Kobayashi, A., and L. Peake. 2000. Racism out of place: Thoughts on whiteness and an antiracist geography in the new millennium. *Annals of the Association of American Geographers* 90 (2): 392–403.

Kocher, A. 2017. Notice to appear: Immigration courts and the legal production of illegalized immigrants. PhD dissertation, Ohio State University.

Koh, J. L. 2008. Immigrant rights signed away? *New America Media*, 4 December. http://news.newamericamedia.org/news/view_article.html?article_id=6766c8f6d7910a3125de6ac586049fc9 (last accessed 4 December 2008).

———. 2013. Waiving due process (goodbye): Stipulated orders of removal and the crisis in immigration adjudication. *North Carolina Law Review* 91 (2): 475–548.

Korovkin, T. 1997. Indigenous peasant struggles and the capitalist modernization of agriculture: Chimborazo, 1964–1991. *Latin American Perspectives* 24 (3): 25–49.

Koser, K. 2001. Asylum policies, trafficking and vulnerability. *International Migration* 38 (3): 91–109.

———. 2007. *International migration: A very short introduction.* New York: Oxford University Press.

———. 2008. Why migrant smuggling pays. *International Migration* 46 (2): 3–26.

Kremer, J. D., K. A. Moccio, and J. W. Hammell. 2009. *Severing a lifeline: The neglect of citizen children in America's immigration enforcement policy.* Report by Dorsey and Whitney LLP for the Urban Institute. http://www.dorsey.com/files/upload/DorseyProBono_SeveringLifeline_web.pdf (last accessed 1 June 2017).

Kyle, D. 2000. *Transnational peasants: Migrations, networks, and ethnicity in Andean Ecuador.* Baltimore: Johns Hopkins University Press.

Kyle, D., and J. Dale. 2001. Smuggling the state back in: Agents of human smuggling reconsidered. In *Global human smuggling: Comparative perspectives*, ed. D. Kyle and R. Koslowski, 29–57. Baltimore: Johns Hopkins University Press.

Kyle, D., and B. Jokisch. 2005. Leaving Ecuador. *Berkeley Review of Latin American Studies*, Spring: 45–48.

Kyle, D., and R. Koslowski. 2001. Introduction. In *Global human smuggling: Comparative perspectives*, ed. D. Kyle and R. Koslowski, 1–25. Baltimore: Johns Hopkins University Press.

Kyle, D., and Z. Liang. 2001. Migration merchants: Human smuggling from Ecuador and China to the United States. In *Controlling a new migration world*, ed. V. Guiraudon and C. Joppke, 200–221. New York: Routledge.

Kyle, D., and C. A. Siracusa. 2005. Seeing the state like a migrant: Why so many non-criminals break immigration laws. In *Illicit flows and criminal things: States, borders, and the other side of globalization*, ed. W. van Schendel and I. Abraham, 153–176. Bloomington: Indiana University Press.

Lawson, V. A. 1998. Hierarchical households and gendered migration in Latin America: Feminist extensions to migration research. *Progress in Human Geography* 22: 39–53.

Lazare, S. 2017. Obama's lethal deportation machine: Trump's anti-immigration measures are intense, but nothing new. *Alternet*, 11 February. http://www.salon.com/2017/02/11/obamas-lethal-deportation-machine-trumps-anti-immigration-measures-are-intense-but-nothing-new_partner/ (last accessed 1 June 2017).

Lee, E. 2007. *At America's gates: Chinese immigration during the exclusion era, 1882–1943*. Chapel Hill: University of North Carolina Press.

Leitner, H., J. Peck, and E. S. Sheppard. 2007. Squaring up to neoliberalism. In *Contesting neoliberalism: Urban frontiers*, ed. H. Leitner, J. Peck, and E. S. Sheppard, 311–327. New York: Guilford Press.

Lind, A., and J. Williams. 2012. Engendering violence in de/hyper-nationalized spaces: Border militarization, state territorialization, and embodied politics at the U.S.-Mexico border. In *Feminisms in North America: Identities, citizenship, human rights*, ed. A. S. Runyan, M. Marchand, P. McDermott, and A. Lind, 156–170. Farnham, UK: Ashgate.

Lowen, M. 2016. Intimate encounters with immigrant criminalisation in Arizona. In *Intimate economies of immigration detention: Critical perspectives*, ed. D. Conlon and N. Hiemstra, 187–202. London: Routledge.

Loyd, J. M., M. Mitchelson, and A. Burridge, eds. 2013. *Beyond walls and cages: Prisons, borders, and global crisis*. Athens: University of Georgia Press.

Luibhéid, E. 2002. *Entry denied: Controlling sexuality at the border*. Minneapolis: University of Minnesota Press.

———. 2014. Sexuality and international migration. In *A global history of sexuality: The modern era*, ed. R. M. Buffington, E. Luibhéid, and D. J. Guy, 119–150. Malden, Mass.: Wiley-Blackwell.

Lykes, M. B., E. Sibley, K. M. Brabeck, C. Hunter, and Y. Johansen-Méndez. 2015. Participatory action research with transnational and mixed-status families: Understanding and responding to post-9/11 threats in Guatemala and the United States. In *The new deportations delirium: Interdisciplinary perspectives*, ed. D. Kanstroom and M. B. Lykes, 193–225. New York: New York University Press.

Mainwaring, C. 2012. Constructing a crisis: The role of immigration detention in Malta. *Population, Space and Place* 18: 687–700.

Mainwaring, C., and S. J. Silverman. 2017. Detention-as-spectacle. *International Political Sociology* 11 (1): 21–38. https://doi.org/10.1093/ips/olw016.

Maldonado, R., and M. Hayem. 2015. *Remittances to Latin America and the Caribbean set a new record high in 2014.* Washington, D.C.: Multilateral Investment Fund, Inter-American Development Bank.

Marconi, S. 2001. A modo de introducción. In *Macroeconomía y economía política en dolarización*, ed. S. Marconi, 11–15. Quito: Ediciones Abya-yala.

Marosi, R., and A. Becker. 2011. Surge of immigrants from India baffles border officials in Texas. *Los Angeles Times*, 6 February. http://articles.latimes.com/2011/feb/06/nation/la-na-border-indians-20110206 (last accessed 1 June 2017).

Marrero, P. 2004. Immigration shift: Many Latin Americans choosing Spain over U.S. *IMDiversity*. http://imdiversity.com/villages/hispanic/immigration-shift-many-latin-americans-choosing-spain-over-u-s/ (last accessed 1 June 2017).

Martin, L. 2012. "Catch and remove": Detention, deterrence, and discipline in U.S. noncitizen family detention practice. *Geopolitics* 17 (2): 312–334.

———. 2015. Noncitizen family detention: Spatial strategies of migrant precarity in U.S. immigration and border control. *Annales de Géographie* 702–703: 231–247.

———. 2016. Discretion, contracting and commodification: Privatisation of U.S. immigration detention as a technology of government. In *Intimate economies of immigration detention: Critical perspectives*, ed. D. Conlon and N. Hiemstra, 32–50. London: Routledge.

Martin, L. L., and M. L. Mitchelson. 2009. Geographies of detention and imprisonment: Interrogating spatial practices of confinement, discipline, law, and state power. *Geography Compass* 3 (1): 459–477.

Martínez, F. 2015. Cifra récord de migrantes detenidos en México; casi 200 mil al cierre de 2015: SG. *La Jornada*, 27 December. http://www.jornada.unam.mx/2015/12/27/politica/004n1pol (last accessed 1 June 2017).

Massey, D. S., J. Durand, and N. J. Malone. 2002. *Beyond smoke and mirrors: Mexican migration in an era of economic integration.* New York: Russell Sage Foundation.

McDowell, L. 1999. *Gender, identity and place: Understanding feminist geographies.* Minneapolis: University of Minnesota Press.

Megoran, N. 2006. For ethnography in political geography: Experiencing and reimagining Ferghana Valley boundary closures. *Political Geography* 25: 622–640.

Meissner, D., D. M. Kerwin, M. Chishti, and C. Bergeron. 2013. *Immigration enforcement in the United States: Rise of a formidable machinery.* Washington, D.C.: Migration Policy Institute.

Menjívar, C. 2000. *Fragmented ties: Salvadoran immigrant networks in America.* Berkeley: University of California Press.

———. 2006. Liminal legality: Salvadoran and Guatemalan immigrants' lives in the United States. *American Journal of Sociology* 111: 999–1037.

Menjívar, C., and L. J. Abrego. 2012. Legal violence: Immigration law and the lives of Central American immigrants. *American Journal of Sociology* 117: 1380–1421.

Menz, G. 2013. The neoliberalized state and the growth of the migration industry. In Gammeltoft-Hansen and Sørensen, *Migration industry*, 108–127.

Meyer, P. J., and C. R. Seelke. 2015. Central America Regional Security Initiative: Background and policy issues for Congress. Congressional Research Service, R41731, 17 December. https://fas.org/sgp/crs/row/R41731.pdf (last accessed 22 June 2017).

Meyer, P. J., R. Margesson, C. R. Seelke,, and M. Taft-Morales. 2016. Unaccompanied children from Central America: Foreign policy considerations. Congressional Research Service, R43702. https://fas.org/sgp/crs/homesec/R43702.pdf (last accessed 22 June 2017).

Miller, T. A. 2003a. Citizenship & severity: Recent immigration reforms and the new penology. *Georgetown Immigration Law Journal* 17 (4): 611–666.

———. 2003b. The impact of mass incarceration on immigration policy. In *Invisible punishment: The collateral consequences of mass imprisonment*, ed. M. Chesney-Lind and M. Mauer, 214–238. New York: New Press.

Mitchelson, M. L. 2014. The production of bedspace: Prison privatization and abstract space. *Geographica Helvetica* 69: 325–333.

Moloney, D. M. 2012. *National insecurities: Immigrants and U.S. deportation policy since 1882*. Chapel Hill: University of North Carolina Press.

Moran, D., N. Gill, and D. Conlon, eds. 2013. *Carceral spaces: Mobility and agency in imprisonment and migrant detention*. Farnham, UK: Ashgate.

Morawetz, N. 2005. Detention decisions and access to habeas corpus for immigrants facing deportation. *Boston College Third World Law Journal* 25: 13–33.

Morris, J. 2016. In the market of morality: International human rights standards and the immigration detention "improvement" complex. In *Intimate economies of immigration detention: Critical perspectives*, ed. D. Conlon and N. Hiemstra, 51–69. London: Routledge.

Moss, P., and I. Dyck. 2002. *Women, body, illness: Space and identity in the everyday lives of women with chronic illness*. Lanham, Md.: Rowman and Littlefield.

Mountz, A. 2003. Human smuggling, the transnational imaginary, and everyday geographies of the nation-state. *Antipode* 35: 622–644.

———. 2004. Embodying the nation-state: Canada's response to human smuggling. *Political Geography* 23 (3): 323–345.

———. 2007. Smoke and mirrors: An ethnography of the state. In *Politics and practice in economic geography*, ed. E. Sheppard, T. Barnes, and J. Peck, 38–48. Thousand Oaks, Calif.: SAGE.

———. 2010. *Seeking asylum: Human smuggling and bureaucracy at the border*. Minneapolis: University of Minnesota Press.

Mountz, A., K. Coddington, R. T. Catania, and J. M. Loyd. 2013. Conceptualizing detention: Mobility, containment, bordering, and exclusion. *Progress in Human Geography* 37 (4): 522–541.

Mountz, A., and N. Hiemstra. 2012. Spatial strategies for rebordering human migration at sea. In *A companion to border studies*, ed. T. M. Wilson and H. Donnan, 455–472. Malden, Mass.: Blackwell.

———. 2014. Chaos and crisis: Dissecting the spatiotemporal logics of contemporary migrations and state practices. *Annals of the Association of American Geographers* 104 (2): 382–390.

Mountz, A., and J. Loyd. 2014. Transnational productions of remoteness: Building onshore and offshore carceral regimes across borders. *Geographica Helvetica* 69: 389–398.

Mountz, A., and R. A. Wright. 1996. Daily life in the transnational migrant community of San Agustín, Oaxaca, and Poughkeepsie, New York. *Diaspora* 5 (3): 403–428.

Nairn, K. 2002. Doing feminist fieldwork about geography fieldwork. In *Feminist geography in practice: Research and methods*, ed. P. Moss, 146–159. Oxford: Blackwell.

Nast, H. J., and S. Pile, eds. 1998. *Places through the body*. London: Routledge.

National Immigrant Justice Center. 2010. Isolated in detention: Limited access to legal counsel in immigration detention facilities jeopardizes a fair day in court. http://www.immigrantjustice.org/isolatedindetention (last accessed 1 June 2017).

Nelson, L. 1999. Bodies (and spaces) do matter: The limits of performativity. *Gender, Place and Culture* 6 (4): 331–353.

Nevins, J. 2007. Dying for a cup of coffee? Migrant deaths in the U.S.-Mexico border region in a neoliberal age. *Geopolitics* 12 (2): 228–247.

———. 2008. *Dying to live: A story of U.S. immigration in an age of global apartheid*. San Francisco: City Lights.

———. 2010. *Operation Gatekeeper and beyond: The war on "illegals" and the remaking of the U.S.-Mexico boundary*. New York: Routledge.

Ngai, M. M. 2005. *Impossible subjects: Illegal aliens and the making of modern America*. Princeton: Princeton University Press.

Nguyen, T. 2005. *We are all suspects now: Untold stories from immigrant communities after 9/11*. Boston: Beacon Press.

NNIRR (National Network for Immigrant and Refugee Rights). 2009. Guilty by immigration status: The impact of immigration laws and enforcement on immigrant families, workers and communities. Human Rights Immigrant Community Action Network (HURRICANE), September. http://www.nnirr.org/~nnirrorg/drupal/sites/default/files/guiltybyimmigrationstatus2008_0.pdf (last accessed 1 June 2017).

Núñez-Neto, B. 2008. Border security: The role of the U.S. Border Patrol. Congressional Research Service, RL32562. 20 November. http://digitalcommons.ilr.cornell.edu/cgi/viewcontent.cgi?article=1577&context=key_workplace (last accessed 29 May 2018).

Nuñez-Neto, B., A. Siskin, and S. Viña. 2005. Border security: Apprehensions of "other than Mexican" aliens. Congressional Research Service, RL33097. 22 September. http://trac.syr.edu/immigration/library/P1.pdf. (last accessed 1 June 2017).

O'Neill, H. 2012. U.S.-born kids of deported parents struggle as family life is "destroyed." *Huffington Post*, 25 August. http://www.huffingtonpost.com/2012/08/25/us-born-kids-deported-parents_n_1830496.html (last accessed 28 September 2015; no longer available).

Pain, R. 2010. The new geopolitics of fear. *Geography Compass* 4 (3): 226–240.

Palmer, C. G. W. 2009. United States Coast Guard migrant interdiction experiences in the Caribbean. Unpublished paper. Panel by U.S. Coast Guard, Conference on Undocumented Hispanic Migration, New London, Conn., 18 October.

Peaco, E. 2012. ICE partnering to fight crime on a global scale. *American Board for Certification in Homeland Security*. http://www.abchs.com/ihs/SUMMER2012/ihs_articles_cover.php (last accessed 1 June 2017; no longer available).

Peck, J., and N. Theodore. 2015. *Fast policy: Experimental statecraft at the thresholds of neoliberalism*. Minneapolis: University of Minnesota Press.

Peck, J., and A. Tickell. 2007. Conceptualizing neoliberalism, thinking Thatcherism. In *Contesting neoliberalism: Urban frontiers*, ed. H. Leitner, J. Peck, and E. S. Sheppard, 26–50. New York: Guilford Press.

Peet, R., and E. Hartwick. 2009. *Theories of development: Contentions, arguments, alternatives.* New York: Guilford Press.

Perreault, T., and P. Martin. 2005. Geographies of neoliberalism in Latin America. *Environment and Planning A* 37: 191–201.

Peutz, N. 2006. Embarking on an anthropology of removal. *Current Anthropology* 47 (2): 217–241.

———. 2010. "Criminal alien" deportees in Somaliland: An ethnography of removal. In De Genova and Peutz, *Deportation regime*, 371–409.

Peutz, N., and N. De Genova. 2010. Introduction to De Genova and Peutz, *Deportation regime*, 1–29.

Pratt, G. 1998. Inscribing domestic work in Filipina bodies. In *Places through the body*, ed. H. J. Nast and S. Pile, 283–304. London: Routledge.

———. 2004. *Working feminism.* Philadelphia: Temple University Press.

Pratt, G., and V. Rosner. 2006. Introduction: The global and the intimate. *Women's Studies Quarterly* 34 (1/2): 13–24.

Precil, P. 1999. Criminal deportees and returned teens: A migration phenomenon, a social problem. *MediaNet Bulletin: Briefing on Haiti*, no. 2, May. https://www.monroecollege.edu/uploadedFiles/_Site_Assets/PDF/Criminal-deportees.pdf. (last accessed 1 June 2017).

Preston, J. 2011. U.S. pledges to raise deportation threshold. *New York Times*, 17 June. http://www.nytimes.com/2011/06/18/us/18immig.html?_r=1. (last accessed 1 June 2017).

Pribilsky, J. 2004. "*Aprendemos a convivir*": Conjugal relations, co-parenting, and family life among Ecuadorian transnational migrants in New York City and the Ecuadorian Andes. *Global Networks* 3 (3): 313–334.

Price, M., and D. Breese. 2016. Unintended return: U.S. deportation and the fractious politics of mobility for Latinos. *Annals of the Association of American Geographers* 106 (2): 366–376.

Radcliffe, S. A. 1999. Race and domestic service: Migration and identity in Ecuador. In *Gender migration and domestic service*, ed. J. H. Momsen, 83–97. London: Routledge.

Ramírez, J., and S. Álvarez. 2009. "Cruzando Fronteras": Una aproximación etnográfica a la migración clandestina ecuatoriana en tránsito hacia Estados Unidos. *Confluenze* 1 (1): 89–113.

Reich, O., and E. Vazquez Ger. 2012. How Ecuador's immigration policy helps al Qaeda. *Foreign Policy*, 2 April. http://foreignpolicy.com/2012/04/02/how-ecuadors-immigration-policy-helps-al-qaeda/ (last accessed 1 June 2017).

Ridgley, J. 2011. The legacy of war: Migration-related detention and the restructuring of the INS in the 1940s. Unpublished paper. Annual Meeting of the Association of American Geographers, Seattle, Wash.

Riva, S. 2017. Across the border and into the cold: Hieleras and the punishment of asylum-seeking Central American women in the United States. *Citizenship Studies* 21: 309–326.

Rojas, R. J. 2004. Plan Colombia: Conflicto armado, y migraciones forzadas. In *Globalización, migracion y derechos humanos*, ed. Programa Andino de Derechos Humanos, 191–210. Quito: Abya-yala.

Salt, J., and J. Stein. 1997. Migration as a business: The case of trafficking. *International Migration* 35 (4): 467–491.

Sandoval, I. R. 2013. Public officials and the migration industry in Guatemala: Greasing the wheels of a corrupt machine. In Gammeltoft-Hansen and Sørensen, *Migration industry*, 215–236.

Sassen, S. 1988. *The mobility of labor and capital: A study in international investment and labor flow*. Cambridge: Cambridge University Press.

Sawyer, S. 2004. *Crude chronicles: Indigenous politics, multinational oil, and neoliberalism in Ecuador*. Durham, N.C.: Duke University Press.

Schuster, L., and N. Majidi. 2013. What happens post-deportation? The experience of deported Afghans. *Migration Studies* 1 (2): 221–240.

———. 2015. Deportation stigma and re-migration. *Journal of Ethnic and Migration Studies* 41 (4): 635–652.

Sheehan, M. 2005. *International security: An analytical survey*. Boulder, Colo.: Lynne Rienner.

Silverman, S. J. 2010. Immigration detention in America: A history of its expansion and a study of its significance. Centre on Migration, Policy and Society, University of Oxford, Working Paper no. 80.

Silvey, R. 2005. Borders, embodiment, and mobility: Feminist migration studies in geography. In *A companion to feminist geography*, ed. L. Nelson and J. Seager, 138–149. Malden, Mass.: Blackwell.

Sin Fronteras. 2014. La ruta del encierro: Situación de las personas en detención en estaciones migratorias y estancias provisionales. Report Mexico. https://sinfronteras .org.mx/wp-content/uploads/2017/05/inf-ruta-encierro.pdf (last accessed 29 May 2018).

Sinha, A. 2015. Slavery by another name: "Voluntary" immigrant detainee labor and the Thirteenth Amendment. *Stanford Journal of Civil Rights & Civil Liberties* 11 (1): 1–44.

Siskin, A., A. Bruno, B. Nunez-Neto, L. M. Seghetti, and R. E. Wasem. 2006. Immigration enforcement within the United States. Congressional Research Service, RL33351, 6 April. http://digitalcommons.ilr.cornell.edu/cgi/viewcontent.cgi?article=1014& context=crs (last accessed 1 June 2017).

Siskin, A., and R. E. Wasem. 2005. Immigration policy on Expedited Removal of aliens. Congressional Research Service RL33109. 30 September. http://trac.syr.edu /immigration/library/P13.pdf (last accessed 29 May 2018).

Slack, J., D. E. Martínez, S. Whiteford, and E. Peiffer. 2015. In harm's way: Family separation, immigration enforcement programs and security on the U.S.-Mexico Border. *Journal on Migration and Human Security* 3 (2): 109–128.

Smith, D. 1987. *The everyday world as problematic: A feminist sociology*. Toronto: University of Toronto Press.

Smith, F. 2001. Refiguring the geopolitical landscape: Nation, "transition" and gendered subjects in post–Cold War Germany. *Space and Polity* 5 (3): 213–235.

Smyth, T. 2015. Abuse of migrants in Mexico rises even as numbers fall. Reuters, 16 October. http://ca.reuters.com/article/topNews/idCAKCN0SA2J020151016 (last accessed 1 June 2017).

Solano, G. 2014. Ecuador orders U.S. military group to leave. Associated Press, 25 April. https://www.yahoo.com/news/ecuador-orders-us-military-group-leave-233412419 .html (last accessed 1 June 2017).

Sørensen, N. N., and T. Gammeltoft-Hansen. 2013. Introduction to Gammeltoft-Hansen and Sørensen, *Migration industry*, 1–23.

Spener, D. 2001. Smuggling migrants through South Texas: Challenges posed by operation Rio Grande. In *Global human smuggling: Comparative perspectives*, ed. D. Kyle and R. Koslowski, 129–165. Baltimore: Johns Hopkins University Press.

———. 2004. Mexican migrant smuggling: A cross-border cottage industry. *Journal of International Migration and Integration* 5 (3): 295–320.

SPLC (Southern Poverty Law Center). 2016. Shadow prisons: Immigrant detention in the south. November. https://www.splcenter.org/sites/default/files/leg_ijp_shadow _prisons_immigrant_detention_report.pdf. (last accessed 1 June 2017).

Staeheli, L. A., and C. R. Nagel. 2008. Rethinking security: Perspectives from Arab-American and British Arab activists. *Antipode* 40 (5): 780–801.

Stoll, D. 2010. From wage-migration to debt-migration? Easy credit, failure in El Norte, and foreclosure in a bubble economy of the Western Guatemalan Highlands. *Latin American Perspectives* 37 (1): 123–142.

———. 2013. *El Norte or bust! How migration fever and microcredit produced a financial crash in a Latin American town*. Lanham, Md.: Rowman and Littlefield.

Stumpf, J. 2006. The crimmigration crisis: Immigrants, crime, and sovereign power. *American University Law Review* 56 (2): 367–419.

Suárez, X., J. Knippen, and M. Meyer. 2016. A trail of impunity: Thousands of migrants in transit face abuses amid Mexico's crackdown. Washington Office on Latin America, 20 October. https://www.wola.org/analysis/a-trail-of-impunity/ (last accessed 1 June 2017).

Sutton, R., and D. Vigneswaran. 2011. A Kafkaesque state: Deportation and detention in South Africa. *Citizenship Studies* 15 (5): 627–642.

Takaki, R. 2008. *A different mirror: A history of multicultural America*. New York: Back Bay Books, Little, Brown.

Thompson, G., and S. Ochoa. 2004. By a back door to the U.S.: A migrant's grim sea voyage. *New York Times*, 1 June, 13.

Tidd, K. W. 2016. Posture statement of Admiral Kurt W. Tidd, Commander, U.S. Southern Command, before the 114th Congress Senate Armed Services Committee, 10 March. https://www.armed-services.senate.gov/imo/media/doc/Tidd_03–10–16 .pdf (last accessed 1 June 2017; no longer available).

Toal, G. 2000. Dis/placing the geo-politics which one cannot not want. *Political Geography* 19: 385–396.

TRAC (Transactional Records Access Clearinghouse). 2006a. Aggravated felonies and deportation. TRAC *Reports*. http://trac.syr.edu/immigration/reports/155/ (last accessed 1 June 2017).

———. 2006b. Immigration judges. TRAC *Reports*. http://trac.syr.edu/immigration /reports/160/ (last accessed 1 June 2017).

——. 2009. Huge increase in transfers of ICE detainees. TRAC *Reports*. http://trac.syr
.edu/immigration/reports/220/ (last accessed 1 June 2017).

——. 2010. Backlog in immigration cases continues to climb. TRAC *Reports*. http://
trac.syr.edu/immigration/reports/225/ (last accessed 1 June 2017).

——. 2011. New judge hiring fails to stem rising immigration case backlog. TRAC
Reports. http://trac.syr.edu/immigration/reports/250/ (last accessed 1 June 2017).

——. 2013. Legal noncitizens receive longest ICE detention. TRAC *Reports*. http://trac
.syr.edu/immigration/reports/321/ (last accessed 1 June 2017).

——. 2015a. Average time pending cases have been waiting in immigration courts as
of April 2015. TRAC *Immigration*. http://trac.syr.edu/phptools/immigration/court
_backlog/apprep_backlog_avgdays.php (last accessed 1 June 2017).

——. 2015b. Backlog of pending cases in immigration courts as of April 2015. TRAC
Immigration. http://trac.syr.edu/phptools/immigration/court_backlog/apprep
_backlog.php (last accessed 1 June 2017).

——. 2015c. Relief granted by immigration judges as of April 2015. TRAC *Immigration*.
http://trac.syr.edu/phptools/immigration/court_backlog/apprep_relief.php (last
accessed 1 June 2017).

——. 2016a. Immigration backlog still rising despite new judge investitures. TRAC *Immigration*. http://trac.syr.edu/immigration/reports/429/ (last accessed 1 June 2017).

——. 2016b. New data on 637 detention facilities used by ICE in FY 2015. TRAC *Immigration*. http://trac.syr.edu/immigration/reports/422/ (last accessed 1 June 2017).

——. 2018. Immigration court backlog tops 650,000. TRAC *Immigration*. http://trac
.syr.edu/whatsnew/email.180104.html (last accessed 10 January 2018).

Urbina, I. 2014. Using jailed migrants as a pool of cheap labor. *New York Times*, 24 May.
https://www.nytimes.com/2014/05/25/us/using-jailed-migrants-as-a-pool-of-cheap
-labor.html?mcubz=0 (last accessed 1 June 2017).

U.S. Coast Guard. 2015. Total interdictions: Fiscal year 1982 to present. http://www.uscg
.mil/hq/cg5/cg531/AMIO/FlowStats/FY.asp (last accessed 28 September 2015; no
longer available).

U.S. Congress, House of Representatives. 2009. Overview of Coast Guard drug and
migrant interdiction, 2011. Hearing Before the Subcommittee on Coast Guard and
Maritime Transportation of the Committee on Transportation and Infrastructure,
House of Representatives, One Hundred Eleventh Congress. https://www.gpo.gov
/fdsys/pkg/CHRG-111hhrg48204/pdf/CHRG-111hhrg48204.pdf. (last accessed
1 June 2017).

U.S. CBP (Customs and Border Patrol). 2005. DHS expands Expedited Removal authority along southwest border. Press release, 14 September. https://www.hsdl.org
/?abstract&did=477118 (last accessed 29 May 2018).

U.S. DHS (Department of Homeland Security). 2004. Designating aliens for Expedited
Removal. *Federal Register* 69: 48877–48881. https://www.gpo.gov/fdsys/granule/FR
-2004-08-11/04-18469 (last accessed 7 June 2018).

——. 2005. Fact Sheet: Secure Border Initiative. http://www.dhs.gov/xnews/releases
/press_release_0794.shtm (last accessed 20 July 2011; no longer available).

——. 2014. ICE Enforcement and Removal Operations report, fiscal year 2014. https://
www.ice.gov/doclib/about/offices/ero/pdf/2014-ice-immigration-removals.pdf (last
accessed 1 June 2017).

————. 2017. Fiscal year 2017 ICE Enforcement and Removal Operations report. https://
www.ice.gov/sites/default/files/documents/Report/2017/iceEndOfYearFY2017.pdf
(last accessed 4 February 2017).

U.S. ICE. 2012. ICE detention standards. 24 February. http://www.ice.gov/factsheets
/facilities-pbnds (last accessed 1 June 2017).

Villegas, R. D., and V. Rietig. 2015. Migrants deported from the United States and Mexico to the Northern Triangle: A statistical and socioeconomic profile. Migration
Policy Institute, Washington, D.C., September.

Wadhia, S. S. 2015. *Beyond deportation: Prosecutorial discretion in immigration cases*.
New York: New York University Press.

Waever, O. 1995. Securitization and desecuritization. In *On security*, ed. R. Lipschutz,
46–86. New York: Columbia University Press.

Walters, W. 2002. Deportation, exclusion, and the international police of aliens. *Citizenship Studies* 6 (3): 265–292.

————. 2004. Secure borders, safe haven, domopolitics. *Citizenship Studies* 8 (3):
237–260.

————. 2008a. Bordering the sea: Shipping industries and the policing of stowaways.
Borderlands 7 (3): 1–25.

————. 2008b. Putting the migration-security complex in its place. In *Risk and the war
on terror*, ed. L. Amoore and M. de Goede, 158–177. London: Routledge.

————. 2016. Flight of the deported: Aircraft, deportation, and politics. *Geopolitics* 21
(2): 435–438.

Weizman, E. 2007. *Hollow land: Israel's architecture of occupation*. New York: Verso.

Welch, M. 2002. *Detained: Immigration laws and the expanding I.N.S. jail complex*.
Philadelphia: Temple University Press.

Wessler, S. F. 2011. U.S. deports 46k parents with kids in just six months. *Colorlines.com*,
2 November. http://www.colorlines.com/articles/us-deports-46k-parents-citizen
-kids-just-six-months (last accessed 1 June 2017).

Wessler, S. F., and J. Hing. 2012. Torn apart: Struggling to stay together after deportation. In *Beyond walls and cages: Prisons, borders, and global crisis*, ed. J. Loyd, M.
Mitchelson, and A. Burridge, 152–162. Athens: University of Georgia Press.

Wheatley, C. 2011. Push back: U.S. deportation policy and the reincorporation of involuntary return migrants in Mexico. *Latin Americanist* 55 (4): 35–60.

Whitten, N. E. 2003. Introduction. In *Millennial Ecuador: Critical essays on cultural
transformations and social dynamics*, ed. N. E. Whitten, 1–45. Iowa City: University
of Iowa Press.

Williams, M. C. 2003. Words, images, enemies: Securitization and international politics. *International Studies Quarterly* 47: 511–531.

Wilsher, D. 2012. *Immigration detention: Law, history, politics*. Cambridge: Cambridge
University Press.

Wimmer, A., and N. G. Schiller. 2003. Methodological nationalism, the social sciences,
and the study of migration: An essay in historical epistemology. *International Migration Review* 37 (3): 576–610.

Wolf, S. 2010. Public security challenges for El Salvador's first leftist government.
NACLA (North American Congress on Latin America) Report on the Americas,
7 July. https://nacla.org/node/6650 (last accessed 1 June 2017).

Wong, T. K. 2015. *Rights, deportation, and detention in the age of immigration control.* Stanford: Stanford University Press.

Wood, G. 2011. A boom behind bars. *Business Week*, 17 March. http://www.businessweek.com/magazine/content/11_13/b4221076266454.htm (last accessed 1 June 2017).

Wright, M. 2006. *Disposable women and other myths of global capitalism.* New York: Routledge.

Xiang, B., B. S. A. Yeoh, and M. Toyota, eds. 2013. *Return: Nationalizing transnational mobility in Asia.* Durham, N.C.: Duke University Press.

Ybarra, M., and I. L. Peña. 2016. "We don't need money, we need to be together": Forced transnationality in deportation's afterlives. *Geopolitics* 22: 34–50.

Zilberg, E. 2004. Fools banished from the kingdom: Remapping geographies of gang violence between the Americas (Los Angeles and San Salvador). *American Quarterly* 56 (3): 759–779.

———. 2006. Gangster in guerilla face: A transnational mirror of production between the USA and El Salvador. *Anthropological Theory* 7 (1): 37–57.

———. 2011. *Space of detention: The making of a transnational gang crisis between Los Angeles and San Salvador.* Durham, N.C.: Duke University Press.

INDEX

GEOGRAPHIES OF JUSTICE AND SOCIAL TRANSFORMATION

CPSIA information can be obtained
at www.ICGtesting.com
Printed in the USA
LVHW030743200722
723942LV00003B/195